By David Crystal in this series

The Story of English in 100 Words

Spell It Out: the Singular Story of English Spelling

Making a Point: the Pernickety Story of English Punctuation

Making Sense: The Glamorous Story of English Grammar

Also by David Crystal

The Gift of the Gab: How Eloquence Works

The Oxford Dictionary of Original Shakespearean Pronunciation

Wordsmiths and Warriors: the English-language Tourist's Guide to Britain

Evolving English: One Language, Many Voices

The Cambridge Encyclopedia of Language

By Ben and David Crystal

Oxford Illustrated Shakespeare

Shakespeare's Words: a Glossary and Language Companion

Sounds Appealing:

The Passionate Story of English Pronunciation

David Crystal

P

PROFILE BOOKS

This paperback edition published in 2019

First published in Great Britain in 2018 by
PROFILE BOOKS LTD
3 Holford Yard
Bevin Way
London WC1X 9HD
www.profilebooks.com

10 9 8 7 6 5 4 3 2

All reasonable efforts have been made to obtain copyright permissions
where required. Acknowledgements appear on page 284. Any omissions
and errors of attribution are unintentional and will, if notified in writing to
the publisher, be corrected in future printings.

A CIP catalogue record for this book is available from the
British Library.

ISBN 978 1 78125 610 7
eISBN 978 1 78283 234 8

Typeset in Iowan by MacGuru Ltd
Printed and bound in Great Britain by
CPI Group (UK) Ltd, Croydon CR0 4YY

Contents

THE LISTENER

9 July 1981 Price fifty pence (IR 70p, USA and Canada $1.50)

David Crystal
Is the BBC still literate?

Geoffrey Robertson
The Contempt Bill: a victory for the lawyers?

Alistair Cooke
Mr Reagan conquers Congress

Hugo Cole
The 1981 Proms

Conor Cruise O'Brien
The achievement of Edmund Burke

August Radio Plans

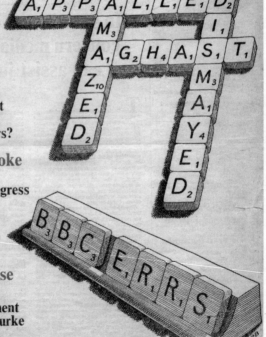

Introduction

In the 1980s, I found myself as the 'voice of language' on BBC Radio 4. It was a time when the range of presenters you would hear on the air in Britain had greatly increased, following the emergence of local radio stations all over the country, and with new voices came new usages and new accents. Many listeners, used to the traditional 'voice of the BBC', with its echoes of wartime authority and pride, were taken aback, and sent letters and postcards in large numbers, expressing concern at what they perceived to be a falling of standards. The comments related to all aspects of spoken language, including vocabulary and grammar, but most were passionate about pronunciation.

The BBC didn't know what to do with the huge postbags that were coming in. There was a Pronunciation Unit that dealt with queries (such as how to pronounce the name of a foreign place or politician), but the range of issues being raised went well beyond its remit, and the small team that staffed it couldn't cope with the quantity. So, as a known linguist who'd already done some broadcasting, it sent them to me.

I went through a month's worth, and wrote what I thought was going to be a single programme about the kind of points being made. It was called 'How dare you talk to me like that', and it was printed in *The Listener* magazine on 9 July 1981. The editor gave it a new and provocative title: 'Language on the air: has it degenerated?' and chose it for the cover illustration that week (p. viii). I was told that it got the largest response of the month. They reprinted it six months later, when the programme was repeated. Another huge response.

For my script, I decided to organize the complaints into a 'top twenty' list. (There were only ever complaints. In the hundreds of letters and cards that I read, nobody once wrote words of praise.) Several were to do with pronunciation – the placing of stress in long words (<u>contro</u>versy or con<u>tro</u>versy), the sounding of 'foreign' words (such as *restaurant*), regional variations (in words like *poor*), the omission of vowels or consonants (as when *February* becomes *Feb'ry*), the insertion of *r* when it isn't in the spelling (as when *drawing* becomes *draw-ring*), and the dropping of final consonants (as in *las' year*).

What really struck me was the intemperate language used by the complainers, and *The Listener* printed some of their emotive adjectives on its cover. People didn't just say they 'disliked' a pronunciation. They used the most extreme words they could think of. They were 'appalled', 'aghast', 'horrified', 'outraged', 'distressed', 'dumbfounded' when they heard something they didn't like. 'Appalled' was the commonest usage. While I was writing my script, in May 1981, news came through that there had been an assassination attempt in Rome on Pope John Paul II. So I ended my piece with a wry comment: if one can be 'appalled' about errors in pronunciation, 'what kind of language is there left to refer to one's feelings when great men get shot?'

Somebody at the BBC noticed the furore, and asked me to do a series – offering an outlet, as it were, for all this pent-up passion. It was called *Speak Out*. Just three episodes. Not enough. The letter rate increased. Another series followed, *English Now*, and this ran for nearly a decade. There was no let-up. After some episodes, I would get as many as a thousand items through the post. Pronunciation was always the main talking point. And here's the interesting thing: the vast majority would have a first-class stamp. Writers evidently felt a sense of urgency. Whatever the point being complained about was, it needed to reach the BBC by tomorrow.

My own pronunciation didn't escape the ire of some listeners. One letter, addressed to the director-general of the BBC, copied to me (thus, two first-class stamps), asked for my immediate removal as presenter on the grounds that programmes to do with pronunciation shouldn't be given to someone who says the word *one* to rhyme with *on* rather than with *sun*. I don't know whether the DG replied, but I did, indirectly, by using the letter in one of the programmes as an excellent illustration of the microscopic way that some listeners actually listen.

What is it about pronunciation that produces such a response? Why does pronunciation get to people in a way that other aspects of speech don't? Why are we so passionate about it? Has it always been that way? Will it always be that way? Is it the same all around the English-speaking world, or is it just a British thing? These are the kinds of questions that this book will explore. The 'why' questions first.

A poetic voice

Ogden Nash cleverly versified his complaints in 'I'll Hush If You'll Hush', published as one of the 'poems of indignation' in *The Primrose Path* (1936).

> Sweet voices have been presented by Nature
> To creatures of varying nomenclature
> The bird, when he unlocks his beak,
> Emits a melody unique;
> The lion's roar, the moo-cow's bellow,
> Are clearly pitched and roundly mellow;
> The squirrel's chatter, the donkey's bray,
> Are fairly pleasant, in their way;
> While even beasts whose noises are awful
> Appeal therewith to their spouses lawful.
> The tomcat's miaow is curdled milk
> To us, but eggnog to his ilk;
> How odd that I cannot rejoice,
> Though human, in the human voice.
> Of sounds I think the furthest South
> Is that which springs from the human mouth.
> No study such despair affords
> As that of human vocal cords.
> So you shudder at the type of larynx
> Whence herrings issue forth as harrinks?
> Do you sometimes wonder which is worse,
> Verce for voice, or voise for verse?
> Then how about the Oxford throat,
> With its swallowed vowels and tweetering note?
> There's little pleasure in the stage
> Since the tired accent became the rage.
> Still, if you think the stage is low,
> Then, what about the radio?

The smooth and oily tongues that drip
With spurious good-fellowship,
That flood your chamber with a spasm
Of cultured cold enthusiasm?
They set my nerves a-leaping skittishly,
These speakers speaking pseudo-wittishly.
Had I of sundry sounds my choice
I should not choose the human voice;
God knows it's bad enough alone,
Without the aid of microphone.
It's a useful means of communication,
But a paltry acoustical decoration.

1
Always there

Pronunciation isn't like the other main areas of spoken language that people complain about, such as grammar or vocabulary. You may not like the way people use a particular word, such as taking *uninterested* to mean *disinterested*, but you are not going to meet that problem frequently in everyday speech. Similarly, if you don't like split infinitives, you are unlikely to hear one very often: you might listen to an entire conversation or radio programme and not encounter a single instance. But every word, every sentence, has to be pronounced, so if you don't like the vowels and consonants of an accent, or the way someone drops consonants, stresses words, or intones a sentence, there's no escape. Pronunciation is always there.

It's such an everyday notion that the term hardly needs a definition, but I'll give one anyway. It is the uttering of the sounds of speech in words and sentences. Some dictionaries prefer terms like 'articulating', 'enunciating', or 'vocalizing', instead of 'uttering', but the effect is the same. When speakers use their vocal organs to communicate meaningfully, we experience pronunciation. It is what enables speech to be intelligible and acceptable, and when people feel that one or other of these qualities fails to be achieved, they become disturbed. In the everyday world of face-to-face conversation, any disturbed feelings usually remain unmentioned. We tend not to say such things as 'I'm appalled to hear the way you just pronounced *February*' to someone's face. But when pronunciation infelicities emerge in a public domain, such as an inaudible stage actor, an unclear announcement on a public address system, or a radio presenter who fails to meet listener expectations of what is appropriate, people can be highly vociferous.

Whether a complaint is justified or misconceived is the subject of later chapters. Both possibilities exist. Sometimes a criticism reflects a state of affairs that everyone would agree about, because it is based on objective fact: if a voice is genuinely inaudible, there is nothing to dispute. But most pronunciation complaints aren't like that: they are matters of opinion and taste, where the viewpoints reflect differing perceptions as to what is appropriate, pleasing, or correct. Audition is as subjective as any other area of sense perception. Beauty, said Shakespeare in *Love's Labour's Lost*, 'is bought by judgement of the eye' – anticipating the much later maxim 'beauty is in the eye of the beholder'. The analysis of pronunciation raises the same consideration. Auditory beauty lies in the ear of the listener.

Pronunciation is always there ... which means that it is ideally placed to meet the demands of each of the two main forces that lie behind the use of language: the need for intelligibility and the need for identity – and both underlie listener unease. Note: two forces, not one. It's often thought that the only function of pronunciation is to facilitate intelligibility; but it is also there to express personal or group identity. When, as speakers of English, we hear someone speak our language, we do not only recognize the words that are said, we recognize who is saying them – often the individual person, and very often the community the speaker belongs to. It is pronunciation, more than anything else, that makes someone sound British, American, or Indian; Scottish, Welsh, or Irish; from Liverpool, Newcastle, or London; from New York, Texas, or Alabama. It is pronunciation, again more than anything else, that gives us a clue about the speaker's social class or educational background, or that allows us to identify the kind of role someone is playing, such as a radio sports commentator or newsreader. Even in the distance, with no words clearly heard, we can tell the difference between a commentary on football, horse racing, or tennis. It's something in the way they speak, as the Beatles almost said.

Of the two criteria, identity and intelligibility, it's issues relating to identity that are the more frequent when it comes to usage criticism. The vast majority of the BBC complainers were not suggesting that they couldn't understand what speakers were saying; they were complaining about the way they were saying it. Some of the criticisms were aesthetic: a pronunciation might be called 'ugly' or 'sloppy'. Some showed dislike of a particular accent. Some acknowledged a historical factor, recalling the 'voice of the BBC' from an earlier broadcasting era. There would be the occasional comment about failed intelligibility, as when presenters dropped their voice at a critical moment or gave a word an emphasis that caused ambiguity. But typically, when people talked about acceptable or unacceptable pronunciation, they were not thinking of the content but the delivery, and in particular the speech habits of the deliverer. We could adapt an old song of Ella Fitzgerald to make the point: 'It ain't what you say but the way that you say it. That's what gets results' – or complaints, in this case.

Exploring the pronunciation dimension in delivery is the subject matter of this book. Some aspects directly affect intelligibility, such as clarity of articulation and speed of speech. Some aspects directly affect identity, such as the way vowels and consonants combine to produce an identifiable accent. It's easy enough to see the importance of pronunciation in relation to intelligibility; but there needs to be a further word of explanation as to why pronunciation is so important in relation to identity. After all, if we want to show our identity, there are many ways in which we can do it. I could, for example, dress in a certain way, wearing some sort of national costume. I could sport a badge or a T-shirt with a message saying 'I am from – Wales, Texas, Melbourne', or wherever. But there are some obvious problems with costumes and badges: they cannot be seen in the dark – or around corners. Speech, on the other hand, can be perceived whether or not we can see the speaker (assuming the speaker is in earshot, of course). And it costs nothing to speak, whereas we have to buy our costumes and badges. It is this easy-to-use universality of speech that prioritizes it as a marker of identity. And pronunciation, as the permanently present manifestation of speech, is what we notice, first and foremost, when issues of identity arise.

Ultimately, intelligibility and identity interact. It's a commonplace that if someone speaks in a very broad local accent, we may not understand them. But a complete breakdown in communication is unusual. Although there's a great deal of regional, social, and personal variation in the way people pronounce their words, most of the time we do understand what they're saying. This is because everyone who speaks modern English makes use of the same basic system of sounds. If we want to understand how pronunciation works, we have to begin with a description of these sounds – and that means understanding how sounds are made. It's all part of the subject of *phonetics*.

Henry Higgins

Rex Harrison and Audrey Hepburn in My Fair Lady

Probably the most famous phonetician, as far as the general public is concerned, is Henry Higgins, the professorial character George Bernard Shaw created in his 1913 play *Pygmalion*, later widely known as *My Fair Lady*. We see Higgins at the beginning of the play (and film) listening to the way Eliza Doolittle speaks, and writing down her Cockney accent in a phonetic transcription. Then, later in the play, as a result of his training, she manages to acquire the 'posh' accent of her day. Most people remember the drills she had to perform, such as to pronounce all her *h*'s – 'In Hertford, Hereford and Hampshire, hurricanes hardly ever happen' – and to replace her vowels so that words like *Spain* don't sound like *spine*: 'The rain in Spain falls mainly on the plain.'

The phoneticians

Phonetics is the study of the way humans make and receive the sounds of speech. *Phoneticians* spend their time analysing how people use their vocal organs in order to speak, how speech sounds are carried through the air, and what happens when people hear them. We don't meet phoneticians in the street very often, but they have been around for a long time.

The study of a language's pronunciation has an ancient history. Around the fifth century BC, the sounds of Sanskrit were being meticulously described by a grammarian and phonetician about whom very little is known other than his name, Panini. In Britain, interest grew in the sixteenth century, with the first attempts at reforming English spelling – a task that requires a detailed appreciation of the sounds of the language. Other writers of the time were interested in developing new systems of shorthand, which again presupposed an understanding of the way English is pronounced. Many of the early writers on phonetics, such as Francis Lodwick, John Wallis, and John Wilkins in the seventeenth century, are little known now, but they helped form a climate of enquiry into the nature of pronunciation that led to the development of the present-day subject in the nineteenth century.

The first recorded use in the *Oxford English Dictionary* of the word *phonetics* is in 1841, and *phonetician* arrived soon after, used primarily in relation to people who wanted to devise a system of phonetic notation that would avoid the irregularities of English spelling. We don't get the modern academic sense of *phonetician* – meaning 'a scholar or student of phonetics' – until we see it in 1877 in a work by Oxford professor Henry Sweet (1845–1912), the most influential writer on this subject in the late nineteenth century. Other suggestions had been *phonetist* and *phoneticist*, but Sweet's usage was the one that caught on.

It took a while before the various professionals involved with language study began to develop the subject in a systematic way. And there were many such professionals – philologists exploring the history of sound change, clinicians investigating speech disorders, and, above all, those teaching foreign languages. In 1886, a group of French language teachers formed an association to promote the use of phonetic script as an aid to language learning and the teaching of reading. They called it *Dhi Fonètik Tîtcherz Asóciécon* (The Phonetic Teachers' Association) and began to publish a journal in which everything was written in phonetic notation. The founder was a language teacher, Paul Passy (1859–1940).

The new association proved to be hugely influential in the development of the subject. It changed its name to the International Phonetic Association in 1897, and the journal's name also changed, to *Le Maître phonétique* (The Phonetic Master). Some of the first articles I wrote as a professional linguist were for that journal, all written in phonetic transcription and reflecting the accent of the writer (p. 20). The abbreviation *IPA* began to circulate; and in due course the Association's first major initiative received the same acronym: the *International Phonetic Alphabet*. The aim was to devise a single set of symbols that could be used to write down the sounds of any language, and it was immediately taken up enthusiastically (and later revised and expanded several times).

English phoneticians soon joined the IPA, and its

membership in Britain grew dramatically in the early 1900s. Among the early members was Daniel Jones (1881–1976), the first professor of phonetics at a British university, and the pre-eminent British phonetician for over 60 years. Anyone who studied English pronunciation in the later decades of the twentieth century owed a debt to Daniel Jones, and that includes me. I was taught phonetics at University College London by Professor A. C. Gimson, a student of DJ (as he was called by his colleagues). Many universities around the world have departments of phonetics nowadays – or at least members of staff in a linguistics or languages department who have been trained in the subject. And the International Phonetics Association is alive and well. Its journal appears three times a year, and a major international conference takes place every four years, attended by around a thousand delegates.

Jones was interested in the sounds of all languages, but his main publications were all about English, including his *English Pronouncing Dictionary*, which went through many editions. He devised the first accurate method for classifying vowels – plotting them on a quadrilateral diagram corresponding to the way the tongue moves up and down, forwards and back. The vowel terminology I shall be using later in this book – close, mid, and open; front, central, and back – stems from this approach. He also popularized the term traditionally used to describe the prestige accent of British English: *Received Pronunciation*, which I'll discuss in Chapter 24.

One of the first things the phoneticians had to do was make it clear in their writing that they were talking about sounds, not letters. Square brackets came to be used to show units in speech: [t] meant the actual sound, to distinguish it from the alphabetical letter. The principle was 'one sound – one symbol', so new symbols had to be devised to show sounds that couldn't be handled by a single letter in the

Roman alphabet, such as [ʃ] for the sound of *sh* in *shoot*. And marks were added above, below, or after a symbol to show different pronunciations, such as [ː] to show that a vowel was long, as in the [uː] of *shoe*. Putting these examples together, we get the full transcription of the word *shoot*: [ʃuːt].

Every audible sound in speech would be transcribed within square brackets. But as linguistic study advanced, it was realized that not every sound is equally important in describing a language. In English, for example, when we say a word like *hat*, we sometimes 'spit out' the [t] – 'hat-uh' – and sometimes we don't. In a really detailed (or 'narrow') phonetic transcription, therefore, we would show the 'uh' effect by using an extra symbol. But whether we spit the sound out or not makes no difference to the meaning of the word: both versions are the same word, *hat*. The consonant remains 'the same', even though it's sounded slightly differently.

How do we capture this notion – that a unit of speech can be 'the same' even though it's sounded differently? A century ago, linguists came up with the concept of the *phoneme* to capture the idea that the sound system of a language is made up of a set of units, each of which can be pronounced with a range of slightly different articulations. So, in the above example, /t/ is the unit that underlies both pronunciations, and we show its underlying identity in a transcription by using forward slashes, not square brackets. You'll see those slashes throughout this book, as when I talk about the 'sounds' of English I mean those underlying units.

We work out the phonemes in a language by showing that they are used to make a difference of meaning. We recognize that /t/ and /d/ are different phonemes in English because there are many pairs of words that are differentiated by them (*minimal pairs*): *tie* vs *die*, *cat* vs *cad*, *bitter* vs *bidder*, and so on. And the same approach is used to identify all the other phonemes that make up the English sound system. If *pat* means something different from *pet*, as it does, then the vowels represented by *a* and *e* in these words must be different phonemes, and we need to give them different symbols: the ones I'm using in this book for these vowels are seen in /pæt/ and /pet/.

It's essential to appreciate that phonemic contrasts such as /t/ vs /d/ exist regardless of the exact way in which we pronounce them, otherwise we'll never be able to explain the differences between regional and social accents. For instance, most people in Ireland pronounce them with the tip of the tongue against their top teeth (p. 28), whereas most people in England pronounce them with the tongue-tip against the ridge behind the top teeth; and most people in India pronounce them with the tongue-tip curled back towards the palate (a *retroflex* pronunciation). But everyone in Ireland, England, and India is making the same contrast, when they are saying *tie* and *die*. They're using the same phonemes, even though they're pronouncing them in slightly different ways. And in a more detailed phonetic transcription, we could draw attention to these tiny differences. For instance, we can show the Irish articulation of /t/ and /d/ by using a bridge-shaped symbol that means 'dental', as in [t̪] and [d̪].

Another way of getting to understand the notion of a phoneme, which I find helpful, is to think of the letters of the alphabet from the same point of view. Letter *t*, for example, is 'the same' letter, regardless of the way you write it in your own handwriting or the way it appears in the many online fonts: T, **t**, *t*, t … We could therefore talk about <t> being a *grapheme*, and indeed this term, and that angle-bracket notation, is often used in linguistic studies of writing.

Early phoneticians experimented with several versions of the phonetic alphabet before settling on the one we know today. Henry Higgins (p. 11) had an idiosyncratic one, which we glimpse at the beginning of *My Fair Lady*. Shaw says in his preface to *Pygmalion* that he wanted to do something to publicize phonetics, which he felt was not being given enough attention at universities like Oxford. He was right: the only phonetics department at the time was one that had been started by Daniel Jones at University College London. Shaw was unequivocal: 'if the play makes the public aware that there are such people as phoneticians and that they are among the most important people in England at present, it will serve its turn.' Eighty years later, novelist Anthony Burgess made a similar point in the epilogue to his language memoir, *A Mouthful of Air*: 'Phonetics, phonetics, and again phonetics. There cannot be too much phonetics.'

Jones gave Shaw advice on the details of English pronunciation, and invited him to see his phonetics department at University College London. The technology used in Higgins's laboratory in the script (and film) is based on what he saw there. Indeed, Higgins might have been called Jones, were it not for the sensibilities of the time. Flattering as the idea might seem at first, we can immediately imagine the real-life source finding aspects of Higgins's character unflattering. The plot contained taboo language (Eliza says 'bloody' at one point), and Higgins – to put it in modern terms – has an affair with one of his students. In *The Real Professor Higgins*, Jones's biographers conclude that he wanted to distance himself from the character and the play, and that Shaw agreed.

According to one of Jones's students, the name of Higgins was borrowed from a London shop sign. It seems that Shaw was travelling on a bus through South London, wondering what name he should give his character, and saw the shop name 'Jones and Higgins'. The student recalled DJ saying, 'he could not call me Jones, so he called me Higgins.'

Actually, Higgins wasn't so much a phonetician, in the modern sense, as an elocutionist. He didn't just want to describe and explain Eliza's pronunciation: he wanted to change it, so that it became more like the cultured speech of society at that time. When Daniel Jones saw the play on its first night, he was furious. He commented drily: 'In *Pygmalion* phonetics is represented as providing a key to social advancement, a function which it may be hoped it will not be called upon to perform indefinitely.' Phoneticians don't go around wanting to change the way people speak.

Burgess's emphasis is warranted. Anyone wanting to engage in the serious study of speech cannot do without phonetics. This book, and others like it, would have been unwritable without it. Phonetics provides the basic tools of the trade – the detailed description of how the vocal organs and auditory mechanisms work, and the symbols enabling us to write down sounds accurately and unambiguously. Showing the differences between accents would be impossible without a transcription. Phonetics also explains many features of pronunciation, such as why some sounds run together in connected speech, and why some disappear. And it has some hugely important applications, not least these days in the fields of speech synthesis and recognition (see further, Chapter 26). When you talk to your computer or phone and it talks back to you, don't forget to thank the phonetic researchers who helped to make it all possible.

Three early phoneticians

Daniel Jones (1881–1967)
Professor of Phonetics,
University College London

Henry Sweet (1845–1912)
Lecturer in Phonetics,
Oxford University

Paul Passy (1859–1940)
Founder of the Phonetic
Teachers' Association

trwazjɛm seri dy m.f.
nymero 122.

lə

mɛːtrə fɔnetik

ɔrgan də l asɔsjasjõ fɔnetik ɛ̃tɛrnasjɔnal

swasɑ̃tdiznœvjɛm ane də l asɔsjasjõ

trwazjɛm seri.—karɑ̃tdøzjɛm ane, ʒyjɛ-desɑ̃:br, 1964

somɛːr

artiklə də fõ.—William F. Stirling† (A. C. G.).—pærə-læŋgwiʒ ənd əðir θiŋz (George L. Trager).—ən əproutʃ tʊ ə rɪplaɪ (David Crystal).—ə fə'netik 'duːdl (W. Stannard Allen).

korɛspõdɑ̃:s.—trænskripʃn in **m.f.** (W. R. Lee).

kõtrɑ̃dy.—*In Honour of Daniel Jones* (D. Crystal).—B. Sundby, *Studies in the Middle English Material of Worcestershire Records* (C. J. E. Ball).—D. Abercrombie, *English Phonetic Texts* (J. C. Wells).—B. Malmberg, *La Fonética* (D. R. Powell).—L. A. Hill and J. M. Ure, *English Sounds and Spellings. Tests* (J. W. Lewis).

parti dez elɛːv.—frɑ̃sɛ.—ˌita'ljaːno.

parti administratiːv.—nuvo mɑ̃:br.—ʃɑ̃ʒmɑ̃ d adrɛs.

uvraːʒ rəsy.

The front page of an issue of Le Maître phonétique
(1964). The French origins of the IPA are clearly seen in the headings. Proper names are not phonetically transcribed.

3
The basic system

How many phonemes are there in the English sound system? That depends a little on the accent people have, but most English accents have 44: 24 consonants and 20 vowels. I'll describe some of the differences later, but to begin with it's easiest to take one accent and use that as the yardstick against which others can be compared. Usually, in British accounts of English speech, this is the one Daniel Jones described as Received Pronunciation – from now on, *RP* – so I'll follow that practice here, referring to differences (such as in American English) as I go along. For people in Britain, and for many abroad, it's the accent traditionally associated with the BBC.

The phoneticians were faced with a major problem when they tried to transcribe these phonemes: there are only 26 letters (graphemes) in the English alphabet. There just aren't enough letters to describe all 44 vowel and consonant phonemes. How is the difference to be handled?

The consonants don't present much of a problem. There are 21 letters of the alphabet to help identify the 24 English consonants, and many of the letters show a relationship with the sounds that makes it easy to grasp their pronunciations. So when we see the consonant phonemes of English written down in a phonetic way, it's not too difficult to 'hear' what is going on, and a good technique is to say the words aloud as you read through the list. (If you are in a public place while reading this, you might get some strange looks – but that is one of the perils of being a phonetician.) There are just seven cases where a special symbol is required:

/p/ as in **p**in, a**pp**le, ri**p**
/b/ as in **b**ig, ta**b**le, ro**b**
/t/ as in **t**op, wri**t**er, po**t**
/d/ as in **d**og, ra**d**ar, be**d**
/k/ as in **k**in, ta**k**ing, ro**ck**
/g/ as in **g**ot, bi**gg**er, hu**g**
/f/ as in **f**at, ri**f**le, o**ff**
/v/ as in **v**an, sa**v**ing, lo**v**e
/θ/ as in **th**in, ear**th**ly, pa**th**
/ð/ as in **th**is, mo**th**er, see**the**
/s/ as in **s**it, ru**s**tic, pa**ss**
/z/ as in **z**ip, bu**zz**er, ha**s**
/ʃ/ as in **sh**op, bi**sh**op, ma**sh**
/ʒ/ as in **g**igolo, confu**s**ion, mira**g**e
/tʃ/ as in **ch**est, bu**tch**er, ca**tch**
/dʒ/ as in **j**est, ba**dg**er, lo**dge**
/h/ as in **h**ot, un**h**and
/m/ as in **m**ap, su**mm**er, di**m**
/n/ as in **n**et, de**n**y, wi**n**
/ŋ/ as in ha**ng**er, si**ng**
/l/ as in **l**ip, po**l**ice, foo**l**
/r/ as in **r**ip, ca**rr**ot, and in many regional accents also after a vowel, as in sta**r**
/w/ as in **w**ell, un**w**illing

Vowels are a different story. English has 20 vowels (in most accents) and there are only five vowel letters in the alphabet: *a, e, i, o,* and *u.* So there are inevitably going to be additional unfamiliar symbols in a phonetic transcription, to capture all the possibilities. Writing about vowels is never straightforward, therefore, and the auditory impressions conveyed are bound to be approximate to anyone who hasn't been trained in phonetics. But even a general impression can be illuminating, and it can be reinforced by using lots of good examples.

We first need to get a clear sense of each of the 20 vowels. The easiest way I know to do this is to say a set of words that differ only in the vowel they use, and get into the habit of associating the vowels with their symbols. In RP, where /r/ is not pronounced after vowels, almost all of the 20 can be heard within the frame *b--d*. In saying them aloud, bear in mind that there will be some regional variations, which I'll describe later. They are shown in the table below, using the order most often found in phonetics textbooks, and illustrating some of the ways phoneticians have transcribed them to avoid the ambiguities that arise from the way English is normally spelled. The reason there are alternative symbols is that in phonetics, as in any subject, there are schools of thought that differ in their views about the best way of analysing vowels. But each school uses its symbols in a consistent way. In this book I will use only the symbols shown in the first column.

b--d frame	Symbols used in this book	Other symbols
bead	iː	ii, ij
bid	ɪ	i
bed	e	ɛ
bad	æ	a
bud	ʌ	
bard	ɑː	aː, aa
bod (as in *odd bod*)	ɒ	o
bored[1]	ɔː	oo

b--d frame	Symbols used in this book	Other symbols
book[2]	ʊ	u
booed	u:	uu, uw
bird	ɜ:	ə:, əə, ər, ɜr[3], ɝ[3]
ga<u>ber</u>dine	ə	ər[3], ɚ[3]
bayed	eɪ	ei, ɛɪ, ej
bide (my time)	aɪ	ai, aj
buoyed (me up)	ɔɪ	ɔi, oi, ɔj
bode (well)[1]	əʊ	əu, oʊ, ou, əw
bowed (my head)	ɑʊ	au, aw
beard	ɪə	iə, ir[3]
bared	ɛə	eə, er[3], ɛr[3]
boor[2]	ʊə	uə, ur[3]

1 In some regional accents illustrated later in the book, these vowels are pronounced with the lips more closely rounded (Chapter 14), and given the symbol /o:/.

2 These are the two vowels which don't easily fit into the *b--d* frame in RP, unless we accept an abbreviation like *Bud* (with a short rounded vowel, for *Budapest*) and imagine a verb *I boored* (from *to boor*); but of course they have their own contrasts in other frames: *book* contrasts with *back*, *bake*, etc., and *boor* with *beer*, *bare*, etc.

3 These symbols would be used in accents where /r/ is always pronounced after vowels.

You'll notice that the first twelve vowels in this list are represented by a single symbol and the other eight have two. Each letter represents a particular auditory quality, so the difference between the two groups is that the former have a single quality, whereas the latter have two. Pronounce /i:/, for example, and hold it for a few seconds: it is the same sound throughout. By contrast, pronounce /aɪ/ slowly – as in an emphatic *why* – and you'll hear the sound change from an /a/ quality similar to that in *man* to an /ɪ/ quality similar to that in *sit*. Vowels that maintain the same auditory quality throughout are called *pure vowels* or *monophthongs* – a term that originated in Greek, meaning 'having a single sound'. Those that change their quality are called *diphthongs* – 'having two sounds' – a word that has two pronunciations: 'dip-thong' (the earliest one) and 'dif-thong' (following the spelling). Whether a vowel has one or two qualities is a really important factor when it comes to discussing the differences between regional accents (Chapter 12).

It's admittedly a rather artificial exercise, to sound out vowels in a frame, or to find contrasts such as *tie* and *die*. These techniques do have a value, because they help us develop a sense of how the sound system (the *phonology*) of a language works. But they are a long way from the realities of everyday speech, as encountered in conversations, political speeches, radio broadcasts, advertising slogans, the names of aliens and cartoon characters, and all the other circumstances where we find pronunciation at work. The study of pronunciation comes alive only when we fill the descriptions with lots of real and interesting examples. Thinking of the vowel contrast between *bod* and *bed* is one thing; thinking of it in relation to *Tom and Jerry* is another.

'Description' is the crucial word in all this. Behind every symbol lies a description – of the way the phoneme is articulated. It isn't possible to make much headway in explaining English pronunciation without being able to describe exactly how the various sounds are made. So this is where all studies of phonetics need to begin, with the vocal organs.

Auditory check 1

Hearing whether vowels have one auditory quality (a monophthong) or two (a diphthong) is going to figure prominently in later chapters, so it's as well to check that you can tell the difference now. Here are sixteen words: eight of them have monophthongs in RP, and eight have diphthongs. You can check your decisions on p. 277.

It's important to note that this is a quiz about how these sounds work in RP. If you have a different accent, you may treat these sounds differently (as described in Chapter 12). If your decisions don't agree with those on p. 277, that will probably be a clue about one of the distinctive features of your accent.

	Monophthong	Diphthong
my		
soon		
car		
round		
men		
fur		
mean		
toy		
toe		
sit		
sure		
law		
clear		
say		
hat		
there		

4

How sounds are made

When Lucy was about three, she complained that she had a sore throat. I looked inside her mouth to see which part was inflamed. Naturally enough, she wanted to see it too, so I got a big mirror and told her to look while she opened her mouth as widely as she could. She stared intently for a few seconds, then said: 'There's an awful lot in there.' No phonetician has ever made a wiser remark.

The diagram on the following page shows how right she was. It is the sort of thing we will see in any phonetics textbook: the configuration of the vocal organs inside the mouth and throat as seen from the side – the lips, teeth, and tongue, the two parts of the palate, the two parts of the throat – the pharynx and the larynx – and the vocal folds located behind our Adam's apple. But we see not only the mouth and throat: the nose, ears, skull, and chest are there as well. We might not think of these other parts of the body as 'vocal organs', but they are intimately involved with pronunciation, and mustn't be ignored.

The diagram is static and rather unexciting on the page. It shows the anatomy of the vocal organs, but gives no hint about their physiology – their movement. These days, that can be easily seen online, thanks to films of speech activity using X-rays, ultrasound, or magnetic resonance imaging. Find one showing some natural speech and look at it, before you read much further. Just type 'film of vocal organ movements' into a search engine, and then click on 'videos', and several examples will come up (see References, p. 279). What will you see?

The most noticeable movements involve the tongue and lips. They seem to be performing a beautifully choreographed dance. The tongue rises and falls with great rapidity, sometimes shooting forward towards the teeth and lips like a fish darting for a piece of food. We see the lips protruding and receding. We see the soft palate rising towards the back of the throat to close off the passageway to the nose, then lowering to allow air through. It's the intricate coordination of lips, tongue, and soft palate that is the most impressive feature – everything moving at the same time. Phoneticians call it *coarticulation*.

But the other impressive feature is the scale of the

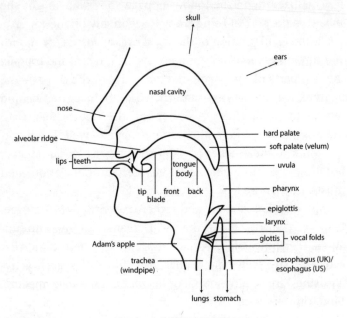

Side view of the vocal organs

operation. Lucy thought the tongue was very small, when she looked at it from the front. From the side we see it is actually very large, its movements controlled by muscles that stretch down in the throat. Normal speech is quite fast – about four or five syllables articulated every second – and it seems extraordinary that such a bulky object can be so flexible and move so fast. That's why we need to include the whole of the head, in any account of the vocal organs, for the coordination is all controlled by the brain. And we need to include the ears, for as we speak we are constantly listening to our pronunciation, partly through the air and partly through the bones of our skull.

We mustn't forget the chest in interpreting our diagram, for without the lungs nothing would happen at all. We can make some speech sounds as we breathe in – a common experience if we try to talk while running, for example – but most speech is produced while we breathe out. The air comes up from the lungs, and passes through the vocal folds before reaching the tongue, nose, and lips, which combine to 'shape' the sounds. The one thing you can't see in the films of mouth movement is the way the vocal folds move and vibrate while air is passing through them. For that, a different technology is required.

You can see film of that too online (see References). The traditional technique is to use mirrors, or to film through a special device such as a laryngoscope; more recently, ultrasound pictures are available. And what we see explains immediately why these vocal organs are called *folds*, instead of the traditional name *vocal cords* (the spelling *vocal chords* has been a popular misspelling for many years). They aren't like cords at all, with its suggestion that they are like taut pieces of vibrating string. They are two stretches of flexible tissue (technically: mucous membrane) that come together and separate rhythmically in a wave-like motion, sometimes gently, sometimes rapidly. It's difficult to describe precisely the nature of the movement: they swell and recede, they ripple, they undulate ... but when we see them in action there's no doubting their sophisticated mobility. They can clash together, as in a cough (or a glottal stop, p. 130). They can come very close together, as when we speak in a whispery or breathy way. They can vibrate at a remarkable number of speeds, ranging from just a few vibrations a second (technically: cycles per second) to several hundred, and this rate controls the intonation and loudness of our speech (p. 34). And when we lose control of them – as happens in a variety of medical conditions – we affirm their fundamental role in pronunciation: we say we have 'lost our voice'.

Writers have made some vivid descriptions of the whole process. My favourite, which captures the spirit of the exercise rather than its precise details, is from Eugène Ionesco's one-act play *The Lesson* (1951), here in Donald Watson's translation. The professor explains how sounds are made to a pupil:

> Air has to be pitilessly forced out of the lungs and then made to pass gently over the vocal cords, lightly brushing them, so that like harps or leaves beneath the wind, they suddenly start quivering, trembling, vibrating, vibrating, vibrating or hissing, or rustling, or bristling, or whistling, and with a whistle set everything in motion: uvula, tongue, palate, teeth ... lips ...
>
> Finally words come out through the nose, the mouth, the ears, the pores of the skin, bringing in their train all the uprooted organs of speech we've just named, a powerful, majestic swarm, no less than what we improperly call the voice, modulating in song or rising in terrible symphonic wrath, a regular procession, sheaves of assorted blossoms,

of sonorous conceits: labials, dentals, plosives, palatals, and the rest, some soft and gentle, some harsh and violent.

This description wouldn't get you high marks in an academic phonetics exam; but it certainly captures the potential evocative power of the voice when it articulates speech – something that those who complain about small points of pronunciation tend to ignore. If there are things to be criticized in someone's pronunciation, there is invariably also a great deal that could be praised.

What are the scientific correlates of the vocal effects that Ionesco impressionistically identifies? The two dimensions – what we say and how we say it – are there. 'Labials, dentals, plosives, palatals …' – these must be referring to consonants, and his description of 'some soft and gentle, some harsh and violent' can be made more precise, as we shall see in later chapters. His reference to modulation in song and rising in wrath clearly refers to our tone of voice. He doesn't separately identify vowels, though I suppose they are hidden within his 'sonorous conceits'.

All of these features – vowels, consonants, tones of voice – are taking place simultaneously when we speak. Any word or sentence can be divided into its vowel and consonant segments; but they can't be spoken without giving them some tone of voice. 'It ain't what we say, but the way that we say it': that's what makes the real impact, whether in a political speech, a religious homily, a stage performance, or just an everyday conversation. 'It's the way you tell 'em,' as comedians like to say about the effectiveness of a joke. So, to explore what is involved in pronunciation in detail, tone of voice is where I like to begin.

5

'Tain't what we say …

… it's the way that we say it. The expression acts as a reminder that there are two dimensions to the sounds of speech. People often think of pronunciation solely in terms of vowels and consonants, and the way these combine into syllables. It's a legacy of the written language. We know what vowels and consonants are because the letters of the alphabet represent them. But 'the way that we say' those vowels and consonants? There are no letters for that.

Punctuation hints at this other dimension. When we see a question mark, we know, if we were to read the sentence aloud, that we should speak it in a questioning way. An exclamation mark? Some sort of exclamatory force. If a word is in capitals or underlined, we make it louder. The everyday term 'tone of voice' is often used to sum up everything that we can do to words to vary their impact. We say such things as 'Don't talk to me in that tone of voice'.

The tone of voice we use often outweighs the meaning conveyed by the vowels and consonants. Whatever a word or sentence might mean, its effect can be altered by changing the tone. We can make an utterance sound routine, surprised, sarcastic, polite, rude, hesitant, and a host of other attitudes and emotions. We can alter the nature of our interaction by changing the tone. If I say, 'I did the right thing, didn't I,' with a definite falling pitch on *didn't*, I'm telling you firmly: I did the right thing. It's a statement, and I might even end it with an exclamation mark. But if I give the word a clearly rising pitch, I'm asking for your advice. I need a question mark. Did I? It's a totally different kind of conversation now.

What are the factors that make up 'tone of voice'? How many such tones are there in English pronunciation? The second question can't be easily answered. The voice can be stretched to express attitudinal nuances in an apparently inexhaustible number of ways – not so much in everyday conversation, unless it gets very emotional, but certainly on stage and screen, where actors push their voices to the limit. No two actors render a speech in exactly the same way: the syllables are the same, but the delivery varies. And even the same actor can vary a performance from one occasion to the next. The variation is what makes a speech fresh and interesting – and what makes speech as a whole fresh and interesting.

Authors do their best to capture the effects. Here are some descriptions:

Jeeves, having said 'Very good, sir', in P. G. Wodehouse, *The Code of the Woosters* (1938), Chapter 1:
He spoke with a certain what-is-it in his voice, and I could see that, if not actually disgruntled, he was far from being gruntled, so I tactfully changed the subject.

Mrs Pardiggle, in Charles Dickens, *Bleak House* (1852–53), Chapter 3:
Always speaking in the same demonstrative, loud, hard tone, so that her voice impressed my fancy as if it had a sort of spectacles on too.

Mr Wyvern, in George Gissing, *Demos* (1886), Chapter 1:
His voice was very deep, and all his words were weighed in the utterance. This deliberation at times led to peculiarities

of emphasis in single words. Probably he was a man of philological crotchets; he said, for instance, 'pro-spect'.

A New Yorker, in Charles Dickens, *Martin Chuzzlewit* (1843–44), Chapter 16:
[Martin smiled], partly occasioned by what the gentleman said, and partly by his manner of saying it, which was odd enough, for he emphasized all the small words and syllables in his discourse, and left the others to take care of themselves: as if he thought the larger parts of speech could be trusted alone, but the little ones required to be constantly looked after.

Ralph Nickleby, in Charles Dickens, *Nicholas Nickleby* (1838–39), Chapter 10:
If an iron door could be supposed to quarrel with its hinges, and to make a firm resolution to open with slow obstinacy, and grind them to powder in the process, it would emit a pleasanter sound in so doing than did these words in the rough and bitter voice in which they were uttered by Ralph.

Fergus, as described by Maud, in Antonia Byatt's *Possession* (1990), Chapter 14:
He's one of those men who argues by increments of voice – so that as you open your mouth he says another, cleverer, louder thing.

The variations seem to be infinite, but they can in fact be analysed into just six interacting factors.

Pitch

This is an attribute of auditory sensation that allows us to describe sounds on a scale from 'high' to 'low'. We can say something high up or low down, or mix the two levels, or gradually ascend or descend through our pitch range. Most of the time we speak using the lower third of our range. We 'raise our voices' from our norm when there is some emotional involvement, such as surprise or excitement. Or we can 'lower our voices', as when we make a parenthetic remark or want to sound conspiratorial. Each language has its own range of tones and tunes that perform these roles and make up its *intonation* system. Intonation is the linguistic use of pitch. We notice it mainly when it varies among languages or among accents. We talk about them using such terms as 'musical', 'monotone', or 'sing-song'. And when a new use of intonation comes along, it can cause headlines – such as 'uptalk'. I'll explore this further in Chapter 6.

Loudness

This is an attribute of auditory sensation that allows us to describe sounds on a scale from 'loud' to 'soft'. We can say something at various level of loudness, which in music would be described using the terms *forte* and *piano* (or *fortissimo* and *pianissimo*). And, again as with music, we can change these levels suddenly or gradually, as with the notions of *crescendo* and *diminuendo*. Each language has its own way of making its syllables, words, and sentences relatively loud or soft. In English, word meanings can often be distinguished by the loudness of a particular syllable, as when we distinguish the noun *record* from the verb: *I'm going to record a record*. The same applies to *increase* and *increase*, *permit* and *permit*, *rebel* and *rebel*, and many more such pairs. The contrast is said to be one of *stress*, or (in a different sense of the word from earlier) *accent*. It's one of the features of English pronunciation that foreign learners of English find challenging, along with the stress pattern of every other English word, which is far from predictable. And it's one of the features that can change quite quickly over time, so that complaints about stress – such as saying *research* as *research* – always figure in any usage list. I'll explore this further in Chapter 7.

Rate

This is an attribute of auditory sensation that allows us to describe sounds on a scale from 'fast' to 'slow'. The speed at which we speak is also sometimes called *tempo*, and here too there is an analogy with musical terms. Fast speech: *allegro* and *allegrissimo*. Slow speech: *lento* and *lentissimo*. Gradually increasing speed: *accelerando*. Gradually decreasing speed: *rallentando*. Everyone has a normal speech rate: some are naturally fast speakers, some slow. Accents too have their norms: some are spoken at a faster rate than others. But everyone varies their speed, usually based on the emotion of the moment – for example, speeding up when excited, or slowing down to make a Really – Interesting – Point. I'll explore this further in Chapter 6.

Rhythm

This is our perception of regularity in speech – or its absence, irregularity. It relies on a combination of pitch, loudness, and rate. If we are speaking rhythmically, we are speaking at a regular rate, within which we make certain syllables louder or higher than others in a regular way. In short, we give speech a 'beat', just as in music. I suppose most of us were first introduced to the rhythms of English in school, through the metres of traditional English poetry. The rhythm of famous lines helps them stay in the mind: 'The curfew tolls the knell of parting day ...' , 'Not a drum was heard, not a funeral

<u>note</u> ...' But rhythm goes well beyond poetry. Everything we say has a certain rhythm to it, which we especially notice when someone departs from the norm and begins to speak unrhythmically, as when drunk or in an uncertain frame of mind. I'll talk about this in Chapter 7.

Pause

It's easy to forget about pause, when talking about pronunciation. Pause is, after all, basically silence. But it is a critical factor, because it defines the boundaries of what we pronounce, and can itself influence the way we perceive speech to be acceptable or not. If people pause too much, we talk about them being 'non-fluent' or 'hesitant'. If they don't pause enough, they are said to 'gabble' or 'clutter'. Either way, erratic pausing can cause difficulties of intelligibility, and can be strongly criticized in public settings where we expect speakers to be in control. A politician who pauses too much is going to give a poor impression. And if people give frequent voice to their pauses – in English usually written down as *er* or *erm* – the effect can seriously impede communication. The occasional *er*(*m*) is natural and universal; but if we punctuate every sentence with an *er* or an *um*, something is going very wrong. That's the subject of Chapter 10.

Everything we say has to be spoken with a certain pitch, loudness, rate, and rhythm, and be demarcated by pauses, so it's handy to have a way of referring to all of these factors at once. They are often called the *prosodic features* of speech – or *prosody*, for short. I'll be referring to *prosody* quite a lot in later chapters. When I do, remember that I'm talking about speech in general, and not just poetry. There's a long history of the term *prosody* being used only in relation to the metrical structure of poetic lines. Poetic prosody is indeed part of the general study of prosody, as we'll see in Chapter 9, but it isn't the whole story.

Timbre

Prosody accounts for most of 'the way that we say it', which is why the above five factors will each be explored in a separate chapter. But there is a further group of vocal effects that enter into any description of tone of voice, and they aren't covered by those headings. In my literary quotations above, we can see how pitch, loudness, rate, rhythm, and pause are present in the characterizations of Jeeves, Pardiggle, the American, Fergus, and Wyvern – but what about Pardiggle's 'hard voice' or Nickleby's 'rough and bitter voice'? That is more a matter of the overall sound of the voice – what is often described as *timbre*. Here are some other examples of timbre effects:

- Somebody says 'look out' in a whisper – a conspiratorial tone of voice.
- A famous female film star says 'Do come in' in a breathy or husky way – a sexy tone of voice.
- M tells off her secret agent saying 'Oh Bond, Bond, Bond' in a creaky or gravelly way – a disparaging tone of voice.
- Somebody addresses their loved one with lips pouting and rounded (p. 97), and says, as if in baby talk, 'Aw, did it hurt then' – a teasing tone of voice.

Similarly, we can add a nasal twang to our pronunciation, spread our lips to produce a 'smiling' tone of voice, or add a spasmodic effect, as when we speak while laughing, giggling, sobbing, or crying.

In all these cases, the effect is one-off: we switch on the

whisper, the breathiness, the creak, the lip-rounding, the giggling for a short time, and then resume our normal voice. Of course, some people always talk in a breathy or creaky voice; it's part of their *voice quality* – the permanently present background characteristic in their voice that allows us to recognize who they are. But most of us deliberately add these features to our speech to make an effect as occasion arises. They aren't as central a part of English pronunciation as are the prosodic features, therefore. Phoneticians call these occasional tones of voice *paralinguistic* features – from Greek *para*, meaning 'alongside, beside'. They are features that seem to act along with the rest of the pronunciation system, rather than play a central role in it.

So, technically, our perception of tones of voice is the result of the way people combine prosodic and paralinguistic features. All the vocal organs play a part, with the vocal folds crucially involved, vibrating in different ways. Intonation relies primarily on the frequency of vocal fold vibration: the faster the vibrations, the higher the voice. Loudness relates to the intensity of the vibrations. M's creaky effect is produced by letting the folds vibrate very slowly. The sexy film star gets her breathiness by keeping them further apart than in normal speech, so that extra breath from the lungs passes through them. When we whisper, the folds aren't vibrating at all. And all the spasmodic effects rely on the way pulses of air from the lungs are repeatedly stopped and released.

When we say we've 'lost our voice', what we mean is we've lost the ability to make our vocal folds vibrate. We find ourselves able to speak only in a whispery, husky way. Such speech doesn't just sound odd; it can actually be quite difficult to make ourselves understood. This is because the vocal folds are also critically involved in the production of the individual speech sounds of English – all of the vowels and half of the consonants. We'll explore those in later chapters, after looking in greater detail at what is actually involved in 'the way that we say it'.

6

High and low

Intonation is the use of pitch to convey meaning in a language. It has been described as the music or melody of speech. That gets the basic idea across, but it's not a perfect analogy. In music, whether instrumental or vocal, we notice when players or singers are 'out of tune', and the performers take great pains to ensure that this doesn't happen. But people do not speak out of tune (unless they suffer from certain kinds of disability). We do not need to tap a tuning fork before we begin a conversation to ensure that our speech is in the right key or at the right pitch.

So it would be misleading to transcribe the melody of speech using a musical stave and a key signature, as I've sometimes seen. When we acquire a language, we learn to make our voice rise and fall in pitch in a limited number of ways to express various meanings, but nobody is checking to make sure that each of these variations is at exactly the same pitch level as everyone else's. As long as the variations roughly correspond, we'll understand what's being said well enough.

The important word to note is 'limited'. In theory we have an indefinite number of pitches at our disposal, within the limits of our voice range. Say 'ah' at the lowest pitch you can make, and then glide upwards to your highest pitch. Most people have a voice range (or *vocal register*) of up to two octaves. We could take any word or sentence and say it at any of the levels within that range. In practice, we tend to speak at certain levels, and we vary the pitches in just a small number of ways.

People find it most comfortable to talk in the lower third of their voice range. If they get excited or angry or surprised, they will then 'raise their voices' – which means increasing both their pitch and loudness. It doesn't happen the other way round. If people are physically and psychologically normal, they don't speak routinely in a high-pitched and loud voice, and lower it only from time to time. (I know there are exceptions!)

Usually, when we're talking, what we're saying doesn't require much pitch variation. What we want to talk about can be said in a 'matter-of-fact' tone of voice, and in most English accents that basic everyday tone is heard as a low falling pitch at the end of a sentence. Imagine being asked when your next dental appointment is: *It's three o'clock on Monday*. Unless you have some particular reason to be surprised about this, that piece of information will be communicated in an unemotional way, with the pitch gradually descending from the beginning to the end of the sentence, and with a final falling glide on *Monday*, making that the most prominent word in the sentence. Most of our sentences are pronounced in a similar way.

Of course, if we have a special reason to do so, we can make a different word the most prominent one. If somebody has just suggested your appointment was at four, you could reply with *It's three o'clock on Monday*. Any sentence has to be seen in context in this way. Bringing the prominence forward in a sentence always tells us something:

> In the garden was a man in a grey coat. Implies: Nothing remarkable.
> In the garden was a man in a grey coat. Implies: Not green, red …

In the garden was a <u>man</u> in a grey coat. Implies: Not a woman, child …

In the <u>garden</u> was a man in a grey coat. Implies: Not in the house, street …

Emphasizing the wrong word can be misleading, therefore, as learners of English as a foreign language soon discover: *I've just been talking to your <u>beautiful</u> daughter* (implication: not the plain one.)

Emphasizing the wrong word can also be distracting, and this is one of the behaviours that irritated my Radio 4 listeners. Presenters often try to make their voices more interesting by adding extra pitch variation, and if they're not careful they can end up making an unimportant word prominent. Prepositions are the commonest cases. Here are two examples I heard recently, one from a weather forecast, the other from a music programme:

The rain will spread <u>into</u> Scotland by tomorrow morning.

That was symphony number five <u>by</u> Gustav Mahler.

In neither case is there any kind of semantic contrast. And the risk is that, by stressing the wrong word, the listener's attention is taken away from the important words, especially if the presenter lowers the voice pitch immediately afterwards – another common complaint – so that in the second example we strain to catch the name of the composer.

Moving the emphasis 'horizontally' – backwards and forwards in a sentence – is one way of changing the meaning. The other way is to change the pitch on a particular word – ringing the 'vertical' changes. The most frequently occurring of all these changes is the way a statement can be turned into a question by replacing the low falling tone with a high rising one: *It's three o'clock on Monday?* The punctuation mark gives us the required clue in writing; in speech the intonation conveys the grammatical contrast.

Several grammatical constructions need intonation to express their meaning. For instance, tag questions (such as *isn't it, aren't they, won't we*) depend on it. They're called questions because, from their grammatical shape, they seem to be asking about something – but whether they have a questioning force depends on how they are said. With a rising tone on the verb, they 'ask'; but with a falling tone, they 'tell'. Where's Michael?

> He's in the garden, isn't he? (I'm asking you in order to find out.)
> He's in the garden, isn't he! (I'm telling you that's where he is. Silly of you to ask!)

Sometimes people don't articulate the tone clearly enough, which elicits the reaction: 'Are you asking me or telling me?' (There are some other examples in my Appendix chapter, p. 275.)

This grammatical function of intonation has led to it being called 'the punctuation of speech'. But that captures only a small part of what intonation does. Its other main function is to express emotion, and here it far exceeds punctuation, which isn't fit for purpose as far as emotional nuance is concerned. A sentence such as *She'll be there by three o'clock* can be said in many different tones of voice – angry, irritated, reassuring, surprised, and so on – but there's no punctuational way of showing the differences. Writers have to gloss the semantics: 'he said angrily / in a surprised tone / with just a hint of irritation …'

I said above, 'in most English accents'. In some parts of the English-speaking world, the everyday 'matter-of-fact' tone is expressed through a rising pitch, not a falling one.

When people talk of a Welsh accent as being very melodic, what they are hearing is the way statements are given a rising lilt. Similar effects can be heard in other Celtic parts of the British Isles, in various cities in northern England (such as Newcastle and Liverpool), in some parts of the USA (especially the south), and in several countries where English is spoken as a foreign language, and where the intonation has been influenced by the speakers' mother tongues (such as the Philippines).

Variation in intonation is also very noticeable when we listen to occupations that rely on speech for their impact. We need only think of the auditory impression conveyed, when exercising their profession, by sports commentators, newsreaders, church ministers, auctioneers, and drill sergeants. Then there's the range of expression we encounter in television advertisements and on the stage, where the overall effect is heavily dependent on intonation, along with the other features described in the previous chapter. Individuals too may have their prosodic distinctiveness: the way we use intonation can be one of the critical features that allow others to recognize us from our voice alone.

The link between intonation and music becomes most noticeable when we introduce a musical quotation into our speech, to convey a general meaning, just as we might use a literary quotation from literature in our writing. I've heard people sometimes say *Hallelujah!* when a satisfactory outcome has been achieved, but instead of saying it they sing it – not necessarily in tune – as the opening bars of the chorus from Handel's *Messiah*. I've heard a vocal rendition of orchestral fragments, such as the theme from *Jaws*. The jocular expression of what the speaker anticipates will be a dangerous social situation is conveyed by the dramatic sounding out of the film's ominous low-pitched glissando quavers. I've come across people simulating the themes from *The Twilight Zone*, *Doctor Who*, *Dragnet*, *The Prisoner*, the shower-room scene in *Psycho*, Laurel and Hardy's clumsy walk music, the alien tone-sequence in *Close Encounters of the Third Kind*, the whistled motif from Clint Eastwood's spaghetti western films, the chase music from a Keystone Kops film, and the opening notes of Beethoven's Fifth Symphony.

The extracts are usually highly stereotyped and brief. An allusion may be just a couple of notes, but that is all that is needed. Someone who arrives in a room with something special to show may accompany it with the fanfare from a racecourse, or just a simple stylized tune, *Ta-daa*. Some of these tunes cross the generations, and fall halfway between music and speech, such as the sing-song call to eat, *Come and ge-e-t it* or the children's catcalling tune, *Nah nah na nah-nah*. There are even intonational idioms, where the pitch pattern is fixed by tradition, as in the pantomime exchange when something dangerous appears behind the actors: 'Oh no there isn't', says an actor; 'Oh yes there is', howl the audience.

Children home in on these effects because intonation, along with rhythm, is the earliest linguistic feature to be acquired. At around nine months of age, the various cries, coos, and babbles, which have no linguistic content, are replaced by vocalizations that are language-specific. It's at this age that babies begin to 'sound English' or 'sound French' or 'sound Chinese', conveying in their primitive utterance the basic prosodic features of the language or languages they are in the process of learning. Soon after, they make their 'first words', spoken with intonation patterns that mark them out as one-word sentences. *Mama!* says the child, with a definite falling tune, meaning 'There's Mummy'. *Mama?* says the child, with a definite rising tune, hearing some footsteps, meaning 'Is that Mummy?' *Mamaaa*, says the child, with an extended level tone, meaning 'Pick me up, Mummy'. And before long these tunes are being reinforced by the catchy intonations and rhythms of nursery rhymes and interactive games such as 'Pat-a-cake' and 'This little piggy'. It will take several years before all the tones and tunes are acquired, with all their meaningful nuances, but the foundation of a language's intonation system is well established by the time a child enters its third year. If you take three-year-olds to a pantomime, you will hear them scream 'Oh yes there is' as loudly and confidently as any of their older siblings.

Why is intonation so important for young children? Because it is an essential way of making sense of the flow of adult utterance they hear around them. We speak in bursts, limited by the amount we can say in a breath, and by the structure of the sentences we are saying. We-do-not-speak-in-long-sentences-like-this-which-are-organized-into-several-grammatical-constructions-with-no-pauses-between-them-because-if-we-did-that-our-listen-ers-would-have-great-difficulty-trying-to-take-everything-in. We break sentences down into chunks, such as phrases and clauses that are easier for our brains to process, both as speakers and as listeners. Punctuation is partly a guide to this organization in writing. In speech, intonation, along with rhythm and pause, does the same job.

It is easy to show the valuable role intonation plays in our ability to remember what has been said. Ask a partner to repeat exactly what you say. Speak a sequence of numerals, beginning with a sequence of two, then three, then four, and so on. Make sure that each one is said with a falling tone and is separated by a pause: 6, 3, 8, 5, 7, 4, 9, 2 ... Listeners have no difficulty remembering and repeating a sequence of three or four numerals at a time, but after five most begin to have some trouble, and many give up altogether. However, if you bring the numerals together into rhythmical intonational 'chunks', you will find they can remember quite long stretches: 6385 / 7492 – like a telephone number. Children need the same strategy when they are learning to decode, remember, and eventually repeat the speech they hear around them; and caretaker adults instinctively break their speech down into smaller chunks that they know their children will find easy to follow.

Intonation, along with its associated prosodic features, is much more than the melody of speech; it is the primary organizational principle underlying spoken discourse. And it must have had an early evolutionary status, crossing the human–animal communication barrier, judging by the role it plays when we train dogs, for example, to respond to commands. In the beginning, perhaps, was the tune.

Uptalk?

You're familiar with uptalk? It's the use of a high rising tone at the end of a statement? As a way of checking that your listener has understood you? For those who speak this way habitually, and for their listeners, it sounds like a never-ending series of questions. Inevitably – as with any linguistic feature that is used with great frequency – it has attracted some criticism.

When did it start? The popular view is that it's a very recent thing, and until I started to research the matter I thought so too. In fact, 'I wuz there' when it first came to public attention. It was 1980. I was in Perth, Western Australia, speaking at a convention of the Australian Association of Speech and Hearing. The local television channel asked me for an interview, which I assumed was going to be about the conference, children's language, and suchlike. But all that the interviewer wanted me to comment on was 'this recent upward inflection that has come in from New Zealand'.

Certainly, the phenomenon became increasingly noticed during the 1980s, and in the UK came to the attention of a wider audience through the Australian soap *Neighbours*. But British people were already familiar with uptalk because of American films and television, where it had been around from at least the days of the Californian hippies in the 1960s (you know?). And in Britain, it had an even longer history, for several regional accents of the British Isles have always been associated with a rising lilt on statements, especially in the Celtic fringe. When people describe, say, the Welsh accent as 'musical', that's what they're noticing. We hear it strongly in Scotland and Northern Ireland too. And in view of the known presence of Celtic speakers of English among the first immigrants to Australia, that's probably how it got into the Antipodean accent in the first place.

I searched for earlier references to uptalk, and eventually found one in 1775. This was in Joshua Steele's essay on *The Melody and Measure of Speech* (1775) – the first attempt I know of to transcribe intonational patterns using a musical notation. It would be very useful, he says, to develop an exact notation to describe 'how much the voice is let down in the conclusion of periods, with respect both to loudness and tone, according to the practice of the best speakers ... for I have observed, that many speakers offend in this article; some keeping up their ends too high.' He clearly didn't like it.

The spread of uptalk has been interesting. At first it was largely confined to young women, especially teenagers, but then it spread to young men, and since has been steadily working its way up the age range. Although many people still say they dislike it, its value lies in its succinctness: it allows someone to make a statement and ask a question at the same time. If I say *I've just visited my friend Peter?*, the rising intonation acts as a comprehension check: I'm assuming you know who Peter is, but I want to make sure. It's the equivalent of an unspoken question ('Do you know who he is?'). If you do know, you will simply nod and let me continue. If you don't, my intonation offers you a chance to get clarification ('Who he?'). I don't need to spell out the options. If there are several people listening to me, I am offering all of them the opportunity to intervene.

Uptalk also has an important social role, as it's an easy way of establishing rapport. If I use it, I assume you know what I'm talking about, so we must know each other well enough. Among a group of friends, who share a common social milieu, each instance of a rising tone on a statement says, in effect: 'Of course you know what I'm talking about, because we're mates.' That's probably the main reason it caught on so much among teenagers: it affirmed, in a trim and easy way, mutual recognition as members of a circle.

7

Loud and soft

When the poet Samuel Rogers died in 1855, anecdotes from his famous breakfast-time conversations were published as *Recollections of the Table-talk of Samuel Rogers*. One of them reads:

> The now fashionable pronunciation of several words is to me at least very offensive: _contemplate_ – is bad enough; but _balcony_ makes me sick.

Balcony is of course the normal pronunciation today; nobody would pronounce it in any other way. But in Rogers' time it was pronounced _balcohny_. And people in fashionable society pronounced *contemplate* as *contemplate*.

That has always been the story of English stress: it changes, over relatively short periods of time. Our great-grandparents would have been part of the society where Rogers' pronunciations were normal. Go back a further generation and the contrast with the present-day becomes even more noticeable. We find hundreds of examples in John Walker's *Critical Pronouncing Dictionary and Expositor of the English Language* (1791): *advertise*, *etiquette*, and *inopportune* all with stress on the final syllable; *cement*, *centenary*, and *explain* all with stress on the first syllable; and *concentrate*, *demonstrate*, and *denigrate* (the *i* pronounced as in *pine*), all with stress on the second. Walker adds the occasional note, recognizing that not everyone uses stress (he calls it *accent*) in the same way, and anticipates Rogers in his note on *contemplate*:

> There is a very prevailing propensity to pronounce this word with the accent on the first syllable; a propensity which ought to be checked by every lover of the harmony of language.

But in other notes he recognizes (reluctantly) the unavoidable role of language change and customary usage. This is what he has to say about *commendable*:

> This word, like *Acceptable*, has, since Johnson wrote his Dictionary [1755], shifted its accent from the second to the first syllable. The sound of the language certainly suffers by these transitions of accent. However, when custom has once decided, we may complain, but we must still acquiesce. The accent on the second syllable of this word is grown vulgar, and there needs no other reason for banishing it from polite pronunciation.

But what pronunciation does polite society use today? *Commendable*. The 'vulgar' one. And in another three generations' time – who knows?

Over the centuries, stress in English words has moved backwards and forwards depending on a range of factors. Part of the variation is due to the way in which two different stress systems came into contact with each other in the early Middle Ages. In Old English, spoken in Britain from the fifth to the eleventh centuries, the main stress occurred on the first syllable in a word, with only a few exceptions. But from the eleventh century, following the Norman Conquest, French became the language of power, and thousands of French words came into English, stressed in a different way. The effect was seismic.

There's a huge difference between the two languages, as can be clearly heard today. English is a language where the rhythm is basically an alternation of strong and weak stresses – what is informally described as a 'tum-te-tum' rhythm, and technically as a *stress-timed* rhythm. The stresses fall at roughly regular intervals in the stream of speech – and if you say this sentence aloud you'll hear that effect:

> The <u>stress</u>es <u>fall</u> at <u>rough</u>ly <u>reg</u>ular <u>int</u>ervals <u>in</u> the <u>stream</u> of <u>speech.</u>

It's an effect that is most noticeable in the rhythm of traditional poetry, such as the iambic pentameter (p. 69). By contrast, French is a language where *each* syllable has a stress – what is informally described as a 'rat-tat-tat' rhythm, and technically as a *syllable-timed* rhythm – with the main emphasis falling on the last syllable of a word. A French speaker would say *Cana<u>da</u>* and *Norman<u>die</u>* whereas an English speaker says *<u>Cana</u>da* and *<u>Nor</u>mandy*.

When new words arrived in English, in the Middle English period, many quickly adapted to the English stress pattern; but the poetic texts of the period, with their regular metre, show that the French pronunciation was not forgotten. Chaucer uses both in the General Prologue to *The Canterbury Tales* – for example, in *virtue*. In line 4 (shown here in modern spelling) we hear the stress on the second syllable:

> Of <u>which</u> vir<u>tue</u> engen<u>dered</u> <u>is</u> the <u>flower</u>,

and in line 307, in describing the Clerk of Oxford, we hear it on the first, as today:

> <u>Sound</u>ing in <u>mor</u>al <u>vir</u>tue <u>was</u> his <u>speech</u>

We would expect usage to favour one or the other over time,

and this is what happened to *virtue*. But the examples in Walker, and in earlier dictionaries, show that many words retained a double pronunciation, with different regions and social groups making different choices, for quite some time. He repeatedly draws his readers' attention to the alternatives, for example describing <u>dec</u>orous as 'uneducated' and de<u>co</u>rous as 'learned', and adds usage notes where he reflects on the reasons.

He has an especially long note about *academy*, which he observes was pronounced <u>aca</u>demy by Shakespeare and Johnson – a pronunciation that was still around in his day, though a<u>ca</u>demy had become the norm:

> That it was accented on the first syllable till within these
> few years, is pretty generally remembered.

Why the change? He thinks it was due to French influence:

> it may be conjectured with some probability, that a fondness
> for pronouncing like the French has been the occasion of
> the alteration. As the English ever suppose the French
> place the accent on the last syllable, in endeavouring to
> pronounce this word after their manner, the stress must
> naturally fall on the second and last syllables, as if divided
> into *a-cád-a-míe*; and from an imitation of this, it is probable
> the present pronunciation of the word was produced.

Not only words from French were affected: thousands of Latin loanwords entered English in the sixteenth century and later, along with thousands more from other languages, such as Spanish and Italian, as English began its global spread. Many acclimatized quickly to their new linguistic environment, and followed the normal English stress pattern; but others retained the stress pattern of the source language – as in *gui<u>tar</u>*, *la<u>goon</u>*, and *casta<u>net</u>* – making the English stress

system increasingly irregular. Words also influenced each
other, in a process called *analogy*, which operated in unpredictable ways, as it still does in modern English. We hear
Word X and feel the need to make it sound like Word Y. So
indisputable, as recommended by Walker, has become *indisputable*, probably because of the influence of the verb *dispute*.

Walker also acknowledges the basic rhythm of English:
he comments in his *academy* note that 'we commonly place
an accent on alternate syllables' (the 'tum-te-tum' effect),
and recognizes that this is an underlying force that accounts
for many pronunciation changes. It is a force that remains
with us today, as heard in several words where usage varies
(and is complained about). The relatively new pronunciation of *controversy* was often referred to in the BBC letters
I described in my introduction. This has long had its stress
on the first syllable, but in British English over the past 50
years or so the stress on the second syllable has become
the more frequent usage, presumably because the word
appeared often in sentences like *the controversy that arose …*,
where four unstressed syllables occur after *con*. In *the controversy that arose …* the number is reduced to three, making
the word conform more to the 'tum-te-tum' pattern. The
change hasn't taken place in American English, because in
that variety the word has two stresses, *controversy*, reflecting
the greater energy being given to the *ver* syllable, with its /r/
pronounced.

Evidence that people are aware of the stress-timed nature
of English comes from the way they unconsciously switch
their pronunciation as they move words about a sentence.
We would normally say:

I have a meeting this afternoon.
I have an afternoon meeting.

The change takes place because we find it uncomfortable to put two stressed syllables together:

I have an after<u>noon</u> <u>mee</u>ting

It's not impossible. Some speakers will say it without it feeling odd; but research studies have shown that they are a minority. Most people try to preserve the 'tum-te-tum' pattern, and the faster they speak the more this is likely to happen. Some other examples:

That's an <u>i</u>deal choice. *vs* <u>That</u>'s i<u>deal</u>.
I'll order some <u>Chi</u>nese food. *vs* We'll eat Chi<u>nese.</u>
The house has an <u>out</u>side shed. *vs* It's cold out<u>side.</u>
I have <u>six</u>teen <u>pa</u>ges to read. *vs* He's six<u>teen</u>. (And
similarly with all the other *teen* numerals, as well as
compounds – *thirty-three, forty-one*, etc.)

There are also regional variations in stress, as the *controversy* example illustrates. It's one of the most noticeable differences between American and British pronunciation. Compare the following pairs:

British	*American*
ad<u>dress</u>	<u>a</u>ddress
ad<u>ve</u>rtisement	adver<u>tise</u>ment
<u>ba</u>llet	bal<u>let</u>
<u>ca</u>fe	ca<u>fe</u>
ciga<u>rette</u>	<u>ci</u>garette
maga<u>zine</u>	<u>ma</u>gazine
<u>pre</u>mier	pre<u>mier</u>
trans<u>late</u>	<u>tra</u>nslate
week<u>end</u>	<u>week</u>end

As already noted (p. 56), British pronunciation has for some time been influenced by American; so any of the above might be heard in Britain these days, especially among young people, with some words more susceptible to the change than others. The influence has been widespread in *debris* (such as might be found on a road following an accident), which is now generally pronounced in radio traffic reports as *debris*; *research* is increasingly heard as *research*; and for the generation that grew up watching episodes of *Star Trek*, there is only one way to pronounce *frontier*, and that is as in 'Space: the Final Frontier'.

Other regional varieties sometimes stress words differently. Scottish and Irish English have many examples where the stress is placed later in the word, as in *advertise*, *realize*, *educate*, *triangle*, and *safeguard*. The metre in *The Phoenix in the Hall*, an eighteenth-century Irish ballad, illustrates this kind of stress in a series of *-ate* verbs:

> I being quite captivated and so infatuated
> I then prognosticated by sad forlorn case;
> But I quickly ruminated – suppose I was defaited,
> I would not be implicated or treated with disgrace;
> So therefore I awaited with my spirits elevated,
> And no more I ponderated let what would me befall.

Varieties of global English of more recent origin display even more radical stress shifts, as many of them use a syllable-timed rhythm, of the kind illustrated above in relation to French. When each syllable is given the same 'beat', the resulting pronunciation, especially when spoken at speed, can be extremely difficult to be understood by people who are used to listening only to traditional stress-timed speech.

Years ago a doctor told me a story of a misunderstanding that arose as a result of conflicting stress patterns (stressed syllables are shown with a preceding '). It seems that a South

Asian woman now living in England went to see him to ask for his advice about her husband. 'What's wrong with him?' he asked. The woman replied: 'He's /ɪmˈpoːˈtent /'. 'Yes, but what's wrong with him?' he repeated. 'I've just told you,' replies the woman, 'he's /ɪmˈpoːˈtent /'. Eventually they worked it out. The woman's stress on the second syllable of *impotent* was enough to make the doctor hear the word as *important*.

Laboratory or lavatory?

The BBC had been in existence for less than five years when in 1926 it set up a committee to advise on the spoken English to be used in broadcasting, under the chairmanship of the poet laureate, Robert Bridges, and with members including George Bernard Shaw and Professor Daniel Jones (p. 17). Its first official publication was in 1929, a pamphlet giving advice to announcers: *Broadcast English: Recommendations to announcers regarding certain words of doubtful pronunciation*.

The committee secretary was Arthur Lloyd James, who in his introduction discussed several examples of confusion that had already arisen, including this now famous case:

> *Laboratory* when broadcast with the stress on the first syllable is liable to be heard by a listener as *lavatory*.

The committee concluded that it was necessary to recommend a pronunciation with the stress on the second syllable. The pamphlet listed 333 words where there had been uncertainty. Most were to do with the pronunciation of individual vowels or consonants (as in *bade, chagrin, furore*), but stress is marked on all words of more than one syllable, and over 60 recommendations concerned where to place the stress.

on the 1st syllable	on the 2nd	on the 3rd
accessory	Allies	apparatus
alabaster	aspirant	artisan
altercate	coincidentally	commandant
antiquary	construe	Deuteronomy
applicable	decrease *verb*	indisputable
armistice	diocesan	
capitalist	disputable	

on the 1st syllable	on the 2nd	on the 3rd
chastisement	environs	
comparable	epistolatory	
conjugal	import *verb*	
controversy	importune	
costume	irreparable	
decrease *noun*	irrevocable	
despicable	laboratory	
dioceses	lapel	
elongate	perfect *verb*	
eyrie	peremptory	
formidable	precedent *adjective*	
gondola	progress *verb*	
gustatory	project *verb*	
import *noun*	research	
lamentable	reverberatory	
obdurate	romance	
octopus	saline *adjective*	
ordure	tattoo	
precedent *noun*	viola [*instrument*]	
progress *noun*		
project *noun*		
saline *noun*		
temporarily		
viola [*flower*]		

It's interesting to see how many have changed since the 1920s. Today, people find it surprising that there was ever any uncertainty about such words as *octopus* and *tattoo*, but that is the thing about stress: we quickly get used to new forms, and forget the old ones. However, while the changes are ongoing, some people do feel disturbed, or even outraged, and – as I reported in my introduction – write in to complain about it.

Even though the Committee had some members who would be happy to describe themselves as pedants, it adopted a resolutely fair-minded position:

> Most of the words that follow admit of more pronunciations than one; they are all words that have caused difficulty to announcers, or words that have given rise to criticism from listeners. The Advisory Committee on Spoken English has discussed each word on its merits, and it recommends that announcers should use the pronunciations set out below. It is not suggested that these pronunciations are the only 'right' ones, and it is not suggested that any special degree of authority attaches to these recommendations. They are recommendations made primarily for the benefit of announcers, to secure some measure of uniformity in the pronunciation of broadcast English, and to provide announcers with some degree of protection against the criticism to which they are, from the nature of their work, peculiarly liable.

It's remarkable that Lloyd James should feel the need to talk about 'protection', with the BBC less than five years old. He would presumably not have been surprised by the extremely worded criticisms of pronunciation that came my way, 50 years later.

8

Fast and slow

In Chapter 25 of *The Pickwick Papers*, Charles Dickens gives us an account of Mr Pickwick's manner of speaking:

> 'And such a man to speak,' said Mr Muzzle. 'How his ideas flow, don't they?' 'Wonderful,' replied Sam; 'they comes a pouring out, knocking each other's heads so fast, that they seems to stun one another; you hardly know what he's arter, do you?' 'That's the great merit of his style of speaking,' rejoined Mr Muzzle.

By contrast, in Chapter 3 of Dickens' *Bleak House*, we are told how Conversation Kenge speaks:

> [He] appeared to enjoy beyond everything the sound of his own voice. I couldn't wonder at that, for it was mellow and full, and gave great importance to every word he uttered. He listened to himself with obvious satisfaction, and sometimes gently beat time to his own music with his head, or rounded a sentence with his hand.

Some people are naturally fast speakers, like Mr Pickwick; some naturally slow, like Mr Kenge. There are risks attached to both: if we talk too quickly, people will have difficulty understanding us; if we speak too slowly, they can lose interest in what we're saying. Either way, the speed at which we speak is a fundamental property of pronunciation, conveying something of our personality as well as providing yet another way – along with intonation and loudness – of adding meaning to what we say.

Most English speakers have a natural speech rate of four or five syllables a second – which might seem a lot until we realize that it takes less than a second to say a four- or five-syllable phrase: *happy birthday; what time is it?; I'm on the train; very interesting*. Mr Pickwick, evidently, spoke faster than that; Mr Kenge spoke slower. There are regional as well as personality differences, which we are quick to sense. People who live in cities tend to speak (and walk) faster than those who live in the countryside – the stereotype of the slow-speaking rustic does have a basis in reality. Some accents are commonly described as 'drawling', such as we hear in parts of Texas or the American South. On the other hand, many South Asian speakers of English have a rapidly spoken, clipped style of speech, reflecting the rhythmical norms of their mother tongue.

Occupations affect speech rate too. Radio newsreaders tend to speak at around 200 syllables a minute, rather than the 250 or so of everyday conversation. And an even more obvious example is sports commentary, where the speed at which the commentator talks is inevitably a reflection of the rate at which the sporting activity takes place. There's a huge difference, for example, between the syllable rate at the beginning of a horse-racing commentary, as the riders leave the starting post, and at the end, as they approach the finishing line. The accelerando is striking, and a defining feature of this genre. Similarly, we can get a reliable indication of dramatic peaks and troughs from the increases and decreases in speed that we hear in a commentary on football, tennis, or any other sport (even in those where the baseline activity speed is slow, such as snooker).

We don't have to be a sports commentator to make use of

the contrasts in meaning conveyed by speed variation. That's the interesting thing about speech rate: we don't speak at exactly the same rate all the time, but speed up and slow down depending on the meaning we want to express. A slowing down usually adds greater import to what is being said. It's difficult to convey in writing, but there are several ways of doing it:

- respelling: just a leetle longer, I'm soooo happy
- adding hyphens: ve-e-ry interesting
- adding dashes: I – don't – know
- adding capital letters: that's a Very Significant Point

As already mentioned in Chapter 5, the slowing down can be a sudden switch to lento or lentissimo, or a gradual rallentando. The latter is very common when we want to signal that we are coming to the end of a speech or a recitation. The last few words, or sometimes sentences, are spoken more slowly. The impression is of the speaker 'winding down'. If it is an interaction, the rallentando acts as a cue to listeners that it is their turn to speak. Often lento speech simply conveys the fact that the speaker is processing the language slowly – thinking of what to say next or pondering the implications of what is being said.

In the same way, speeding up our speech, whether sudden or gradual, conveys different kinds of meaning. In a study of the speech used in interviews, carried out in 1960, a team of researchers found six main reasons why people speak more quickly than usual, and gave each one a neat descriptive label:

- *road hogs*: speakers think they are about to be interrupted, so they speed up in order to let their listener(s) know they don't want it to happen; when several people are competing to speak next, the fastest speaker is usually the winner.

- *hot potatoes*: speakers realize that what they are saying is unpleasant, contentious, or risqué, so they speed up in order to get it over with as quickly as possible.
- *getaways*: speakers realize that they have just said something unpalatable, so they speed up to put as much space as possible between themselves and the distasteful topic – to escape potential embarrassment.
- *smokescreens*: speakers realize that what they have said might be taken the wrong way, so they speed up, presenting new material that they hope will capture the attention of their listeners.
- *greener pastures*: speakers, while saying something, think of something more interesting to say, so they speed up in order to reach the new topic as quickly as possible.
- *rebounds*: speakers realize that, for whatever reason, their speed of speaking has been inappropriately slow (perhaps because they've sensed a growth in listener inattention), so they speed up to correct it, and end up speaking more quickly than they had intended.

These are all very plausible scenarios, and there are still other contexts where we will hear rate changes. A spoken parenthesis, for example, is usually spoken in a lowered pitch and loudness, and at a faster rate. Imagine saying the following sentence:

My uncle John (he's the one I was telling you about the other day) has decided to visit us next week.

Because the information in the parenthesis is 'old news', most people would drop their voices and speed up while saying it.

And obviously, when we are in a highly emotional state, very excited or very angry, we tend to talk faster (as well as louder and higher).

New technology is making us adopt new habits of speech rate. In theory it should be possible to talk to a machine at the same speed that we use when talking to humans. In practice, we have to speak slower, and even 'word – at – a – time', if we want to guarantee total comprehension, or a perfect written version (in speech-to-text applications). The situation will undoubtedly improve, as the technology becomes linguistically more sophisticated; it is already hugely superior to what it was even five years ago. And presumably, at some point, programmers will want to give robotic voices the same self-awareness about rate variation that is illustrated by the bullet points above (see further, Chapter 26). At the moment, Daleks and other aliens tend to speak without varying their speech rate. It's one of the things that identifies them as alien.

9

Strong and weak

If I had to select one feature of speech that explains more about English pronunciation than any other, I would choose rhythm. It is there from the very beginning of child language acquisition, as the frame within which first words and intonation patterns operate (Chapter 6). Why do children in their first year of language learning like to say such things as *doggie* and *horsey* rather than *dog* and *horse*? Why do their carers feed such forms to them in their 'baby talk'? Children seem drawn to words of two syllables, one strong and one weak, heard in dozens of words like *mummy, daddy, teddy, biccy, cookie, bottle* … The pronunciation of the vowels and consonants may be immature – with my fifteen-month-old son Steven, *bottle* came out as *bobo, window* as *wawa* – but the two-beat strong/weak rhythm is there. Everything he said was rough-and-ready, apart from the rhythm. That was as established and confident as his heartbeat.

Infants like the reduplications they hear adults use, when they begin to talk – *bye bye, night night, pee-pee, beep-beep, quack-quack* – and, as with *bobo* and *wawa*, do the same thing themselves. Words of a more complex form are reduced to the same basic pattern: *banana* is universally *nana*. We might expect one-year-olds to start their language learning with words of just one syllable; but typically around half of the first fifty words produced between twelve and eighteen months consist of two, often with the same syllable repeated.

It's a sensible teaching and learning strategy. If the aim is to get your child to speak, then offering them two chances to pronounce a sound is going to be better than one.

Emphatic rhythm permeates the interactions between carers and children during the period from around six to eighteen months. Think of the games that are played – tickling games (*Round and round the garden, This little piggy went to market*), clapping games (*If you're happy and you know it clap your hands*), knee-bobbing games (*This is the way the lady rides, Horsey horsey don't you stop*), repetition songs (*Old MacDonald had a farm, The wheels on the bus go round and round*), and a host of activity nursery rhymes (*Hickory Dickory Dock, Jack and Jill, Humpty Dumpty*). They all have one thing in common: a strong rhythm, usually reinforced by touch and body movement.

We grow up remembering the rhythms of our early childhood. And these rhythms develop a wide range of patterns. As already mentioned in Chapter 7, the basic traditional rhythm of English is stress-timed ('tum-te-tum') – the heartbeat comparison is something more than just a metaphor. But within that steady beat there are several possibilities, all found in nursery rhymes:

- a weak beat followed by a strong beat:
    The <u>grand</u> old <u>Duke</u> of <u>York</u>
- a strong beat followed by a weak beat:
    <u>Pe</u>ter <u>Pe</u>ter <u>pump</u>kin <u>eat</u>er
- a strong beat followed by two weak beats:
    <u>Hick</u>ory <u>dick</u>ory <u>dock</u>
- two weak beats followed by a strong beat:
    Oranges and lemons
    Say the <u>bells</u> of Saint <u>Clem</u>ent's
- two strong beats together:
    <u>Tom</u>, <u>Tom</u>, the piper's son

There are other possibilities, of course, such as having a sequence of three or more weak beats (*One* potato, *two* potato) or having three or more strong beats (*Ding, dong, bell*), but these are unusual by comparison with the 'top five'.

And it's those five patterns that have become the reference norms when we listen to the rhythmical units that form the metre of a poem. Literary scholars have given them learned names, and readers may well remember their first encounter with the terminology in school English lessons. The memory may not be a particularly pleasant one, I'm sorry to say. I well recall my own school introduction to prosody, which was no more than learning a series of Greek technical terms and mechanical 'counting' exercises of lines of verse I didn't understand. Boredom was the result. But these terms can be given life, if we know their etymology, and if they are related to lines that are exciting and involving, such as these:

- a weak beat followed by a strong beat – an *iamb*, or *iambic* rhythm (from Greek *iambos*, a type of verse in this rhythm, with a probable link to *Iambe*, a deity in Greek mythology; it was felt to be the default metre for poetry, being most like the rhythm of everyday speech)

    Once <u>more</u> un<u>to</u> the <u>breach</u>, dear <u>friends</u>, once <u>more</u>,
    Or <u>close</u> the <u>wall</u> up <u>with</u> our <u>Eng</u>lish <u>dead</u> …
    (William Shakespeare, *Henry V*)

- a strong beat followed by a weak beat – a *trochee*, or *trochaic* rhythm (from a Greek word for 'running' or 'tripping along')

    <u>Dou</u>ble, <u>dou</u>ble, <u>toil</u> and <u>trou</u>ble,
    <u>Fire</u> <u>burn</u> and <u>caul</u>dron <u>bub</u>ble …
    (William Shakespeare, *Macbeth*)

- a strong beat followed by two weak beats – a *dactyl*, or *dactylic* rhythm (from a Greek word for a finger, which consists of one long bone and two short ones)

  <u>Can</u>non to <u>right</u> of them,
  <u>Can</u>non to <u>left</u> of them,
  <u>Can</u>non in <u>front</u> of them
  <u>Voll</u>eyed and <u>thund</u>ered …
  (Alfred, Lord Tennyson, *The Charge of the Light Brigade*)

- two weak beats followed by a strong beat – an *anapaest*, or *anapaestic* rhythm (from a Greek word meaning 'struck back' or 'reversed' – that is, the opposite rhythm to a dactyl)

  Not a <u>drum</u> was <u>heard</u>, not a <u>fun</u>eral <u>note</u>
  As his <u>corpse</u> to the <u>ram</u>part we hurried …
  (Charles Wolfe, *The Burial of Sir John Moore at Corunna*)

- two strong beats together – a *spondee*, or *spondaic* rhythm (from a Greek word meaning 'solemn drink-offering', during which syllables were pronounced slowly and evenly)

  <u>Blow</u>, <u>winds</u>, and crack your cheeks! <u>rage</u>! <u>blow</u>!
  (William Shakespeare, *King Lear*)

We use all these rhythms in everyday speech, but in a much less predictable way than in traditional poetry (though even in poetry there are alternative ways of saying some of the above lines).

Here's an extract from a conversation, with the strong syllables underlined, short pauses marked by a dot, longer pauses by a dash, and the intonation units divided by slashes. It's taken from recordings I made for the Survey of English

Usage at University College London, in which the speakers were unaware that they were being recorded (they were told later!). We are being given an account of a holiday abroad where the Channel crossing was evidently a success:

> but it was <u>love</u>ly / <u>our</u> one / with the <u>night</u>club / and we
> <u>had</u> a . we <u>had</u> a <u>super cab</u>in / which was <u>just</u> be<u>low</u> the
> <u>night</u>club / – <u>utt</u>erly <u>sound</u>proof / . you know <u>when</u> you
> <u>think</u> what <u>hous</u>es are <u>like</u> / – when we <u>shut</u> our <u>cab</u>in
> <u>door</u> / . you <u>would</u>n't <u>know</u> there was <u>any</u>thing out<u>side</u> /
> and <u>yet</u> there was a <u>night</u>club / <u>pound</u>ing <u>mus</u>ic a<u>way</u> / .
> just <u>one</u> – im<u>med</u>iately <u>over</u><u>head</u> / and <u>we</u> were the <u>cab</u>in
> <u>next</u> <u>to</u> it – and you <u>could</u>n't <u>hear</u> it / . at <u>all</u>/

The most noticeable contrast with the poetry examples is the way the spontaneous choice of words results in a continuously varying rhythm. Poets spend a great deal of time finding the right word, especially when they commit themselves to a particular metre. They may even invent a word to fit the metre, if one doesn't exist. The Chorus in Shakespeare's *Henry V* asks, 'Can this cockpit hold the vasty fields of France?' There was no such word as *vasty* in English before that, but to use the word that did exist, *vast*, would have destroyed the regular rhythm of the line at that point. So he made one up.

No such considerations bother us in everyday conversation. As my extract illustrates, we find all the rhythm units used in sequences of varying lengths and rubbing up against each other in random ways. We can try to identify particular patterns – iambic (*our <u>cab</u>in <u>door</u>*), trochaic (*<u>pound</u>ing <u>mus</u>ic*), dactylic (*<u>hous</u>es are*), anapaestic (*when we <u>shut</u>*), spondaic (*<u>next</u> <u>to</u>*) – but it's sometimes ambiguous where one unit ends and the next begins. Any regularity is interrupted by false starts (*we had a . we had a*), extra thoughts (*you couldn't hear it / . at all /*), and changes of mind (*just one* [floor above us] becomes *immediately overhead*). The underlying stress-timed rhythm nonetheless comes across.

We do sometimes make our everyday speech more metrical. Imagine a situation where someone says in an extremely irritated tone, *I <u>really</u> <u>think</u> it's <u>time</u> you <u>cleaned</u> the <u>car</u>*. The likelihood is that this sentence will come out with the stressed syllables very strong, so that the effect is like a regular iambic line (*Once more unto the breach, dear friends, once more*). To make the sentence even more irritated, each unstressed syllable can be said with a high pitch, giving a 'spiky' effect. A rather less irritated version would pronounce each stressed syllable with a falling glide, continuing into the unstressed syllable, resulting in a 'glissando' effect: *I re-e-ally thi-ink it's ti-ime ...*

There's a general point here, which applies to poetry as much as to everyday speech. Rhythmical change is there for a reason. A change in metre can correlate with a change in mood, atmosphere, or subject matter. It can reflect the sounds of the real world. It can bring auditory freshness to a poem, a speech, or a conversational story. Just as in music, when we notice and respond emotionally to a particular rhythm or rhythmical change, so it is in the way we speak.

The point applies just as much to unrhythmical speech. A sudden lack of rhythm usually suggests that a speaker is uncertain, unconfident, not sure what to say. It's the sort of effect that political speakers, or anyone engaged in an argument, should avoid at all costs, for a more fluent participant will sense the hesitancy and make capital out of it. Maintaining rhythmical speech, in these circumstances, has a rhetorical force. Hesitant speech isn't always interpreted negatively: it may mean that the speaker is being profoundly thoughtful. It may also, of course, mean simply that the speaker is drunk.

Rhythm sells

Advertising slogans like to be short, simple, and memorable, so they use all the tricks of the linguistic trade, such as alliteration, rhyme, and – above all – rhythm. One of the most effective techniques is to take a short sentence and repeat its construction, using exactly the same rhythm:

> Save money. Live better. (Walmart)
> Expand your mind, change your world. (*New Statesman*)
> Your vision. Our future. (Olympus)

Even more effective is to make the repeated rhythm one beat shorter, so that there is an extra punch at the end:

> Live in your world. Play in ours. (PlayStation)
> Share moments. Share life. (Kodak)
> Double your pleasure. Double your fun. (Doublemint gum)

A double repetition is more difficult, but very powerful when it's achieved:

> Buy it. Sell it. Love it. (eBay)
> Outwit. Outplay. Outlast. (*Survivor* TV series)

10

Filled and unfilled

In the final volume of her letters and diaries, *War Within and Without* (1980), Anne Morrow Lindbergh describes American secretary of state John Foster Dulles' conversational style:

> Thoughts die and are buried in the silences between sentences.

When somebody pauses a lot, or makes their pauses very long, we notice.

When I say 'a lot', I mean 'in unexpected places' or 'in unexpected ways'. Nobody notices natural short pausing, required when we need to take a breath within a long utterance, or when we want to show we've reached the end of a sentence, or to mark the boundaries of a grammatical construction. In the following sentence, said at a normal unemotional conversational speed (Chapter 8), there would be very slight pauses between the rhythm units, shown here separated by slashes. Nobody would pay special attention to them, because they simply reinforce the points where the sentence construction changes. They help us grasp what is being said.

> Actually / if you don't mind me saying so / I think all of us / and I include Mum and Dad in this / believe it was definitely the right decision.

But what if that sentence were said in this way? (A dot shows a short pause and the number of dashes shows increasingly longer pauses.)

> Actually / -- if you don't . mind me . saying so / I think
> - all of us / -- and I include mum --- and dad --- in this /
> believe it was definitely the right decision.

The emotional temperature has hugely risen. What is it about Dad that has caused the speaker to separate him out in this way? Is it because Dad is seriously ill? Or has Dad finally come round to the idea after a heated argument? And why is the speaker so hesitant? Is he unhappy about the decision? Is he feeling it isn't his place to say such a thing? If he had paused again before *me*, that would suggest the latter even more.

When there's no grammatical reason for them, pauses always mean something, and they become a noticeable feature of pronunciation. We don't expect professional speakers to pause outside these norms, and if they do, listeners quickly become irritated or bored. Some of the BBC letters I referred to in my introduction criticized announcers who (according to the complainers) paused in the wrong places. And if politicians making an important speech begin to pause erratically, we would wonder whether they were in control of all their facts or convinced about their own arguments. That was one of the main criticisms levelled at Donald Trump during the election campaign.

A pause can add a nuance that its pauseless equivalent lacks. What would you make of this sentence?

> John and his friend have just bought a new car.

There's no implication; the sentence just means what it says. But add pauses:

John and his – friend – have just bought a new car.

Now there's something significant about the friend. A criminal? A lover?

Pauses are influenced by a wide range of factors. An unexpected pause in a sentence might be the result of speakers taking a drink, wiping their nose, turning a page, checking a text message, or, as in this observation by William Cowper, in his long poem *Conversation* (1782), puffing on a pipe:

> The pipe, with solemn interposing puff,
> Makes half a sentence at a time enough;
> The dozing sages drop the drowsy strain,
> Then pause, and puff – and speak, and pause again.

Many a film star has timed a pull on a cigarette to make a dramatic point.

These are all silent pauses – or, as phoneticians call them, *unfilled* pauses. Their presence becomes even more noticeable when we turn them into *filled* pauses, usually by saying *er* /ə:/ or *erm* /ɜ:m/. The length of the *er*(*m*) varies: it can be extremely short (more an *uh* than an *er*), or it can be lengthy (*errrm*). The longer the syllable lasts, the more we are making it mean something. Take the following exchange:

> A: I'll get the first train in the morning.
> B: Errr --

B means something like: 'Excuse me, but I think there's a problem with that, which I'll articulate as soon as I can get my thoughts in order.'

As with unfilled pauses, the location of a filled pause in a sentence can affect the meaning, or give a poor impression. We could replace the silent pause before *friend* by an *er* in the above example, and achieve the same effect. And if a politician were to introduce an *er*(*m*) before a numerical fact, it would give us a distinct feeling that the speaker wasn't on top of the subject:

> So this means a total of errm 20 per cent of the
> population will benefit ...

Vote for me?

Filled pauses are different from unfilled pauses in one crucial respect: they can be repeated. We can say *er*(*m*) several times in succession – though the more we do, the more non-fluent we will sound, and the more listeners will switch off. In fact most speakers use a filled pause just once, at any given moment. Saying it two or three times in succession makes the speaker sound like a bonging Big Ben.

There's one exception to this. A speaker can vary the pro-nunciation of the sound that fills the pause. I once heard a scientist at a conference asked a question that he obviously found really interesting, but difficult to answer. He couldn't stay totally silent, as he thought out what to say; that would suggest he was nonplussed. He didn't want to waffle. So he used filled pauses to convey to his questioner that he was actively processing a reply. In quick succession he said: *mmm*, /əməməm/, *yeah-yeah-yeah*, blew noisy air between rounded lips, and then trilled the tip of his tongue between them. It gave the impression of someone who was quite excited at the way he was being made to think.

There is nothing unusual about this, other than the fact that people don't normally do such things in front of a large audience. In private conversation I imagine everyone from time to time uses idiosyncratic hesitation patterns. I know someone who often hesitates with a nasal noise that reminds me of the way Bugs Bunny talks when he says *eeee* (*What's up, Doc?*). A famous lexicographer of my acquaintance always hesitated with the sound /aɪ/, that he frequently repeated; it was as if he were saying *I* all the time.

Used well, of course, pauses can be extremely effective, and are often encountered in literature in such phrases as a *pregnant pause*, a *dramatic pause*, a *momentary pause*, an *awkward pause*, a *pause for thought*, and a *pause for effect*. Anyone who watches competition or award events on television (*Strictly Come Dancing*, the Oscars) will be familiar with the last of these, used predictably whenever someone is being announced: 'and the winner is …' The pause is supposed to heighten anticipation before the Great Reveal. As Mark Twain once said in a speech: 'The right word may be effective, but no word was ever as effective as a rightly timed pause.' Actors love them: 'The most precious things in speech are pauses,' said Ralph Richardson. And indeed, when we compare different actors giving the same speech, the most important variable is their pausing.

Some writers exploit pause. Repeatedly in Harold Pinter's plays we encounter the well-timed pause. It's sometimes a character note, sometimes a means of creating atmosphere, especially a mood of uncertainty or menace. Here's Aston in *The Caretaker*, making Davies feel uneasy:

> Of course, there's a lot to be done to this place. What I think, though, I think I'll put in a partition … in one of the rooms along the landing. I think it'll take it. You know … they've got these screens … you know … Oriental. They break up a room with them. Make it into two parts. I could either do that or I could have a partition. I could knock them up, you see, if I had a workshop.
> *Pause.*
> Anyway, I think I've decided on the partition.
> *Pause.*

English punctuation gives us various ways of showing a pause – a short or long dash, or (as here) ellipsis dots. Pinter seems to be using a hierarchy of pauses: presumably *Pause* is longer than three dots, and three dots longer than a dash (which he also uses). How to interpret the pauses, and what 'business' to introduce along with them, always generates a lively discussion in the rehearsal room.

Novelists love them too, especially crime writers. Interrogation and reveal scenes are full of significant pauses. Here's Lawrence Cavendish in court, in Agatha Christie's *The Mysterious Affair at Styles* (Chapter 6):

> Just as he was about to step down, he paused, and said rather hesitatingly: 'I should like to make a suggestion if I may?'

It seems *de rigueur* for everyone to pause, at some point or other, in a crime novel, whether they're innocent or guilty. The novelist doesn't usually explain the reason for the pause. That's for the reader to work out.

As so often in this book, I go to Charles Dickens to find vivid descriptions of pronunciation features; and in *Our Mutual Friend* (1864–65, II, Chapter 12) he gives us as clear an example of a meaningful pause as we might hope to find:

> The Secretary, working in the Dismal Swamp betimes next morning, was informed that a youth waited in the hall who gave the name of Sloppy. The footman who communicated this intelligence made a decent pause before uttering the name, to express that it was forced on his reluctance by the youth in question, and that if the youth had had the good sense and good taste to inherit some other name it would have spared the feelings of him the bearer.

11

The value of vowels

In the twelfth century, an anonymous Icelandic scholar, today known as 'the first grammarian', wrote a perceptive analysis of his language in which he recognizes a priority of vowels over consonants, for, as he says: 'In the name of every consonant there is a vowel, because the consonants can neither be named nor pronounced without a vowel.' It certainly applies to English: each consonant letter in the written alphabet needs a vowel in order to be articulated: 'bee, dee, eff, emm, ess …' In the case of *r*, in some accents a vowel alone is enough to identify it: 'ah'.

Vowels provide the core element on which consonants depend. It's possible to have words whose pronunciation consists only of vowels: *I, a, awe* (/ɔ:/ – ignore the irregular spelling), letter *e, owe*, exclamatory *oi*, and, in accents where /r/ isn't pronounced, *are, err, ear, air, or, our, ire*. By contrast, there are no words that consist only of consonants, unless we count such interjections as *shh* and *mm*. And as syllables become more complex, we can see the way the vowel retains its central role, with the consonants functioning at the edges.

> consonant + vowel: *go, we, you*
> consonants + vowel: *true, spy, free*
> vowel + consonant: *at, on, inn*
> vowel + consonants: *ask, asks, angsts*
> consonant + vowel + consonant: *cat, sock, peel*

consonant + vowel + consonants: *cats, pant, sixth*
consonants + vowel + consonant: *clip, tram, string*
consonants + vowel + consonants: *strings, cramps, twelfths*

I'll describe these patterns in more detail in Chapter 21.

The role played by vowels has been repeatedly affirmed in the history of language study. Two quotations illustrate, from different literary traditions. First, the German philologist Jacob Grimm, in his *Germanic Grammar* (1819, section 1):

> One may view the vowels as the necessary colouring or animation of all words, as the breath without which they would not even exist. The real individuality of the word rests on the vowel sound: it affords the finest relationships.

Then, 175 years later, novelist Anthony Burgess makes the same point, more vividly, in *A Mouthful of Air* (1992, Chapter 4):

> There is no doubt something gross and brash and materialistic about consonants: they are noises made by banging things together, rubbing, hissing, buzzing. Vowels, on the other hand, are pure music – woodwind to the consonantal percussion – and, because they are produced by the creation of space between the tongue and the hard or soft palate, and these spaces are not measured scientifically but arrived at by a sort of acoustic guesswork, they tend to be indefinite and mutable. The history of the sound-changes of a language is mainly a history of its vowels.

And, I would add, the story of its regional and social dialects.

Phoneticians have found ways of getting round the acoustic guesswork. It is now routinely possible to show the precise physical characteristics of each vowel, including any individual variations, using modern acoustic technology. We can also see the way the tongue moves, as described in Chapter 4.

And with an appropriate amount of ear-training, anyone can learn to hear the differences between vowels, and identify exactly where in the mouth space we hold our tongue when we pronounce them.

Jacob Grimm's account gives vowels a primeval status when he describes them as the breath that gives existence to words. In the beginning was the vowel? Certainly in children, vowel-like sounds are there from the very start in cries and then in babble, and the set of vowels in a language is acquired long before the set of consonants is complete – in English, all usually present by around age two, or soon after. A typical set of words produced by a two-year-old is shown below: all twenty of the vowels described in the table on pp. 23–4 are in use – with some immature pronunciations, of course, but each one was pronounced in a way that showed that the child was aware of its distinctive identity.

iː	see
ɪ	milk
e	teddy
æ	daddy
ʌ	done
ɑː	car
ɒ	dog
ɔː	more
ʊ	look
uː	shoe
ɜː	bird
ə	banan<u>a</u>
ɛɪ	<u>ba</u>by
aɪ	night

ɔɪ	toy
əʊ	no
aʊ	down
ɪə	ear
ɛə	there
ʊə	poor

All English vowels have certain features that distinguish them from consonants. They are all voiced (which makes them unlike the voiceless consonants, p. 121). They are all oral (which makes them unlike the nasals, p. 149). They are all sounded without any audible friction (which makes them unlike the fricatives, p. 132). They are all continuants – we can keep them going for as long as we have breath (which makes them unlike the plosives, p. 119). The only similarity in pronunciation is with the small group of approximants, especially /w/ as in *we* and /j/ as in *you*, which are sometimes called 'semi-vowels' (p. 159). But these sounds function as consonants, not vowels, being used only at the edges of syllables.

Each vowel is the result of a set of factors that work together to produce its separate identity. To pronounce a vowel accurately we need to control its length, the part of the tongue involved, the tongue height, the position of the lips, and whether the sound retains the same auditory quality throughout or whether this quality changes. We need to explore each of these factors to understand how vowels work in English pronunciation, and a good place to begin is with the factors that are easiest to perceive.

The Tyger puzzle

William Blake

Generations of children have learned the opening stanza of William Blake's 'The Tyger':

> Tyger Tyger, burning bright,
> In the forests of the night;
> What immortal hand or eye,
> Could frame thy fearful symmetry?

And all have puzzled over how the vowel at the end of the last word should be pronounced.

The couplet has generated quite a lot of ink. Some commentators say it is simply an eye rhyme. That, to my mind, is the lazy solution. At a time when the spelling system was becoming standardized, eye rhymes were certainly a possibility, and some poets used them a lot, but why have just one eye rhyme in a poem where all the other rhymes are exact pronunciation partners?

An explanation in terms of sounds is much more likely. Blake is recalling an earlier pronunciation of final –*y*, which did in fact rhyme with words like *eye* (see further, Chapter 27). A classic example is Oberon's speech in *A Midsummer Night's Dream* (3.2.102), where we find *dye, eye, espy, sky*, and *by* mixed in with *archery, gloriously*, and *remedy*:

Flower of this purple dye,
Hit with Cupid's archery,
Sink in apple of his eye.
When his love he doth espy,
Let her shine as gloriously
As the Venus of the sky.
When thou wakest, if she be by,
Beg of her for remedy.

Eye rhymes are not a viable explanation in Shakespeare's time, as the spelling system wasn't stable enough to guarantee them, and the writers on pronunciation at the time (the orthoepists) always stress the auditory value of rhyme. Some of these writers actually try to capture the phonetic quality of those -*y* words. John Hart, for example, writing in the 1570s, transcribes *boldly* as *boldlei*, *certainly* as *sertenlei*, and so on. Clearly he is trying to convey some sort of diphthong here. In my work on Shakespearean original pronunciation (OP), I transcribe this as /əɪ/. It's a pronunciation that lasted into the eighteenth century in educated speech, and can still be heard in some regional accents today.

By the time that Blake was writing, the everyday pronunciation had shifted to its modern form, like a short 'ee'. This is how John Walker, for example, describes *symmetry* in his *Pronouncing Dictionary*, published just three years before Blake's poem: he rhymes it with *me*. The pronunciation with the final diphthong would have sounded distinctly old-fashioned by then. But wouldn't that suit someone who begins a poem with a spelling of *tyger* that was also archaic?

The phonaesthetics of the stanzas adds further support for an explanation in terms of sounds rather than spellings. The same diphthong turns up in *tyger*, and is then echoed at the end of all eight lines of the opening two stanzas: *bright, night, eye, symmetry, skies, eyes, aspire, fire*. To my ear, this adds the same kind of mystical atmosphere that we hear when Oberon's speech is read in an OP way.

People do remember long-gone pronunciations – *wind* to rhyme with *mind*, for example. And if I pronounce *lord* as 'lahd', perhaps in a parody of upper-class speech, I am actually producing the normal pronunciation of this word as it was a century ago. Daniel Jones (p. 17), writing in the 1910s, locates it in the place where today in RP we would find the vowel of *far*. Nobody says 'lahd' any more, but if I were to write a rhyming poem in which I had the following lines, I think readers would have no difficulty in 'hearing' the old pronunciation despite the modern spelling:

The butler looked all round the yard:
'There's no one in the grounds, my lord.'

Some writers would opt for a nonstandard spelling here (such as 'lahrd') but such alternatives often are not available in the orthography – as in the case of *symmetry*. There was no archaic spelling for Blake to fall back on, in this case, to help the reader. And so we have the spelling that has come down to us.

12

One quality or two?

As pointed out in Chapter 3, one of the most noticeable regional variations in vowels arises from whether they have one quality (a *monophthong*) or two (a *diphthong*). In some accents, speakers turn a pure vowel into a diphthong (the technical term is a bit of a mouthful – to *dipthongize*); in others, it's the other way round (to *monophthongize*). Probably the most widely heard example of monophthongization (for British listeners) is in pop music, where singers who don't normally pronounce /aɪ/ as /ɑ:/ (in words like *I* and *my*) do so when they're singing, adopting a mock-American sound so that they come out as 'ah' and 'mah'. Similarly, most pop singers will turn the /əʊ/ in words like *no* and *go* into /o:/ – a pronunciation that is in any case widely heard in Scottish, Welsh, and northern England accents as well as in North America (and Shakespeare).

Scottish English is one of the best examples of an accent where the diphthongs of RP (p. 14) have become pure vowels. Words like *say* and *take*, /eɪ/ in RP, are pronounced with a long /e:/ vowel. And words like *house* and *now*, which have a wide /ɑʊ/ diphthong in RP, come out with a long /u:/ vowel – often written as 'hoose' and 'noo'. Back in 1958, the pop group Lord Rockingham's XI had a hit single called 'Hoots Mon', which parodied a Scottish accent, and included the famous line, 'There's a moose loose aboot this hoose.'

In Liverpool there's a hairdressing salon called *Him and*

Hair. It's an accent pun that only works if you know how the classical Scouse accent sounds. The /ɛə/ diphthong in such words as *bared* has the same quality as the /ɜ:/ vowel in *bird*, so *hair* and *her* sound the same. When people try to write Scouse down, they usually try to convey this using a *u* spelling: *fair hair* becomes *fur ur*.

It's difficult to capture these differences using normal English spelling, but writers do sometimes manage it. Alongside the Scots respellings, we find examples in the way northern accents in England are portrayed: *take*, for example, might be written *tek* or *tehk*, to suggest the way words with an /eɪ/ phoneme in RP are pronounced with an /e/, sometimes short (*tek*), sometimes long (*tehk*). The same spellings turn up in representations of local speech from other parts of England, the southern USA, the Caribbean, and in fact all over the English-speaking world. 'I'd tek care,' says Kitty in George Eliot's *Scenes of Clerical Life* (1857, Chapter 21). 'An business men mek loadsa cash', writes Benjamin Zephaniah in his poem 'Talking Turkeys!' (1994).

The opposite effect, where a pure vowel becomes a diphthong, is also heard in Liverpool – not least, in the name of the city itself. The long /u:/ in words like *soon* has a first element that sounds like a short 'ee', so *Liverpool* locally comes out as 'Liverpiwl'. But diphthongization is widespread around the English-speaking world. We will hear words like *be* and *see* beginning with a short central vowel (schwa, p. 117), so that they sound like 'buh-ee' and 'suh-ee', in London (Cockney), Australia, and the southern USA. An accent like Cockney is notable for its diphthongs, compared to RP: *bought* becomes more like 'bohwt' /bɔʊt/, *moon* more like 'muh-oon' /məʊn/.

Dialect humour books rely greatly on diphthongs to convey regional accents. In Jim Everhart's *Illustrated Texas Dictionary of the English Language* (1968, volume 2) we are introduced to *banes* (defined as 'large, smooth kidney-shaped, edible seeds'), and many other local words in which /iː/ is replaced by /eɪ/, such as *whalebarahs* (in the garden), *paypal* (human beings), *grain* (a colour), and *stale* (to thieve). He also teaches us another diphthongization, heard regionally across the southern USA, in which /ɑː/ also becomes /eɪ/: the auxiliary verb contraction for *can not* – *kaint*. In Sam Llewellyn's *Yacky dar moy bewty!* (1985), several British regionalisms are glossed in a similar way, and show diphthong substitutions, such as Devon's *two crame tays* and Birmingham's *yow'll soy* (you'll see).

Nor does RP escape the humorist, especially the very conservative, 'far back' accent. That description comes from the way words such as *lord* /lɔːd/ were pronounced (well into the twentieth century) with a vowel further back in the mouth as /lɑːd/ (p. 87). I once heard this effect multiplied over three different vowels: someone was talking about a car hire company near Tower Bridge in London and pronounced it 'tah cah hah' /tɑː kɑː hɑː/, instead of the more usual /taʊə kɑː haɪə/. These pronunciations were relentlessly parodied in the pages of *Punch* (such as the *evah* spelling of *ever* reported on p. 164). In a cartoon of May 1876, a gentleman described as a 'languid swell' asks a barmaid, 'Sthawa Wifl'caw Heaw?' She apologizes that she doesn't speak French. (The editor thoughtfully provides a gloss: 'Is there a rifle corps here?')

Getting the difference right between pure vowels and diphthongs was a major focus of traditional elocution. We hear an example in *Pygmalion* (p. 11) when Henry Higgins attempts to get Eliza to say 'How now, brown cow' with full /aʊ/ diphthongs, instead of her natural /ɑː/. It has become the most famous speech-training sentence in the English language.

13

Long or short?

Another factor that is quite easy to perceive is vowel length, which is an important distinction in the pure vowels. Compare the vowels in *bid, bed, bad, bud, bod, book,* and *gab-erdine* with those in *bead, bard, bored, booed,* and *bird.* The first seven are all relatively short; the other five are relatively long.

It's an auditory contrast that writers love to exploit when they name their characters, especially if they want to convey a light-hearted, friendly, or humorous tone. The choice that seems to appeal most is one where the two parts of a name differ, with the stressed syllable in the first name having a different length from the stressed syllable in the second. We hear a long vowel followed by a short vowel in J. M. Barrie's *Peter Pan,* Barbara Todd's *Worzel Gummidge,* Douglas Adams' *Arthur Dent,* and Roald Dahl's *Charlie Bucket, Bruce Bogtrotter, George Kranky,* and *Veruca Salt.* The first name can be a title, as in Lawrence Sterne's *Corporal Trim* and *Parson Yorick,* or Charles Dickens' *Sergeant Buzfuz,* and the effect even carries over into a pair of characters, such as Shakespeare's *Snare* and *Fang,* or television duos such as *Starsky* and *Hutch, Beavis* and *Butt-head,* and *Mork* and *Mindy.* The opposite effect, of short followed by long, is heard in the duos *Laurel* and *Hardy, Lennon* and *McCartney,* and *Thelma* and *Louise.*

Diphthongs are also relatively long, and often replace long pure vowels in regional speech (Chapter 12), so it's not surprising to find them contrasting with short vowels in the same way. We find the short vowel coming second, in such names as Herman Melville's *Moby-Dick*, F. Scott Fitzgerald's *Jay Gatsby*, J. K. Rowling's *Seamus Finnigan*, and Terry Pratchett's *Perspicacia Tick*. We find it coming first in such duos as *Jekyll* and *Hyde* and *Chip 'n' Dale*.

Charles Dickens is a writer who thoroughly exploits the phonaesthetic potential of vowel length in his character names. It's the short vowel that has a special appeal: I analysed one comprehensive list of his characters and found that 62 per cent had a short vowel in the stressed syllable of the first name and 63 per cent had one in the surname. The typical Dickensian name is short + short: *Oliver Twist, Samuel Pickwick, Bob Cratchit, Vincent Crummles, Leicester Dedlock, Mr Fezziwig, Lizzie Hexham, Seth Pecksniff, Daniel Quilp, Harold Skimpole, Augustus Snodgrass* ... If the name can be reinforced by using the same short vowel and/or by repeating initial consonants (*alliteration*), as in *Nicholas Nickleby*, so much the better. Long + short is heard with pure vowels in *Martin Chuzzlewit, Paul Dombey, Barnaby Rudge, Newman Noggs, Cornelia Blimber, Herbert Pocket, Clara Peggotty, Louisa Chick* ...; and with diphthongs in *David Copperfield, Amy Dorrit, Abel Magwitch* ...

Many famous literary or cinema names show the same preferences for short-vowel use: *Tristram Shandy, Huckleberry Finn, Binx Bolling, Atticus Finch, Hannibal Lecter, Billy Bunter, Forrest Gump, Bilbo Baggins, Harry Potter* ... Longer sequences are heard in Terry Pratchett's *Sacharissa Cripslock* or Roald Dahl's *Amanda Thripp*. The *Nicholas Nickleby* pattern is there in J. K. Rowling's *Filius Flitwick* and *Florean Fortescue*. A short vowel followed by a /g/ is a recurrent motif: alongside Dickens' *Montague Tigg* and *Silas Wegg* we find Pratchett's *Jason Ogg*, Rowling's *Arabella Figg*, and Stephen King's *Randall Flagg*.

A noticeable feature of these names is the way most of them follow the traditional stress-timed rhythm (Chapter 7) of English, consisting of a sequence of alternating heavy and light syllables. This rhythm is especially evident in strictly metrical poems, such as those using lines of iambic pentameter, which (in their most regular form) consist of five units, each containing a light + heavy syllable. It's an interesting exercise to explore the way these syllables interact with vowel length. Poets have a large vocabulary at their disposal, with many auditory effects to choose from, and finding the 'right' word is a matter not only of meaning but also of sound. It has to 'mean right', but it also has to 'sound right'.

Long vowels by their nature tend to cause a natural slowing of pronunciation; short vowels tend to speed it up. So we might expect to find a preponderance of long vowels and diphthongs in poems where there is leisurely description or an elegiac mood, as in the opening stanza of Thomas Gray's *Elegy Written in a Country Churchyard*, where almost all of the ten stressed syllables in the four lines contain a long vowel or diphthong – the exception is *knell* (where the continuant consonants /n/ and /l/ compensate for the lack of vowel length, and maintain the leisurely pace):

> The curfew tolls the knell of parting day,
> The lowing herd wind slowly o'er the lea

By contrast, we might expect to find a preponderance of short vowels in poems dealing with rapidly passing or dramatic events, as in the opening lines of Robert Browning's 'How They Brought the Good News from Ghent to Aix':

> I sprang to the stirrup, and Joris, and he;
> I galloped, Dirck galloped, we galloped all three

Nothing is totally predictable in poetry, of course, but it is certainly a genre where contrasts of vowel length have a value that transcends their basic role in differentiating the meaning of words.

It is a short step from poetic rhythm to sung musical rhythm, where the contrast between short and long is at times very noticeable, especially in jazz and popular music. The terminology reflects it, in such labels as *be-bop* and *boogie-woogie*. Scat singing routinely varies vowel quality (p. 106), but without length contrasts it couldn't exist at all: *doo-be-doo-be-dah* ... The nonsense names of many popular songs also rely on it, such as Disney's *Zip-a-dee-doo-dah*, Gene Vincent's *Be-bop-a-lula*, the Beatles' *Ob-la-di, ob-la-da*, the Crystals' (no relation) *Da Doo Ron Ron*, and innumerable variants of the *Sha-la-la*, *Shoo-be-doo* type.

There are some interesting regional variations in the use of vowel length. One of the most famous in England, along with a change in vowel quality, is the north vs south distinction illustrated by *bath*: short in northern /baθ/, long in southern /bɑːθ/. A similar change differentiates British and American English: the long /ɑː/ of Received Pronunciation (p. 21) in such words as *ask*, *bath*, *France*, and *plant* becomes a short /æ/ in General American speech. Then there is Scotland, where we find a number of length differences compared to RP: in many accents, words that contrast in length in RP sound the same in most Scottish English, such as *full* and *fool*, *Pam* and *palm*, *cot* and *caught*; and several pairs of words that have vowels the same length in RP show a difference, with *greed* shorter than *agreed*, *tide* shorter than *tied*, and *brood* shorter than *brewed*.

Length has also been affected by changes in pronunciation over time, some quite recent. Refined RP speakers in Victorian England began to say *off* and *across*, /ɒf, əˈkrɒs/, with a long vowel, /ɔː/ – 'awff, acrawss', and it can still be heard today. *Room* was usually pronounced with a short vowel, as

/rʊm/, in the early twentieth century. Today it has largely been replaced by the long vowel /ru:m/, though many people who say /ru:m/ also say *bedroom* with the short vowel, /ˈbedrʊm/. Regional variation in the use of /ʊ/ and /ʊ:/ goes in both directions. Short can become long, as when *book* and *look* /bʊk, lʊk/ are pronounced /bu:k/ and /lu:k/ (e.g. in Lancashire). Long can become short: when I lived in the south of England, my dentist fixed my *tooth* /tu:θ/; in North Wales he fixes my /tʊθ/.

Undoubtedly the best-known of the pronunciation changes affecting length in the history of English is the group of changes that began in Middle English around the start of the fifteenth century, which affected most of the long vowels in the speech of the time. What triggered the changes is unknown, but the phenomenon is known as the Great Vowel Shift. When, 200 years later, we hear Shakespeare spoken in original pronunciation (Chapter 27), the language presents few difficulties, despite the differences. When we hear Chaucer spoken in original pronunciation, it's much harder, because the long vowels have unfamiliar values. A sentence such as 'take time to go to see the moon now' would have sounded something like:

tahk teem to gaw to seh the mohn noo
/tɑ:k ti:m tʊ gɔ: tʊ sɛ: ðə mɔ:n nʊ:/

When *moon* sounds like *moan* and *time* like *team*, the comprehension problem for the modern listener is obvious. But only the long vowels of Middle English were affected; the short vowels have stayed the same, with hardly any changes. Indeed, if we were able to time-travel even as far back as Anglo-Saxon times, we would have no difficulty recognizing such words as *in*, *on*, *well*, and *man*. It's the long vowels and the diphthongs that give earlier periods of English their distinctive auditory character.

Auditory check 2

Here are twelve words each containing a vowel with a single auditory quality in RP, but five are long and seven are short. Can you hear the contrast? You can check your decisions on p. 277.

As with other quizzes in this book, this is an exercise about how these vowels work in RP. If you have a different accent, you may treat these sounds differently (as described in Chapter 13). If your decisions don't agree with those on p. 277, that will probably be a clue about one of the distinctive features of your accent.

	Long	Short
moon		
pit		
fell		
see		
tap		
put		
her		
pot		
cup		
palm		
the		
saw		

14
Spread or rounded?

There are two very noticeable visual differences among the English vowels. One relates to the height of the tongue (p. 28), which can be seen in the degree of mouth opening. The other relates to the configuration of the lips while we pronounce a vowel: they can be spread or rounded. We can see and feel the difference easily if we say 'eeoo': the lips are spread for the 'ee' /i:/ and rounded for the 'oo' /u:/.

These are the two extremes of lip movement, with the tongue high. With vowels that are pronounced lower in the mouth, the amount of rounding is much less noticeable: look in a mirror while saying *loo*, *look*, *law*, *lock* and you will see the jaw dropping further with each vowel, and the lips progressively becoming less noticeably rounded.

A distinctive feature of the RP vowel system is that only vowels made at the back of the mouth have lip-rounding – the four just illustrated, two long, *loo* /u:/, and *law* /lɔ: /, and two short, *look* /lʊk/ and *lock* /lɒk/. In this respect, English is very different from a language like French, which has rounding on vowels made at the front of the mouth too, as heard in *tu* ('you'), *deux* ('two'), and *soeur* ('sister'). As we'll see, some regional English accents do use these sounds, but the prestige accents in both British and American English avoid them. The latter actually has less lip-rounding than in RP: words with the vowel of *lock* (*hot*, *top*, etc) have an unrounded vowel, so that to British ears an American saying *hot* sounds more like *hat*.

A rounded element is also part of four of the RP diphthongs, as can be seen from the vowel table on pp. 23–4. In two cases, heard in *owl* and *old*, the rounding occurs as the second element: /aʊl/, /əʊld/. In the other two, heard in *toy* and *tour*, it occurs as the first: /tɔɪ/, /tʊə/. In conservative RP speakers, the /ʊə/ diphthong is often replaced by a rounded pure vowel, /ɔː/, so that, for example, *sure* and *your* are heard as 'shaw' and 'yaw', /ʃɔː/, /jɔː/. They pronounce *sure* and *Shaw* in exactly the same way.

There is a great deal of regional variation in the use of lip-rounding. Some accents seem to go in for it, increasing the number of rounded vowels, compared with RP, and pronouncing them more fully; others seem to shy away from it. Scottish English is a prominent increaser: words with a high back vowel, as in *moon* and *use*, are pronounced further forward in the mouth, but keeping the lip-rounding, so that the effect is a sound like the *u* in French *tu*. This can also be heard in Northern Ireland, where the rounding additionally affects the /aʊ/ diphthong heard in words like *now*. Many speakers there pronounce the first part of this phoneme higher than in RP or Scots, so that it sounds more like the 'he' in *hen*, and they lip-round the first element as well as the second, so that it resembles the vowel in the French word *soeur*. Keep your lips firmly rounded throughout while saying *now* and you'll capture the effect.

Probably the most noticeable of the accents that increase rounding are those heard throughout the north of England, where the RP /ʌ/ vowel in words like *cup* and *luck* is replaced by a rounded one, /ʊ/. As many words containing /ʌ/ rank in the top hundred or so in word-frequency lists (e.g. *but*, *come*, *just*, *much*, *one*, *some*, *such*, *up*, *us*), any variation is going to be highly distinctive. It's one of the most prominent features whenever a northern accent is respelled in dialect literature, such as writing *some* as *soom*.

There is no rounding at all in the RP /aɪ/ diphthong, in words like *right* and *nice*. This contrasts with its use in Irish English, where it has a rounded first element, often shown in Irish dialect literature as a respelling: *royt* for *right*. In an Irish version of *The Griffin*, one of Grimm's fairy tales, we encounter a leprechaun with a strong Irish accent: ' "Foine," sez the leprechaun, "roight yez are," sez he.' But this pronunciation is by no means restricted to Ireland. A similar rounding will be heard, for instance, in Birmingham and East Anglia.

Then there are the accents that decrease the amount of lip-rounding on certain vowels. Scotland and Ireland figure again. In Scottish English, many words that are lip-rounded in RP lose their rounding – *go* is often written as *gae*, *stone* as *stane*. And in Irish English, words such as *join* and *boy* have a diphthong more like RP *my*, as seen in such spellings as *jine*. The same thing happens in most West Indian accents, so that *toy* and *tie* sound the same. And it's there in Shakespeare too: *groin* rhymes with *swine* in *Venus and Adonis* (line 1116):

> And nuzzling in his flank, the loving swine
> Sheathed unaware the tusk in his soft groin.

Elsewhere, we see rounding lost in Cockney pronunciation of words like *window* and *fellow*, often spelled *winder* and *feller* /ˈwɪndə/, /ˈfelə/ in representations of the accent; and many Cockneys replace the /aʊ/ diphthong by a pure vowel in words like *now* and *town*, often spelled *nah* and *tahn* /naː/, /taːn/.

We might expect to hear a change in lip-rounding in regional accents, where the speakers want to distance themselves from the 'posh' connotations of RP, as heard in the very marked rounding that refined RP speakers use in such words as *do*, *book*, and *caught*. How can one achieve such distance? A widely used change is to turn the pure vowel

/u:/ into a diphthong, by starting it with a front vowel, as /ɪʊ/, heard in Cockney, Liverpool, Australia, and many other places, and often written as 'diu' or 'dew' in popular writing: *Dew yew moind*? Another way would be to lose the rounding altogether, common in many American English accents, where the lips are neutrally open or even spread, in words like *book*, and more open than in RP in words like *caught*.

A surprising development in recent years has been to hear this loss of rounding in /ʊ/, in words like *good* and *could* – a vowel that is often extra-rounded, with protruding lips, in refined RP. Young RP speakers today are going in the other direction, saying these words with no rounding at all. The unrounding has even spread to /u:/ in words like *cool* and *school*, which are often pronounced by youngsters with a short vowel, so that *cool* sounds more like *cull* and *school* like *skull*.

The diphthongs with rounded second elements, /əʊ/ as in *no*, and /aʊ/ as in *now*, have also attracted a great deal of variation, both regional and social. In Cockney, Irish English, and Australian English, words like *no* have a very open first element, so that *no* /naʊ/ sounds like RP *now*. In popular Irish writing, we often see it respelled as *ou* or *ow*: *the ould country*. Accents that do this then have to find a way of keeping *no* and *now* distinct, and they do this by pronouncing the first element of *now* further forward in the mouth, in the direction of the vowel in RP *men* /nɛʊ/ – 'ne-oo'. The same need to keep the words distinct is heard in Birmingham, where (to change the example) *float* has a more open onset, so that it sounds like RP *flout*. *Flout* then has the /ɛʊ/ vowel.

In Canadian English, /aʊ/ has a very individual quality. In words like *house*, *south*, and *out* (where the diphthong is followed by a voiceless consonant, p. 121) the first element is formed higher in the mouth than in General American speech, with a quality like the *u* in RP *mud*. That is why

Americans parody a Canadian accent by saying 'oot' for *out*, stressing the /ʊ/ element. To British ears, the effect isn't so strange, as a similar quality (with *out* sounding more like RP *oat*) can be heard in many West Country or Irish accents.

Of course, if most RP speakers say *no* as /nəʊ/, anyone wanting to show that they belong to a higher social class has the option of saying it differently, and this is what we hear when refined speakers say such words with a very open and fronted first element: /nɛʊ/. To maintain the difference with *now*, they then say that word with a 'further back' pronunciation, /nɑʊ/, where the first element has the quality we normally hear in words like *car*. An alternative way of showing refinement is to do away with the diphthong and rounding altogether, so that *no* comes out as /nə:/ – 'ner'. There's an accent joke based on this shift. A very posh head teacher was giving a farewell speech to the boys about to leave his school. He hoped that they would all go out into the world with a /gə:l/ before them. To get the joke, we have to appreciate that, for the head, /gə:l/ meant *goal*; for the not-so-posh lads, it meant *girl*.

These are some of the ways in which lip-rounding is used to show differences in meaning in words. And that might seem to be the end of the rounding story. But there is another dimension to rounding in English that falls under the heading of the 'paralinguistic' tones of voice described in Chapter 5. We can exaggerate lip-rounding over a whole utterance or completely avoid it.

Exaggerated lip-rounding is most often encountered in baby talk. When carers talk to a baby, one of the things they often do is keep their lips rounded when saying such things as 'Who's a lovely little baby then?' – as well as making babyish consonant changes, such as 'lickle' for *little* and 'den' for *then*. The same effect can be heard when we talk to non-threatening animals, such as pet cats and birds. And it is there again when we talk to our intimates as if they were a baby. I remember a social occasion when a husband complained jocularly to his wife, who had been handing round some biscuits, that he hadn't been offered one. 'Aw, did he want a biscuit then?' said his wife, with marked lip-rounding. The tone of voice caused some hilarity, but no incomprehension. Evidently it is the sort of thing that everyone does from time to time.

Why do we lip-round when talking to babies? It's a way of gaining their attention and achieving a response. Lip-rounding is not a major feature of English; as we saw above, few vowels actually use it. So if someone lip-rounds a whole utterance, it makes that utterance stand out. It's unusual linguistic behaviour. The speakers are being playful with the language, and that is always a means of getting people to notice you – which of course is what parents of an infant want. They love the baby, and they want the baby to love them back – but you can't love someone if you don't notice them. Along with other features of baby talk (such as wider pitch range), lip-rounding is one of the means carers employ to obtain the response they desire.

Lip-spreading throughout an utterance is not so commonly encountered. Because there are many vowels that are not normally rounded, the effect of lip-rounding, when we do come across it, is immediately noticeable. But as only a handful of vowels are normally rounded, lip-spreading is going to be less evident, and will depend very much on the choice of words. I remember hearing it very noticeably in a television advertisement for the washing powder that was described as 'new blue Daz'. The speaker was smiling as she said it, and the result was to turn the two rounded /uː/s into spread versions. It can be effective, but it can also give a 'soapy', insincere, or patronizing impression. If people sound as if they're always smiling, the 'meaning' of the smile dissipates. The negative effect is particularly strong when there's no visual context, and is thus something that radio presenters who have been instructed to 'sound friendly' need to be aware of. There's no need for a smiling tone when introducing Mahler's Ninth Symphony.

Auditory check 3

Here are eight words each containing a vowel with a single
auditory quality in RP, but four are pronounced without any
rounding of the lips and four have some degree of rounding.
Can you hear the contrast? You can check your decisions on
p. 277.

As with other quizzes in this book, this is an exercise
about how these vowels work in RP. If you have a different
accent, you may treat these sounds differently (as described
in Chapter 14). If your decisions don't agree with those on
p. 277, that will probably be a clue about one of the distinctive features of your accent.

	Rounded	Unrounded
look		
men		
feel		
paw		
bird		
true		
lot		
sit		

Prunes and prism

Mrs General

Maintaining a pleasing lip-shape, it seems, was fashionable, at least in Dickens' day. Here is Mrs General, a genteel widow who has set herself up as a 'companion to ladies', in *Little Dorrit* (Chapter 41), having heard Amy address Mr Dorrit as 'Father':

> 'Papa is a preferable mode of address,' observed Mrs General. 'Father is rather vulgar, my dear. The word Papa, besides, gives a pretty form to the lips. Papa, potatoes, poultry, prunes, and prism are all very good words for the lips: especially prunes and prism. You will find it serviceable, in the formation of a demeanour, if you sometimes say to yourself in company – on entering a room, for instance – Papa, potatoes, poultry, prunes and prism, prunes and prism.'

15

Close or open? Front or back?

We can get a clear idea of the way the tongue moves up and down, when pronouncing vowels, just by looking at the speaker's mouth: the more open the mouth, the more open the vowel. That's why a doctor asks us to 'say ah', /ɑː/, when wanting to examine our throat. It's one of the vowels that has maximum openness, so phoneticians call vowels in this position *open* or *low* vowels. And, as it's pronounced with the back of the tongue in its lowest position, it makes the largest opening and thus gives the best view of the pharynx, where our sore throat is likely to be.

A wide open mouth means a big resonant sound. There's nothing blocking the air on its way out from the lungs. It's thus the primeval sound for a cry: babies go *waaaa*, not *weee* or *wooo*. The primeval laugh is *ha ha ha* (and its variants, such as *har har*). And if we want to shout, we're more likely to be heard if our mouth is wide open. Not surprisingly, therefore, quite a few of the more excited, emotional, and noisy inter-jections make use of it, or the equivalent maximally open vowel made at the front of the mouth: *ah, aargh, alas* (and *alack*), *alleluia, amen, avast, ay, bah, bastard, blah blah blah, blast, bravo, crap, damn, drat, ga-ga, hah, halloa, hurrah, huzzah, lah-di-dah, pah, rah-rah-rah, rat-tat-tat, shazam, ta, ta ta, ta dah, tra la la, yah boo, yadda yadda, zap.*

When the tongue is at its highest position in the mouth, close to the roof of the mouth, we hear the two long vowels

/i:/ as in *tea* and /u:/ as in *too*. Phoneticians accordingly call them *high* or *close* vowels. They leave the smallest aperture for sound to escape. Their short vowel partners, /ɪ/ as in *pit* and /ʊ/ as in *put*, are made with the tongue not quite so high. You can feel the tongue and the jaw lowering slightly if you say the two front vowels several times in quick succession: /i: ɪ i: ɪ .../. The same thing happens if you say the two back vowels in sequence, /u: ʊ u: ʊ .../, but the lip-rounding makes it harder to feel the movement.

A good way of getting a feel for the close front vowels is to listen to words that seem to have a sound symbolic meaning of smallness (p. 124). We hear the short vowel in *tinkle*, *mini*, *midget*, *dinky*, and the long vowel in *wee*, *teensy*, *petite*, and reduplicated words such as *teeny-weeny*, *easy-peasy*, and *heebie-jeebies*. We often emphasize the closeness of the /i:/ vowels when we want to stress the smallness, and this is sometimes reflected in the spelling. When Mrs Mann offers Mr Bumble a glass of gin (in *Oliver Twist*, Chapter 7) she is very persuasive: 'Just a leetle drop, with a little cold water, and a lump of sugar.' Tininess is there in Jonathan Swift's *Lilliput*, Disney's *Jiminy Cricket*, Lewis Carroll's *Tweedledum* and *Tweedledee*, and J. K. Rowling's game of *quidditch*, in which players chase a very small golden *snitch* (replacing the *snidget*). We hear it in some nursery rhymes, such as *Wee Willie Winkie*, *Eeper Weeper*, *chimney sweeper*, and *Incy wincy spider* ... (aka *Itsy bitsy spider* ...). The interjections that use high front vowels are also generally minimal or moderate in their exclamatory force, often effete, euphemistic, or childlike: (with the long vowel) *eek*, *tee hee*, *sheesh*, *gee*, *dear(y) me*, *jeez*, *jeepers-creepers*; (with the short vowel) *flip*, *fiddlesticks*; and (with both short and long) *fiddle-de-dee*. The contrast with the open vowels can be seen in the way writers represent laughter: there's something full-blooded about *ha-ha-ha* which is missing in *he-he-he*.

The close back long vowel behaves similarly: *boo, boo hoo, boom-boom* (as a joke reaction), *coo, cooee, cootchie-cootchie, deuce, oof, ooh, oops(y), phew, phooey, pooh, shoot* (avoiding *shit*), *strewth, super-duper, whew, whoops(y), whoosh, woo hoo, yaroo, yoo-hoo*. In cartoon names such as *Scooby Doo, Boo-Boo, Goofy, Snoopy, Droopy*, and *Mr Magoo*, or Roald Dahl's *Oompa-Loompas* and *Augustus Gloop*, smallness is still there, but now with a suggestion of bulk or ineptness.

Of course most uses of a vowel have no symbolic meaning. It doesn't make sense to ask 'What is the meaning of /i:/ or /u:/?', or any other phoneme. But choosing examples where the sounds do have some symbolic force is a useful way of remembering them, and in my view rather more interesting than the usual textbook method of giving a random selection of words that just happen to contain them. This approach also brings to light some pertinent juxtapositions. Pronunciation is not just a matter of learning individual sounds; it is learning to distinguish sounds from each other.

Because of the nature of the vowel space that the tongue makes beneath the palate, there can be no greater auditory contrast than between close and open – /i:, ɪ, u:, ʊ/ vs /a, ɑ:/ or between close front and close back: /i:, ɪ/ vs /u:, ʊ/. The contrast between /ɪ/ and /a/ is especially noticeable in reduplicated expressions, most of which also suggest smallness or unimportance, such as *bric-a-brac, chit-chat, dilly dally, kitty cat, knick knack, fiddle faddle, mishmash, pit-a-pat, riffraff, tit for tat*. Brand names can rely on it: *Kit Kat, Tic Tac*. Several cartoon names and nursery rhymes use it: *Bambi, Simba, Dick Dastardly, Pink Panther, Jack and Jill, Jack be nimble Jack be quick*. Fictional place names use it: *Illyria, Atlantis, Minas Tirith, Shangri-La*. Its appeal has a long history: Shakespeare has *bibble-babble, pibble-pabble, tilly-fally, skimble-skamble, snip-snap*.

We can get a good sense of the four corners of the vowel

area by listening to the following set of names from the world of fiction (when a name has more than one syllable, the stressed syllable is underlined):

/æ/ and /iː/ Anne <u>Stee</u>le (*Sense and Sensibility*)
/æ/ and /uː/ in Ba<u>loo</u> (*Jungle Book*)
/æ/ and /ʊ/ in <u>Sar</u>uman (*The Lord of the Rings*)
/æ/ and /ɑː/ Bran Stark (*Game of Thrones*)
/ɑː/ and /uː/ in <u>Pooh</u>-Bah (*The Mikado*)
/ɑː/ and /ʊ/ Charles Muntz (*Up*)
/ɑː/ and /iː/ <u>Char</u>lie <u>Wea</u>sley (*Harry Potter and the Prisoner of Azkaban*)
/ɑː/ and /ɪ/ in <u>Syd</u>ney <u>Car</u>ton (*A Tale of Two Cities*)
/ɪ/ and /uː/ in <u>Win</u>nie the Pooh (*The House at Pooh Corner*)
/ɪ/ and /ʊ/ in <u>Lill</u>iput (*Gulliver's Travels*)
/iː/ and /uː/ Pete <u>Pu</u>ma (*Looney Tunes*)
/iː/ and /ʊ/ in <u>Soot</u>y and Sweep (UK TV series)

It's clear from the above that there are two intersecting dimensions when we describe vowels: the vertical dimension, along which vowels are classified on a scale from close (through mid) to open; and the horizontal dimension, along which vowels are classified on a scale from front (through central) to back. To fill out the vowel picture, we now need to explore what happens in the mid and central areas.

The *mid* vowels are of two broad types. Those made with the front of the tongue have a vowel with some sort of 'e' quality, as in /e/ *bed*, /eɪ/ *bay*, and /ɛə/ *bare*. Those made with the back of the tongue have a vowel with some sort of 'o' quality, as in /ɒ/ *bod*, /ɔː/ *bore*, and /ɔɪ/ *boy*. In between are two vowels that occupy the centre of the vowel space: /ɜː/ as in *bird*, and /ʌ/ as in *bud*. (The unstressed central vowel, schwa, needs separate discussion: p. 117.) Once again, we can hear these contrasts in character names. Front mid vowels: two /e/s in *Henry Jekyll*; two /eɪ/s in *Baby Jane*; two /ɛə/s in *The Hair Bear Bunch*. Back mid vowels: two /ɒ/s in *Olga da Polga*; two /ɔ:/s in *Georgie Porgie*; two /ɔɪ/s – very uncommon, as /ɔɪ/ is the least used vowel in English (p. 176) – in *Gloin* and *Oin*. Central vowels: two /ɜ:/s in *Ernie* and *Bert*; two /ʌ/s in *Bugs Bunny*. And a short and long mid back vowel contrast in *Lord Voldemort*.

More commonly, writers like to juxtapose vowels from different parts of the vowel area. If they're thinking vertically, they contrast a mid vowel with one of the close or open options (I illustrate here from just the pure vowels, with stressed syllables underlined where necessary):

mid front and close:
/i:/ and /e/ in Peter Pevensie
/e/ and /ɪ/ in Henry Higgins;
/e/ and /u:/ in Ebenezer Scrooge
/e/ and /ʊ/ in Emma Woodhouse

mid front and open:
/æ/ and /e/ in Hannibal Lecter
/ɑ:/ and /e/ in Arthur Dent

mid back and close:
/i:/ and /ɒ/ in (Zaphod) Beeblebrox
/ɪ/ and /ɒ/ in Willy Wonka
/ɒ/ and /u:/ in Robinson Crusoe
/ɒ/ and /ʊ/ in Robin Hood
/ɔ:/ and /i:/ in Ford Prefect
/ɔ:/ and /ɪ/ in George Wickham
/ɔ:/ and /u:/ in Lorna Doone
/ʊ/ and /ɔ:/ in Bullroarer Took

mid back and open:
/æ/ and /ɒ/ in <u>Dan</u>iel Der<u>on</u>da
/ɒ/ and /ɑ:/ in <u>Jon</u>athan <u>Har</u>ker
/æ/ and /ɔ:/ in Jack <u>Daw</u>kins
/ɔ:/ and/ ɑ:/ in <u>Geor</u>giana <u>Dar</u>cy

central and close:
/ʌ/ and /ɪ/ in <u>Huck</u>leberry Finn,
/i:/ and /ʌ/ in Speed <u>Bug</u>gy
/ʌ/ and /ʊ/ in <u>Jun</u>gle Book
/u:/ and /ʌ/ in Scrooge Mc<u>Duck</u>
/ɜ:/ and /ɪ/ in <u>Vir</u>gil Tibbs
/i:/ and /ɜ:/ in <u>Twee</u>ty Bird
/ɜ:/ and /ʊ/ in <u>Ber</u>tie <u>Woos</u>ter
/u:/ and /ɜ:/ in <u>Ju</u>dah Ben-<u>Hur</u>

central and open:
/æ/ and /ʌ/ in <u>Daff</u>y Duck
/ɑ:/ and /ʌ/ in <u>Char</u>lie <u>Buck</u>et
/æ/ and /ɜ:/ in <u>Cath</u>erine <u>Earn</u>shaw
/ɑ:/ and /ɜ:/ in <u>Mar</u>jorie <u>Durs</u>ley

If writers are thinking horizontally, they can contrast mid front and mid back, or one of these with a central vowel:

mid front and mid back:
/ɒ/ and /e/ in Tom and <u>Jer</u>ry
/e/ and /ɔ:/ in <u>Len</u>nie Small

mid front and central:
/e/ and /ʌ/ in <u>Ben</u>jamin <u>Bun</u>ny
/e/ and /ɜ:/ in Tess <u>Dur</u>beyfield

mid back and central:
/ɒ/ and /ʌ/ in <u>For</u>rest Gump

/ɜː/ and /ɒ/ in <u>Ker</u>mit the Frog
/ɔː/ and /ʌ/ in George of the <u>Jun</u>gle
/ɔː/ and /ɜː/ in <u>Bor</u>gin and Burkes

They can make diphthong contrasts in the same way (<u>Ja</u>mes Bond, <u>Ma</u>ry Poppins, Draco Mal<u>foy</u>, etc.).

These patterns can be extended into a three-way (or more) contrast – too many options to illustrate all of them here, but a general impression of the effect can be gained from such character names as *Lolita, Milly-Molly-Mandy, Bilbo Baggins, Brobdingnag, Svengali, Marivella*, and *Snipp, Snapp, Snurr*. Ringing the changes on a set of vowels has an early appeal: witness nursery rhyme juxtapositions such as *Ding Dong Bell, Eeny Meeny Miny Mo, See Saw Margery Daw, Fee Fi Fo Fum*, and Old MacDonald's *E-I-E-I-O*. And some popular nonsensical expressions continue the effect: *bish bash bosh, bada bing bada boom*, and Spike Milligan's poem 'The Ning Nang Nong'.

Some of these effects won't work in exactly the same way in all accents, because of the way regional variations cause the tongue to take a different vertical or horizontal position for individual vowels. Close or mid vowels can be pronounced lower. The /iː/ vowel, for example, is more open in most Irish accents, so that *tea* /tiː/ comes out as /teɪ/, and is often spelled *tay* in popular writing. (A famous respelling occurs in the title of Seán O'Casey's play, *Juno and the Paycock*.) In Birmingham, the vowel at the end of words like *sorry* and *merry* is a diphthong, /əɪ/, so that we hear 'sorruh-i' – something we hear in Shakespearean English too (Chapter 27). In Cockney, the unstressed /ə/ vowel at the end of words like *copper* is pronounced in a more open way, like 'coppa'. In New Zealand, /ɪ/ usually has a central [ə] quality – an effect that Australians like to parody when they say Kiwis pronounce *fish and chips* as 'fush and chups'. Such distinctions are quite subtle. An RP speaker says the name *Philip* with the two vowels sounding the same. An Australian makes the second *i* sound like the vowel in *the*: 'Phil-up'. A New Zealander gives both vowels a *the*-quality: 'Phulup'.

In the same sort of way, in regional accents low or mid vowels can be pronounced higher; vowels at the front can be pronounced further back; and those at the back can be pronounced further forward. We hear the front/back dimension at work in the way words like *bath* are pronounced. In RP, as we saw in Chapter 13, the tongue is at its lowest back point: /bɑ:θ/. In Australian English it's much further forward, /ba:θ/ – in popular writing sometimes spelled as *baath*. And in the USA, we hear it rising at the front, with various qualities, ranging from /bæ:θ/ to a pronunciation with three distinct qualities /beɪəθ/ – as it were, 'bay-uth'. The front short vowels /æ/ and /e/ are both pronounced higher in the mouth in South Africa, Australia, and New Zealand. *Jack* (RP /dʒæk/) comes out as /dʒek/, 'Jek', and *yes* (RP /jes/) as /jɪs/, 'yis'. There's an old witticism which is actually quite useful to anyone who wants to remember this pair of changes. For South Africans, it's said, *sex* is what you carry coal in, while *six* is needed for procreation!

The articulatory possibilities relating to vertical and horizontal tongue movement are clearly very numerous, and many of the distinctions in regional accents are extremely subtle. They provide English accents with much of the information we need when we hear people speak and try to guess where they're from. It takes phoneticians quite some time to learn to recognize all the possible vowel variations, write them down in a phonetic transcription, and produce them accurately. I'm always impressed by professional impressionists who are able to capture these accent nuances quickly and effectively. Phoneticians aren't impressionists. Before I can 'do' an accent, I have to analyse it, working out the sound system and trying it out on a large number of words, to make sure I'm getting the contrasts right. Which means consonants as well as vowels.

Auditory check 4

Here are eleven words each containing a vowel with a single auditory quality in RP, but the vowels vary in the height of the tongue: four have the tongue in close position, five in mid position, and two in open position. Can you hear the contrast? You can check your decisions on p. 277.

As with other quizzes in this book, this is an exercise about how these vowels work in RP. If you have a different accent, you may treat these sounds differently (as described in Chapter 13). If your decisions don't agree with those on p. 277, that will probably be a clue about one of the distinctive features of your accent.

	Close	Mid	Open
see			
get			
cat			
cut			
shoe			
the			
took			
far			
bird			
pick			
stop			

Here is the same set of words, but this time the task is to identify whether the vowels are made towards the front of the mouth, the centre, or the back: four are front vowels, three are central, and four are back.

	Front	Central	Back
see			
get			
cat			
cut			
shoe			
the			
took			
far			
bird			
pick			
stop			

Schwa

For English readers, probably the most intriguing of all the phonetic symbols is the one that has been called *schwa*. It represents a weak vowel made in the very centre of the vowel area, and is especially relevant for English because of its frequency. It's the vowel used in the normal unstressed pronunciation of *the* and *a*. You'll hear it in the unstressed syllable at the beginning of such words as *above*, *along*, and *today*, and at the end of hundreds of words ending in *-a*, such as *extra*, *idea*, *pizza*, and *sofa*. It's there in the final syllable of words ending in a vowel followed by *r*, when that *r* isn't pronounced (p. 22), such as *actor*, *collar*, *teacher*, and *colour*, and in the comparative of adjectives and adverbs: *big* > *bigger*, *soon* > *sooner*. And it's used as an element in four of the diphthongs in RP (p. 21): *bode* /bəʊd/, *beer* /bɪə/, *bear* /bɛə/, and *boor* /bʊə/.

As the spelling of these examples suggests, several vowels become schwa when they're unstressed – *o* in *actor*, *e* in *teacher*, and so on – and so it is often called the 'neutral' vowel. In fact its actual phonetic value varies across words and accents (as well as among languages). In English, the phonetic quality in the middle of a word (as in *today* and *probable*) isn't exactly the same as at the beginning or end (as in *along* and *sofa*). Sometimes the tongue is noticeably higher or lower in the mouth – an effect that shows up clearly in acoustic studies. In some accents, the variants are more noticeable because schwa is used in a stressed syllable. I pronounce such words as *cup* and *luck* with a schwa – reflecting my early years in North Wales and Liverpool – and this makes me sound very different from RP speakers, who use a more open vowel /ʌ/. But I don't round my lips, as most people from the north of England do.

The unusual name comes from Hebrew, where *sheva* was the name of the sign placed under a consonant letter to show the absence of a following vowel or, in some positions, the sounding of a central vowel. In this sense, there are citations in English from as early as 1582. The term was adopted by nineteenth-century Germanic philologists to identify similar sounds in Indo-European languages: *sheva* became *shva* in German, and was spelled as *schwa* (sometimes *shwa*) when it arrived in English – the first *OED* citation is 1895. It was included in the International Phonetic Alphabet when this was devised in the 1880s, and the 'inverted e' symbol was chosen to show it. Most people pronounce the *w* as /w/, but some reflect the German history and use a /v/.

16

The plosive family

This is Captain Corcoran singing to his crew in Gilbert and Sullivan's *HMS Pinafore*:

> Bad language or abuse,
> I never, never use,
> Whatever the emergency;
> Though 'bother it' I may
> Occasionally say,
> I never use a big, big D—

For the Victorians, *damn* was felt to be such a strong swear word that it was invariably abbreviated in writing to *D---*. It was often softened to *darn* or *dash*, especially by the ladies, but for men it was the default expletive. Probably everyone used it – even the good Captain. Queried by his crew, 'What, never?' his response always raises an audience laugh: 'Hardly ever.'

There's evidently something rather satisfying about those words beginning with *d-*. Or *b-*. Corcoran's *bother it* reminds the modern ear of *bloody*, *bugger*, *bollocks*, *bastard*, and other *b*-words of strong emotional force. Again, they can be softened – *B*, *bosh*, *blimey*, *bozo* – but the common element stays. What is it about /d/ and /b/ that seems to make them the sounds of choice when someone wants to swear or insult?

It's all to do with the way these sounds are made. The speaker is in a heightened emotional state, tense, and – in some circumstances – ready to lash out or hit. Swearing provides a linguistic release of the pent-up tension. It makes the swearer feel a little more relaxed, even when there's nobody around to listen to the utterance – as when, alone in a narrow space, one bangs one's head against some object. It is a rare person who can suffer the indignity in silence (I imagine – empirical evidence is hard to come by).

'Release' is the operative word. When we articulate a /b/ we close our lips tightly. We may not realize it, but we also automatically close off the airway into the nose by raising the back of our palate. As a result, air from the lungs builds up in our mouth behind the closure, so that when we pronounce /b/ it's released in a sudden burst. It's the nearest parallel to an emotional explosion that English pronunciation can provide. It is indeed an explosive sound – a word that lies behind the technical term used by phoneticians: *plosive*. It's also described as a *stop* consonant, for the same reason: the air is 'stopped' by the closure. Because the two lips are involved in making the closure, it's called a *bilabial* plosive. And because the vocal folds are vibrating at the same time, it's said to be *voiced*. So there we have the full phonetic description of /b/: it's a *voiced bilabial plosive*.

/d/ is articulated in exactly the same way, except that the closure this time is made by the tongue against the ridge behind our teeth – the *alveolar* ridge – and the air is compressed in the middle of the mouth. So /d/ is described as a *voiced alveolar plosive*. The explosion, as the air is released, won't be quite as strong as the one made at the lips, as the quantity of air that builds up is in a smaller space. I'd expect there to be far more emotional impact coming from *b*-words than *d*-words, in our swearing scenario.

English has a third voiced plosive sound – the /g/ heard at the beginning of *go*. Here the closure is further back, made by the back of the tongue against the rear part of the roof of the mouth – the part shown as the *velum* in the diagram on page 28. It's therefore called a *voiced velar plosive*. (It's not so easy to feel the place of articulation, though you can get a rough idea if you say /g/ a few times – 'guh-guh-guh' – and sharply breathe in while doing so. You'll feel the cooler air rushing past the velar area in your mouth.) Being so far back, the amount of air compressed behind it is relatively small, compared with /b/ and /d/. I wouldn't expect there to be many swear words or insult words beginning with *g-*, therefore – though there are a few, such as *git* and *goof*. They tend not to be quite as emotionally forceful as those made further forward in the mouth.

In English, each of the voiced plosives has a counterpart where the vocal folds are not vibrating. These *voiceless* plosives are bilabial /p/, alveolar /t/, and velar /k/. They are also articulated in a very tense way – actually more tensely than in the case of the voiced sounds. You can get an impression of the amount of tension involved when these sounds are released by carrying out a simple action. Pronounce a /p/ ('puh'), and while doing so hold the back of your hand in front of your lips. You'll feel a puff of air as the lips open. Phonetician call this *aspiration*. (You don't get this effect with /b/.)

As these sounds are even more full of tension than their voiced equivalents, we'd expect them to be just as often used in emotional expressions, if not more so. And that is what we find. In fact there's a great deal of double use in 'rude' words, with the voiceless sounds occurring not just initially (as in *pisser* and *poof*) but at both the beginning and the end – reinforcing each other. Sometimes it's a repetition of the same sound, as in *tit*, *twit*, *twat*, and *tart*, but more often the words combine different places of articulation, as in *punk*, *prick, puke, prat, twerp, kink, cack, cock, kook, crap, cretin, clot,* and – strongest of all – *cunt.* Combinations of voiced and voiceless plosives also occur, such as *brat, dope, idiot, turd, clod,* and *gook.* And the power of those final plosives can be felt even if the initial consonant belongs to some other phonetic family, as in *wimp, wop, sap, slob, shit, nit, sod, dork, fuck, honk, mug,* and *wog.*

It was ever thus: in Shakespeare's day we find *pish, tush, pox, 'sblood, sot, cuckold, scurvy, caitiff, coxcomb, jack, pander, clotpoll, popinjay, drab, lackey,* and many more. There are 962 headwords in Hugh Rawson's *A Dictionary of Invective* (1989), which has the excellent subtitle: *A Treasury of Curses, Insults, Put-Downs and Other formerly Unprintable Terms from Anglo-Saxon Times to the Present*; and 812 (85 per cent) of these contain a plosive. The items that don't are generally much weaker, and often teasing, such as *fool, heel, lemon, loon, moron, ninny, oaf, swine, wuss* ...

Of course, only a tiny number of words in English are involved in swearing and insults. Most of the words which contain plosives have no such emotive associations. But it's interesting nonetheless to see how poets and dramatists often use these emotionally neutral consonants to build up alliterative sequences – a feature of literary English since Anglo-Saxon times – and they can then pack a considerable descriptive or emotional punch. I'm thinking of such lines as Thomas Hardy's opening to 'At Castle Boterel':

> As I drive to the junction of lane and highway,
> And the drizzle bedrenches the waggonette

Or Hopkins' 'Pied Beauty':

> Glory be to God for dappled things –
> for skies of couple-colour as a brinded cow

Insult sequences, such as those we find in Shakespeare, also illustrate the point: the individual words may not be especially insulting, but in combination the accumulation of plosives produce a phonetic crescendo. All six plosives are used in Hal's harangue to Francis in *Henry IV Part 1* (2.4.68): 'Wilt thou rob this leathern-jer<u>k</u>in, <u>c</u>rys<u>t</u>al-<u>b</u>u<u>tt</u>on, no<u>t</u>-<u>p</u>ate<u>d</u>, aga<u>t</u>e-ring, <u>p</u>u<u>k</u>e-s<u>t</u>o<u>ck</u>ing, <u>c</u>ad<u>d</u>is-gar<u>t</u>er, smooth-<u>t</u>ongue S<u>p</u>anish <u>p</u>ouch?'

Writers often rely on plosives to give their characters names that are sometimes humorous and sometimes menacing. Charles Dickens is a famous case in point. Take some instances beginning with B: *Bayham Badger, Jack Bamber, Barkis, Bill Barley, Cornelia Blimber, Josiah Bounderby, Bumble, Buzfuz* ... In one online list of 400 character names from Dickens, I counted 333 containing a plosive – 84 per cent, including several where they (along with the short vowels, see p. 91) convey the entire sonic effect, as in *Bud, Biddy, Guppy, Peggotty, Pip, Tappertit,* and *Tigg*. It comes as a bit of surprise (to a phonetician, at any rate) to encounter a Dickensian name that lacks these sounds, such as *Samuel Weller* and *Rose Maylie*.

Nonsense verse has always relied greatly on plosives. Famous examples include Lewis Carroll's 'Jabberwocky', in which 20 of the 27 coinages – excluding duplicates, and allowing for some uncertainties of pronunciation – use plosives for effect: *bandersnatch, beamish, borogoves, brillig, burbled, callay, callooh, frabjous, galumphing, gimble, gyre, jubjub, manxome, outgrabe, snicker-snack, toves, tulgey, tumtum, vorpal, wabe* (the exceptions are *frumious, mimsy, mome, raths, slithy, uffish, whiffling*). And then there is Edward Lear's *Pobble* (who has no toes), Spike Milligan's land of the *Bumbley Boo*, and many more.

There's no intrinsic connection between a sound and meaning: we can't sensibly ask 'What does /b/ mean?' Still, over the centuries clusters of words have emerged where the pronunciation does seem to exploit the articulatory character of sounds. It's called *sound symbolism*, and all languages so far studied illustrate it. In literature, the corresponding term is *onomatopoeia*, said of words that reflect some properties of the real world, as in *splash*, *cuckoo*, and *babble*. But the effects go well beyond poetry, as I illustrated in the previous chapter in relation to vowel height. For example, a final /p/, preceded by a short vowel, is very common in words that have a meaning to do with suddenness, such as *blip*, *gap*, *pip*, *hop*, and *tap*. A final /b/ suggests largeness or lack of shape or direction, as in *blob*, *tub*, *club*, *flab*, *jab*, and *lob*. Of course, there are lots of words where the final /p/ or /b/ has nothing to do with these meanings (such as *keep* and *verb*), but it's interesting that when authors make up a nonsense name, these properties come to the surface. How would you name a really fat cartoon character: Mr Nup or Mr Nub?

Child language acquisition must be one of the reasons why young children (and children's authors) like plosives so much. Research has shown how plosives are the first consonant-like sounds to be heard in six-month-old babbling – indeed, the word *babble* is itself a reflection of what they do. And when we look at a typical list of 'first words', we see plosives predominating in the words they are copying from their caretakers. I report three lists in my *Listen to your Child*, and in each case 60 per cent of the words contained them, such as *daddy*, *doggie*, *baby*, *pee-pee*, *car*, *teddy*, *ball*, *dolly*, *bottle*, *down*, *go*, *bye-bye*. The two bilabials are usually the first to be heard, and then the two velars, with the two alveolars last. The voiced consonants usually appear before the voiceless ones. All plosives usually appear at the beginnings of words before they occur at the end. Indeed, it's normal for children in the early second year to pronounce new words without their final consonants, so that *bib* comes out as /bɪ/ and *cat* as /ka/. The word 'usually' is important in all of this, as there are many individual differences in early child speech.

Plosives provide some of the best examples of how consonants work in English, for they show contrasts of meaning in all three positions in the word: initial, medial, and final. Initially, we find such pairs as *pin/bin*, *tip/dip*, and *coat/goat*. Medial examples would be *caper/caber*, *latter/ladder*, and *sacking/sagging*. Final examples: *mop/mob*, *hit/hid*, and *lock/log*. They are also among the sounds foreigners find easiest to learn, because they are very common among the languages of the world. Nobody has yet found a language that has no plosive consonants – though the number of plosives and their place of articulation varies among them.

Another convenience, for those learning English – and I include little children here alongside foreign learners – is that plosives don't vary very much in their articulation from one part of the word to another. The main exception learners have to listen out for is that at the ends of words a plosive may not be released. At the end of the sentence 'Give me a cup' in normal colloquial speech, the lips usually stay closed. We don't say 'cup-uh'. (In really emphatic speech, of course, people do often 'spit out' the final sound.) Similarly, a dog-owner who says *good dog* probably won't release the /d/ in *good*: it'll sound like 'goodog' (see further, Chapter 23).

Another thing that learners have to be aware of, if their English is to sound native, is the way a voiceless plosive changes its pronunciation when preceded by /s/. In words like *spin*, *stick*, and *scone*, the aspiration usually disappears: try the back-of-the-hand trick while saying these words, and in most accents you won't feel the puff of air. (In a few accents, such as Welsh or Irish, it may still be there, as these are accents where aspiration is strongly present.)

Apart from that, /p/ and /b/ hardly vary at all within an accent. The phonemes /k/ and /g/ do a little: when these sounds are used before a front vowel (p. 106) they are articulated a bit further forward in the mouth than when they occur before a back vowel: do the breathing-in trick while saying *keep* and *car* and you'll feel the difference, with the cold air more in the middle of the mouth for *keep*. The greatest variation affects /t/ and /d/, as the position of the tongue is influenced by whatever sounds follow them. In words like *trip* and *drip*, the tongue is pulled back a little, towards the place where /r/ is pronounced (Chapter 20). In *eighth* it's pulled forward, towards the teeth, because that's the place where the *th* /θ/ is pronounced (Chapter 17).

The way the sound is released can also be affected. If you say *not now*, the air released by the /t/ actually comes out through your nose, not your mouth, because of the influence of the following nasal sound. And if you say *little*, the way /l/ is formed makes the air come out around the sides of your tongue. Children take a while before they articulate these sequences in the right way: they will say 'litt-ul', pushing the air out through the front of the mouth.

The sound /t/ is the one that attracts many BBC complaints, because it is very prone to be dropped in colloquial speech, or when surrounded by other consonants. Dickens spotted this in his representations of everyday speech, for instance in *David Copperfield* (Chapter 3): '"I couldn't azackly" – that was always the substitute for "exactly", in Peggotty's militia of words'. In a sequence such as the /ktl/ in the middle of *exactly* the tongue has to move rapidly from the velar position to the alveolar position and then reshape to make the /l/ sound. In slow speech, it's not a problem. In fast speech, we have to make a real effort to avoid dropping the /t/. It would be the same with *cyclists*, where the /sts/ becomes

/ss/, and many more such words. I discuss this kind of omission (*elision*) in Chapter 23.

A related phenomenon affecting /t/ is the way it readily falls under the influence of a following sound. Say *cut price* rapidly, or *not me*. The odds are that you will say something like 'cup price' and 'nop me'. In such cases, phoneticians talk about the way /t/ *assimilates* to the following sound. Again, it takes a real effort to avoid this kind of assimilation. With the slower speech of radio newsreading (p. 64), it's easier to retain the clear articulation of /t/, and most readers do, so that when an assimilation does take place it's often noticed – and complained about. That's discussed in Chapter 23 too.

Is there much variation in the way plosive sounds are pronounced, as we listen to them in the various accents of English? They do vary a little. There is stronger aspiration in most Celtic accents, as mentioned above, so that we often hear a distinct /h/-like sound emerging after the plosive in words like *pig*. On the other hand, northern English accents, such as in Lancashire, tend to reduce the amount of aspiration, so that *pig* can sound almost like *big*. The same happens in Indian English and in South African English. I once misheard someone from Johannesburg who said his name was *Parry*. I heard it as *Barry*. In Liverpool, and related accents, a final /k/ is turned into a fricative, so that *back* comes out with the /k/ sounding like the *ch* in a Scottish pronunciation of *loch* – /bax/.

Once again, /t/ is the plosive that varies most, in regional accents. In much American and South African English, for example, it's replaced in medial position by an /r/-like tap, as in the *r* of *very*, so that *writer* sounds more like *rider*. In Liverpool, where I used to live, and wider afield, I would only ever hear *get off* pronounced as 'geroff'. There's also a change taking place in RP (p. 21), among younger people: they have begun to release their initial /t/s slowly in some words, so that *two* and *time*, for example, come out with a tiny s-like sound (shown here with superscripts) as /tˢuː/ and /tˢaɪm/. But the most famous /t/-replacement, in all accents, is certainly the glottal stop. That deserves a panel to itself.

Auditory check 5

Here are twelve words each containing an initial consonant; six of them are plosives. Can you identify them? You can check your decisions on p. 277.

	Plosive	Not a plosive
fee		
go		
lay		
tie		
key		
joy		
zoo		
pay		
do		
cheer		
bow		
me		

The glottal stop

Youthful Dominie (fresh from a course of phonetics). "BUT THERE'S NO SUCH WORD AS 'WA'ER.' IT'S 'WATER.' SAY 'WATER.'" *Wee Sandy.* "WA'ER."
Dominie. "NO, BOY. I TOLD YOU IT WAS 'WATER.'"
Wee Sandy (with great effort). "WAT-TER."
Dominie (with a sigh of relief). "YES—THAAT'S BE'ER.

It's another plosive, as the word 'stop' indicates, but it's of a different kind from all the others. The six consonants in Chapter 16 routinely change the meaning of the words in which they occur: *pin* vs *bin*, *lock* vs *log*, and so on. They are different phonemes (Chapter 3). But if we replace one of those plosives with a glottal stop, we don't change the meaning: all we get is a different-sounding word.

Most people in most accents use a glottal stop before /n/, in such words as *cotton* and *button*, in normal colloquial speech; they don't say *cot-ton*, *but-ton*. Of course, if they've been trained to speak carefully, the /t/ will be sounded. But even the most careful of RP speakers will often slip a glottal stop into words where two vowels are adjacent, such as in *co-operate* – avoiding 'co-woperate' – or *uh-oh*. And when they emphasize a word, it'll be there: say 'That's awful' with a real stress on *awful*, and you'll hear a glottal stop before the *a*. Singers do this a lot; it's often called a 'hard attack'. So do some television weather forecasters, for a reason that escapes me.

Within words, it usually replaces a voiceless plosive, especially /t/, both in the middle (as in *football*) or at the end (as in *what?*). When the middle consonant is a single plosive, as in *bottle*, the replacement by a glottal stop is regional, with Cockney speakers famous over the centuries for 'dropping the t'. Dropping the /p/ or /k/ is less common, but will be heard at the end of such words as *look* or *cup* (as in *cu' o' tea*). It's by no means restricted to London speech, though: travel to Bristol, Leeds, Tyneside, East Anglia, or into Scotland or Wales, and you'll hear it repeatedly, as well as in English accents around the world – for instance, American pronunciations of *Manhattan*, *Clinton*, and *Batman*.

17

The fricative family

F has become famous in the history of English because it has become an abbreviation in its own right: the 'F word'. Some people use it in speaking, wanting to avoid the full form of *fuck*: they say *eff off*, or simply *efff*, and it has prompted other forms, such as *effing*. More fastidious speakers drop everything apart from the first consonant, and just say *oh fff* – allowing it to be interpreted, if the listener so wishes, as a euphemism, such as *flip*, *fiddle*, *fooey*, or *fudge*. I imagine it wasn't very different in Shakespeare's day, with *fie* and *foh*.

The elongation shown by *fff* is the clue to this family of sounds, and the main point of articulatory difference with the plosives of the previous chapter. We can't 'hold' a plosive for very long – all we'd hear would be silence. By contrast, we can hold /f/ for as long as we want – at least, until our breath runs out. What we're producing is a stream of audible friction, and that is the source of the phonetician's term for sounds like /f/: *fricatives*.

Fricative sounds are much more difficult to produce than plosives. To make the friction noise, we have to hold two of our vocal organs very close together, but without touching, so that the air from our lungs is forced through the narrow gap. This is actually quite tricky to do, as it would be with other movable parts of the body. Make your finger touch the top of a table – an easy action. Then try holding your finger as close as possible above the table, but without touching it

– much more difficult, especially to maintain an even distance between finger and table. That's the kind of action we expect our vocal organs to make in order to produce fricatives.

In the case of /f/, the lower lip is close to the upper teeth, and that is the basis of the phonetician's technical term for this sound: a 'lip-teeth' or *labio-dental* fricative. As with the plosives, it can be made with or without the vocal folds vibrating: the voiceless version is /f/; the voiced version is /v/. I can't think of any rude words that begin with /v/, other than the application of everyday names, such as *villain*, *vixen*, and (in Shakespeare's day) *varlet*. In fact, /f/ has very few too – just a few instances such as *fool*, *fart*, *fink*, *frig*, *oaf*, and *poof* – and the same applies to the other fricatives described below; but when they occur they're quite effective, as the prolonged friction can give them a strong emotional force.

A closure between any two of the vocal organs can produce a fricative, and English makes great use of this option – nine contrasts (as opposed to the six for plosives), causing learners (both children and foreign learners) that little bit of extra difficulty, as some of the distinctions are quite subtle. In phonetics textbooks, it's conventional to start at the front of the mouth and move towards the back, so I'll do the same. In each case, the pathway into the nose is closed off, so that all the air comes out of the mouth.

We can move the tip of the tongue towards the upper front teeth, and that produces the two *dental* fricatives, one voiceless, the other voiced. Both are usually written *th* in everyday spelling, so to distinguish them phoneticians introduced two symbols. They chose a Greek letter to represent the voiceless sound in words like *thin*: theta, whose symbol is /θ/. For the voiced sound, in words like *this*, they went back to Old English, and chose the runic symbol that had the same sound, eth (pronounce the *th* as at the end of *wreathe*, not *wreath*), whose symbol is /ð/. They are quite difficult sounds to make, as the sides of the tongue make a firm contact with the upper side teeth, leaving just a narrow slit in the middle for the air to escape. Some speakers actually put the tip of the tongue between their teeth. You can feel the location of the aperture if you perform the 'breathing-in' strategy (p. 121) while making a *th* sound.

The next pair of fricatives is further back, the distinction between voiceless /s/ and voiced /z/. These are made by the blade of the tongue (the part just behind the tip, p. 28) coming close to the alveolar ridge above the top teeth, so they are called *alveolar* fricatives. The sides of the tongue, meanwhile, make a firm contact with the side teeth, so that the only place for the air to escape is through a narrow groove in the middle of the tongue. It's a very tricky manoeuvre, so it's not surprising that some children get it wrong. If they push their tongue too far forward, they end up making a *th* sound – called a lisp. If they let the tongue slip back, or don't press the sides firmly against the teeth, they get a *sh*-like, 'slushy' sound. And depending on how tightly and narrowly they make the groove, the sound of /s/ can vary from a gentle hiss to one that is quite shrill.

Saying *sin* and *shin* one after the other is a good way of feeling the different place of articulation between the next pair of fricatives, /s/ and *sh*, for which phoneticians have given the symbol /ʃ/. The voiced equivalent can be heard at the beginning of *genre*: its symbol is /ʒ/. For these sounds the front of the tongue has to move close to the front of the hard palate, just above the alveolar ridge, with the sides of the tongue pressing against the top teeth, as they did for /s/ and /z/. The result is another groove, but not so narrow as the one made for /s/ and /z/. The friction that emerges is spread over a wider area, so the sounds aren't so shrill. When we make /ʃ/ or /ʒ/, it feels more relaxed. The technical name points to the difference: /s/ and /z/ are alveolar fricatives; /ʃ/ and /ʒ/ are *palato-alveolar* fricatives. It's a critical difference in English, as there are several pairs of words that are distinguished by the contrast, especially with /s/ – *sea/she, seat/sheet, lass/lash, fasten/fashion, baize/beige*. But it's a subtle difference of configuration, which of course is why we find people playing with it, and making up tongue-twisters such as *She sells sea-shells on the sea-shore*. The tongue is literally twisting.

That leaves one more fricative – an unusual one, /h/, as in *hop*. It's made by producing a strong pulse of air, which we hear as it passes through the glottis (p. 28). The reason it's unusual is that, unlike the other fricatives, it's not used at the end of words. The other fricatives appear in all positions, as we hear with *fat, toffee,* and *stuff; van, govern,* and *leave; sink, basin,* and *peace; zoo, bazaar,* and *breeze; sheep, passion,* and *sash; genre, fusion,* and *beige*. But for /h/ we have only *heart* and *unhappy* – unless we sound an interjection with a strong final puff of air, as in *ahhh*.

The vocal folds don't vibrate, when we sound /h/, and another idiosyncrasy of this fricative is that there is no voiced equivalent. All we get is a contrast of presence vs absence – of the kind we hear between *heart* and *art*. I could of course pronounce *art* with a glottal stop at the beginning – the nearest thing to a voiced sound – by saying it strongly, but I don't thereby change the meaning (the glottal stop isn't a phoneme in English: p. 21); the word simply sounds more emphatic. The only exception I can think of is the contrast between the exclamations *uh-huh* (a noise of agreement) and *uh-uh* (with a glottal stop in the middle – a noise of disapproval or warning).

Fricatives come into their own in exclamatory noises.

When written down, they appear in various spellings, as writers attempt to convey pronunciations that often fall outside the normal sound system. The most diverse example is the use of the velar fricative, /x/, which has no role in English other than in the occasional loan-word from Scottish or Welsh (*loch*, *bach*). The noise of disgust is commonly written *yuck*, and pronounced with a plosive, but a fricative variant is common too, as seen in such spellings as *ach*, *blech*, *yech*, *ugh*, *argh*, *bleurgh*, and *yeurgh* – a regular feature of dialogue in children's comics. Other interjection fricatives include /f/ in *phew*, *phwoar*, *faugh*, *pff*, *phut*, *oof*, *oomph*, and *arf-arf*, /ʃ/ in *shoo*, *shh*, *sheesh*, *shucks*, *shazam*, *pshaw*, *bosh*, *gosh*, *eesh*, *touché*, and *whisht* (also Shakespearean *pish* and *tush*), and /s/ in *sod*, *oops*, and *strewth* – the last particularly unusual, for the *th* phonemes hardly ever occur in interjections. What's notable is that these are all voiceless fricatives. A voiced fricative is very rare in an interjection: *va-va-voom*.

I've left /h/ till last, as it deserves a paragraph to itself. It may be the least of the fricatives, in terms of its ability to contrast, but – perhaps for that reason – it is a major feature of interjections, some of which are very frequent in English (once again, in various spellings), as with greetings (*hello*, *hi*, *hey*, *ahoy*), laughter (*hahaha*, *hehehe*, *hohoho*, *har de har har*), responses (*huh*, *hmm*, *mhm*, *uh huh*, *hear hear*, *humph*, *whoa*), expletives (*heavens*, *heck*, *hell*), task noises (*heave-ho*), joyful expressions (*hurrah*, *hip hip hooray*, *huzzah*, *woo hoo*, *hallelujah*), and a wide range of other attitudes and emotions (*aha*, *ha*, *ho hum*). Many are literary representations: does anyone ever really say *harumph* (the usual way of representing a snort of disbelief, dislike, or annoyance) or *ahem* (clearing the throat to get someone's attention)? Nor does crying sound like *boohoohoo*, unless we are being sarcastic.

The fricatives show enormous differences in terms of

frequency (pp. 175–6). By far the commonest is /s/, because it can be used at the beginning of words in consonant clusters (*spin, step, slip, strip, split* …) and at the ends it has an important grammatical role to play, being used (along with /z/) for plurals (*cat/cats*), possessives (*cat's, cats'*), and the third person singular in verbs (*walks*). At the other end of the frequency scale, /ʒ/ is hardly used at all in English. After /h/, it's the most irregular of the English consonants, having very little contrastive function. It occurs initially and finally in only a few French loanwords, such as *genre, gigue, rouge*, and *prestige*, though it's a little more common in the middle of words, as in *fusion* and *vision*. It doesn't combine with other consonants to form a cluster – unless you're writing an alien language, where names such as *Zhmeen* might occur. In some words the pronunciation has been changed to make them sound more English – which is why *garage* (originally 'garahzh') became 'garridge'. So it's quite hard to find examples where /ʒ/ makes a difference of meaning: the examples given in the phonetics textbooks (such as *Confucian* and *confusion*) are somewhat artificial, as a result. A consequence is that people often vary in their pronunciation of words like *Asia* and *version*, sometimes using /ʃ/ and sometimes /ʒ/, as it makes no difference to the meaning.

Words like *sixths* and *strengths* are fricative-packed, and so, because of the complex articulations involved, these are the words most likely to simplify their pronunciation in colloquial speech, either by dropping one of the fricatives or allowing one to change its phonetic form (Chapter 23). Examples of dropping (*elision*) are heard when we pronounce *clothes* as 'cloze', *twelfths* as 'twelths' or 'twelfs', *what's up* as 'wassup' or 'wazzup', *cup of* as 'cuppa', and *could have* as 'coulda'. Examples of change (*assimilation*) are heard in such sequences as *this year* and *has she*, where the final /s/ becomes a /ʃ/ or /ʒ/ – 'thish year' – or in *have to* and *is there*, where it takes quite an effort to maintain the distinct articulations – as radio presenters and church readers try to do, in the hope of avoiding a rude comment from sharp-eared listeners.

Children learning English have the same problem. They have to distinguish five places of articulation, and it takes them several years to get them all right. The first fricatives to be acquired are usually /f/ and /s/ – voiceless fricatives are much easier to hear, and they are also more frequent in carer speech. A typical error is to hear them replace fricatives by the corresponding plosives (*van* becomes *ban*) or to mix up adjacent fricatives (*fish* becomes *fis*). The last ones to be acquired are the 'th' sounds, which are often not consistently used until well after age five. If five-year-olds are shown pictures of, say, two puppets, one called *thip* and the other called *fip*, and asked 'Which one is thip?', the results are pretty random. But a couple of years later, the distinction is well established – assuming the child is learning an accent that uses the distinction, of course (see further, Appendix).

Within an accent, there aren't many usage variations involving fricatives. The main alternation in RP is in such words as *issue*, where some say 'issju' and some say 'ishu' – similarly with *usual, ratio, appreciate,* and so on. In clusters, some people pronounce *wins* and *winds* or *mince* and *mints* identically; others carefully articulate the /d/ or /t/. *Nephew* allows an alternation between /f/ and /v/. There's rather more variation among regional accents. In the West Country of England, in counties like Somerset, there's an ancient substitution of voiced for voiceless fricatives – /s/ becoming /z/ and /f/ becoming /v/, so that we hear 'Zummerzet' and 'vortnight'. Just as famous is the replacement of dental fricatives by labio-dental ones in Cockney: *thing* becoming 'fing' and *brother* becoming 'bruvver' – something also heard

in southern USA and the Caribbean. In Ireland, dental fricatives are replaced by plosives, so we hear *three* as 'tree' and
this as 'dis'.

The most famous alternation, however, affects /h/, which
throughout its history has been dropped, with varying (but
usually negative) reactions: *hill* becomes *ill*, *happy* becomes
appy. It was especially contentious in the eighteenth century,
when it became a marker of the divide between upper-class
and lower-class speech, and a special target of elocutionists. 'Poor Letter H' was a regular topic in the pages of *Punch*
throughout the following century, and its elision still attracts
opprobrium today. *H*-dropping (and adding, as when *arm*
becomes *harm*) has always been associated with Cockney
speakers, but it goes well beyond London, and travelled as far
afield as Australia. It's even dropped in RP, in such words as
him and *have* when unstressed: *I gave him a lift* and *I could have
done it*. Only the most insecure and self-conscious speaker
would try to pronounce /h/ here.

One result of the variation in the use of /h/ has been
the emergence of a new use of the indefinite article, as in *an
hotel* and *an historical*. *An* has always been used before a word
beginning with a vowel, and *a* is used before a consonant. The
rule therefore gives us *a hotel*. If the /h/ is dropped, as it often
is in unstressed position, it would be *an 'otel*, and in previous centuries that was a perfectly acceptable pronunciation
among the educated classes. Indeed, obligatory, according to
Lady Agnes Grove, in *The Social Fetich* (1907): 'A book', she
says, 'becomes barely readable if the article *a* instead of *an* is
placed before the word *hotel*.' But as antipathy to a dropped
/h/ built up, people started to reinsert it, while retaining the
an, and belief that this was the 'correct' form has led to it
being increasingly encountered in print today.

Front voiceless fricatives have always had an attraction

for children's writers, presumably because they sense the auditory appeal of the high-pitched sounds and their expressive potential. Examples from olden days include *Little Miss Muffet* and *Fee Fie Fo Fum*. Twentieth-century poetry examples include Jack Prelutsky's tale of two giants, *Huffer and Cuffer*, Michael Dugan's 'A Crocodile Named Cedric Sheaf', and – probably the most famous of all – Dick Bruna's *Miffy*.

The /s/ and /ʃ/ also have an attraction because of their sound symbolic properties when used in consonant clusters. Several words beginning with /sw/ express smooth or wide-reaching movement (*swathe, sweep, swerve, swing, swirl, swoop* …); those with a final /ʃ/ swift or strong movement (*bash, crash, dash, flash, lash, push, rush, splash* …). The /sl/ combination suggests a downward movement, direction, or position (*slack, slant, slide, slim, slip, slope, slump* …) or a negative association (*slag, slander, sleazy, slime, slob, slop, sludge, slur, sly* …). The /sn/ combination is especially associated with unpleasantness (*snag, snake, snarl, sneer, snide, snipe, snoop, snot* …). Not all such words can be interpreted in these ways, of course (*swear, sweet, swim* …, *fish, bush, wash* …, *slick, sleek, sleep.., snow, snooker, snug* …), but that there is some basis for these interpretations is shown by the many writers who name their evil or dangerous characters in ways that exploit the associations. I'm thinking of J. K. Rowling's *Salazar Slytherin*, Terry Pratchett's *Mad Lord Snapcase*, or *Slewstone* in Hilary Crystal's *The Memors*. And what is it with V? *Darth Vader, Voldemort* …

Auditory check 6

Here are sixteen words each containing an initial consonant; eight of them are fricatives. Can you identify them? You can check your decisions on p. 278.

	Fricative	Not a fricative
say		
two		
vow		
me		
shy		
they		
lie		
char		
zoo		
fee		
row		
no		
hi		
jay		
thin		
bee		

Poetic friction

When poets develop a penchant for alliteration, fricatives tend to be a major feature, their potential for elongation being well exploited when the works are read aloud. Gerard Manley Hopkins uses all the fricatives except one (/ʒ/) in the opening lines of 'That nature is a Heraclitean fire and of the comfort of the Resurrection' (1888):

> Cloud-puffball, torn tufts, tossed pillows, flaunt forth, then
>   chevy on an air-
> built thoroughfare: heaven-roysterers, in gay-gangs they
>   throng; they glitter in marches.
> Down roughcast, down dazzling whitewash, wherever an
>   elm arches,
> Shivelights and shadowtackle in long lashes lace, lance, and
>   pair.

So does Robert Bridges, in 'London snow' (1890):

> When men were all asleep the snow came flying,
> In large white flakes falling on the city brown,
> Stealthily and perpetually settling and loosely lying,
>   Hushing the latest traffic of the drowsy town;
> Deadening, muffling, stifling its murmurs failing;
> Lazily and incessantly floating down and down:
>   Silently sifting and veiling road, roof and railing;
> Hiding difference, making unevenness even,
> Into angles and crevices softly drifting and sailing.

John Bradburne, by contrast, often uses a single fricative repeatedly, as in 'Brewing' (1978):

> First Eve fell fast for fallen fiend's first fable,
> Foul weather followed for us folk forlorn

Writers readily home in on the expressive potential of fricatives as a means of adding to a character. The Friar in Chaucer's *Canterbury Tales* (Prologue, line 264) has an /s/ affectation:

Somewhat he lipsed, for his wantownesse,
To make his Englissh sweete upon his tonge.

Charles Dickens, in *David Copperfield* (Chapter 21), gives Littimer (Steerforth's servant) a different kind of /s/:

a soft way of speaking, with a peculiar habit of whispering the letter S so distinctly, that he seemed to use it oftener than any other man.

In Aldous Huxley's *Antic Hay* (Chapter 4), a character exploits fricative expressiveness to the full:

'Here's an end to any civilized conversation,' Mr Mercaptan complained, hissing on the *c*, labiating lingeringly on the *v* of 'civilized' and giving the first two *i*'s their fullest value. The word, in his mouth, seemed to take on a special and a richer significance.

18

The affricate family

This may be stretching too far the notion of 'family', in its sense of a group of entities sharing common features, for there are only two affricates recognized in English. The name was coined to capture the difference that can be heard between *tin* and *chin* or *din* and *gin*. These are sounds that start in exactly the same way, but instead of the sharp release of the air that we hear after the alveolar plosives /t/ and /d/ (p. 120), there is a gradual release, sounding like the palato-alveolar fricatives /ʃ/ and /ʒ/ (p. 135). It is this combination of plosive and audible friction that prompted the new term, which comes from a Latin verb meaning 'rub against'. It's not really 'rubbing', but the front of the tongue is certainly very close to the roof of the mouth, just behind the alveolar ridge, after the plosive element is released. Technically, then, they can be described as *post-alveolar* or *palato-alveolar* affricates; but because they are the only ones in English, they are usually referred to simply as 'the affricates', as heard in voiceless *chin* and voiced *gin*.

With the new term came new symbols. There's no single letter in the English alphabet for the first consonant in *chin*: we have to use a digraph, *c* + *h*, and that is ambiguous, as many words beginning with *ch* don't have the affricate sound (such as *character* and *chasm*). Loanwords such as *ciao* and *ciabatta* complicate things further, because although they do have the affricate sound, they are spelled differently. The situation for *gin* is just as bad, as many words with a voiced affricate are spelled with a *j* (as in *jeep*) or with some other combination of letters (as in *ridge*). So the nineteenth-century phoneticians created two new symbols, using the /t/ of *tin* and the /ʃ/ of *shin* for the voiceless affricate, and the /d/ of *din* and the /ʒ/ of *genre* for the voiceless one, giving /tʃ/ and /dʒ/. The two elements should always be written tightly together, to show they are a single sound, and to distinguish them from sequences where /t/ and /ʃ/ or /d/ and /ʒ/ just happen to be next to each other, as in *night shirt* and *good genre*.

The affricates behave in the sound system in a regular way. They can occur in all parts of a word, and they allow a straightforward contrast between voiceless and voiced, as can be seen in such pairs as *chin* and *gin*, *riches* and *ridges*, and *larch* and *large*. But they are by no means as frequent as the members of the related plosive and fricative families: indeed, apart from /ʒ/, they are the least used of all the consonants (see the table on pp. 175–6), though I suspect they would be higher in any frequency count based on very informal speech. /tʃ/ certainly would, because of the way it's used in common interjections such as farewells (*ciao*, *cheers*, *cheerio*, and its derivatives, such as *cheery-bye*), drinking salutations (*cheers*, *chin chin*), endearments (*cootchie-cootchie-coo*), and sound symbolic expressions such as *ouch*, *choo* or *atchoo* (for a sneeze), *choo-choo* (baby talk for a locomotive), *chop chop* (hurry up), and *kaching* or *kerching* (for money, reflecting the bell noise that old tills used to make). Presumably it would rank highly in the speech of photographers: *say cheese*. And it turns up in quite a few colloquial words, such as *chav*, *chump*, *chomp*, *chock* (full), *chips*, *chuffed*, and *bitch*.

/dʒ/ would be more frequent in the speech of those who swear with it (*Jesus* and its euphemistic forms, such as *gee*, *geez*, *jeepers*, *Geronimo*, and *jeesh*) and presumably among *Star*

Wars enthusiasts (*Jedi, Jabba the Hutt, Jar Jar Binks, Jas Emari, Janus Greejatus, Jarrus, Queen Jamillia, Jubnuk*, et al.). It would be higher in a corpus of Judaeo-Christian texts (*Jesus, Joseph, Jew, Jerusalem, Judaea, Judah, Judas, James, John, Jeremiah, Jericho*, and another 200 or so names beginning with *J*). It's a prominent presence in men's first names: according to a survey carried out by the online genealogy site, Ancestry, the top male name over the past 500 years is *John*, followed by *William, Thomas, George*, and *James*. There are three voiced initial affricates out of five here, and a double presence in *George*, so we can hardly say that /ʤ/ is a neglected consonant, despite its relatively low frequency ranking.

There's another factor that would increase the number of affricates in samples of colloquial speech: as we saw in earlier chapters, when a word ending in /t/ is followed by one beginning with /ʃ/, the two sounds can assimilate (Chapter 23) to produce an affricate: *that ship* can sound like 'that chip'; similarly, a word ending in /d/ followed by one beginning with /j/ will readily assimilate, so that *good use* sounds like 'good juice'. In some accents, the assimilation covers several syllables, as in Cockney *Wotcher got?* ('What have you got?') and *Wouldja believe it!* ('Would you …'). These assimilations would of course be carefully avoided in formal speech.

The association of affricates with informal speech may well be the reason for the most noticeable variation in the use of affricates in English: the way some speakers don't use them within words when /t/ or /d/ is followed by /j/. On the one hand, we will hear *statue, question*, and *soldier* pronounced with affricates – /ˈstaʧuː/, /ˈkwesʧən/, /ˈsəʊlʤə/; on the other hand, we will hear these words with the sounds clearly distinguished, so that *statue* sounds like 'stat you' /ˈstatjuː/, and similarly /ˈkwestjən/, /ˈsəʊldjə/. The avoidance of an affricate is most noticeable in very careful speech when the following vowel is /u/, as in *actual*, *gradual*, and *education*, and (in British English) *tune* and *Tuesday*. Pronunciations such as 'act-you-al' /'aktjuəl/ and 'tyoon' /tju:n/ for these speakers will be heard in all styles of their speech, not just the most formal. They will also make a clear contrast between *dune* and *June*.

By contrast, those who use the affricate in these words are likely to take them a stage further in colloquial speech: 'actchual' /'aktʃuəl/ becomes shortened to /'aktʃəl/ and then further to /'akʃl/. Nonstandard spellings reflecting pronunciation are often seen in the representation of local speech, as in 'De po' man acshully bust inter tears' (from Charles W. Chesnutt, *The House behind the Cedars*, 1900, Chapter 23) or 'we never did ackshally reach the town' (from Joseph A. Altsheler, *The Border Watch*, 1912, Chapter 15).

In some contexts, the distinction between /tʃ/ and /ʃ/ can be very difficult to hear, so many speakers go for the easier articulatory option, and use the latter. Because /n/ is made at the same place in the mouth as /t/ and /d/ (p. 120), it makes it very easy to drop the plosive, so that instead of *lunch* /lʌntʃ/ and *strange* /streɪndʒ/ we hear /lʌnʃ/ and /streɪnʒ/.

The mixed identity of /tʃ/ and /dʒ/ – part plosive, part fricative – does seem to make them that little bit more difficult to learn. Children don't acquire them until around age four, well after all the plosives are established and most of the fricatives. Before that, they replace them by plosives: so *chip* comes out as 'tip' and *jar* as 'dar'. I recall one three-year-old child called John who confused someone when asked what his name was: 'Don', he said. 'Hello, Don', said the questioner – to which the child replied crossly, 'Not Don – Don.' It's a familiar phenomenon in studies of language acquisition: the child can hear the distinction but not make it. And there are several other kinds of confusion involving affricates – children regularly muddle pairs like *cheese* and *trees,* for instance. And not only children. That contrast has presented many a foreign learner of English with a challenge in both listening and speaking.

Auditory check 7

Here are nine words each containing an initial consonant; four of them are affricates. Can you identify them? You can check your decisions on p. 278.

	Affricate	**Not an affricate**
show		
char		
see		
jay		
chip		
tie		
do		
row		
joe		

19
The nasal family

Nasal sounds are among the most frequent of all the English consonants, yet are among the least noticed. Or perhaps I should say: they remain unnoticed until we find ourselves unable to pronounce them. Then we realize just how much we depend upon them.

There are only three: /m/ as in *me*, /n/ as in *no*, and /ŋ/ as in *sing*. They form an exact parallel to the series of plosive consonants, in terms of where they're made in the mouth (p. 119). The lips close for /m/, just like /p/ and /b/ – the *bilabial* nasal. The blade of the tongue hits the alveolar ridge for /n/, just like /t/ and /d/ – the *alveolar* nasal. And the back of the tongue hits the back part of the roof of the mouth (the velum), just like /k/ and/g/ – the *velar* nasal. The only difference from plosives is that the soft palate is lowered, so that the air comes out through the nose – hence the name *nasal*. We don't easily feel the raising and lowering, but if you say a word like *button* quickly, so that the n becomes an entire syllable – as /ˈbʌtn/ rather than pronouncing the /t/ clearly as in /ˈbʌtən/ – it's possible to feel the soft palate move.

We only really get a sense of the role of the soft palate when our nose is blocked. That's when we find ourselves unable to pronounce nasal consonants. Novelists make a brave effort to represent the effects, when their characters have a cold. Here's Holpweed, in *The Memors*, apologizing to his boss: 'I'b sorry, but I caa'd go oud.' To interpret this, we have to 'hear' the sentence, and work out the equivalences: /m/ is replaced by /b/ in *I'm*; /n/ is replaced by /d/ in *can't*. We can do it easily enough because we have all had a cold, and know how our speech can get 'clogged' as a consequence. But it's somewhat difficult to read, so novelists tend to use the respelling technique only for short stretches.

There's one big difference between nasal and plosive consonants in English: there are no voiceless nasals that change the meaning, in the way that plosives do (as in *bin/ pin*). Another is that one of the nasals isn't used in words in the same way as plosives: /m/ and /n/ do work in parallel, being found at the beginning, in the middle, and at the end of words (*mad, image, rum; nip, inner, ran*), but /ŋ/ is used only in the middle and at the end (*singer, sing*). There are no words beginning with 'ng', other than in rare foreign imports, such as the name of a type of African drum, *ngoma*, or the first name of the crime writer *Ngaio Marsh* – and most people pronounce such words by adapting them to English, either by replacing the /ŋ/ with /n/ or adding a vowel before the /ŋ/.

The easiest consonant to pronounce of all is /m/, which is probably why it's so frequent: all we have to do is close our lips and make our vocal folds vibrate. It's the default noise of satisfaction, approval, and acknowledgement in everyday conversation, the exact meaning depending on the intonation with which it's said: we can provide feedback to a speaker by making a series of *mm* noises. It can also be used to express hesitation, uncertainty, and interrogation (*mm?*), again depending on the intonation. In fiction it's usually written with a double *m*, but some writers multiply the *m*'s to five or more: in the 'Bells' episode of the BBC sitcom *Blackadder II* (1986) the script reads:

KATE: The word is that your servant is the worst servant in London.

BLACKADDER: Mmmmm. That's true. Baldrick, you're fired.

This ability to elongate is because the nasals, like the fricatives and vowels, are continuant sounds (though lacking the audible friction found in fricatives) – we can keep them going as long as we want, within the limits of our breath, as anyone knows who has hummed a tune. We only use /m/ when we're humming, but it's possible to lengthen all the nasals in the same way. A long /n/ is often heard, as in a very hesitant *nnno* or a really emphatic *nnnever*. I recently heard a dog owner telling her pet to stop doing something, and she kept the *n* of *no* going for a full two or three seconds before pronouncing the vowel. /ŋ/ is least likely to be lengthened in this way, but it can happen, as when a novelist representing a telephone noise might write *ring-g-g*, which we can easily imitate in speech.

Because of its ease, /m/ is often the first consonant to be used by children when they begin to talk. It is already a frequent element in babbling at around six months of age: the typical *mamama* alongside *bababa* has misled innumerable mothers into believing that their child is naming them; but the randomness of the articulation and intonation at that age shows that these are sounds being practised just as sounds, rather than being used meaningfully. A definite-sounding *mama*, that can be heard around the first birthday, is something new, and a *mummy* or *mommy*, with a vowel change between the syllables, is very different from the erratic reduplications heard in babbling.

/m/ turns up in quite a few important (to the child) early words, such as *more*, *my*, and *milk*. /n/ is frequent too, as it is present in action words such as *gone* (or *all-gone*), *done* (or *all-done*), and (*fall*) *down*, as well as everyday concepts such as *nice*, *nose*, *night-night*, and the all-important *no*. Even /ŋ/ occurs in early words, such as *ring* and *sing*. And there are a surprising number of real-world noises that require nasals for best imitative effect, such as *nee-naa* (for an emergency vehicle siren), *meow*, *moo*, *neigh*, and *oink-oink*. Clearly, little ones like nasals, presumably because they are so easy to make. Keeping the soft palate lowered is the default state, as it permits natural breathing; raising it, to shut off the nasal cavity, as required for every other English sound, is what has to be learned.

Not surprisingly, writing aimed at children makes a great use of nasals, especially /m/ and especially in sequences, as in *Mickey Mouse*, *Maid Marian*, *Minerva McGonagall* (in *Harry Potter*), and *Mad Madam Mim* (from Disney's *The Sword and the Stone*). Playground games and nursery rhymes also like them, particularly when /m/ and /n/ alternate, as in *Eeny Meeny Miny Mo*, *One Man Went to Mow*, *The Farmer's in his Den*, *Ring-a-Ring-a-Roses*, and *This Old Man* (who played *knick-knack*). The alternation is noticeable in alien names too, as in *Star Wars' Momaw Nadon*; but aliens for some reason tend to go in for alveolar rather than bilabial nasals – to continue with *Star Wars*: *Queen Neeyutnee*, *Nien Nunb*, *Nuvo Vindi*, and *Ona Nobis*.

/m/ is the most widely used of all the nasals – and not just in English. In a major survey of the phonemes found in 451 of the world's languages, carried out by American linguist Ian Maddieson in 1984, /m/ was the consonant that occurred most often (in 94 per cent of the languages). It turns up in all dialects of English, without any regional variation, and is never dropped, even in rapid speech. Its articulation is extremely stable: the only noticeable shift is when /m/ is followed by /f/, and the labio-dental fricative makes the lower lip retract, as in *comfort* and *triumph*. It's actually quite difficult to maintain a pure bilabial articulation in such words. Also, in a sequence where /n/ is followed by /m/, it's /m/ that is the dominant force, making /n/ change, as when *and* becomes /əm/ in *Sunday and Monday* or *more and more*.

/n/ shows greater variation. It readily adopts the character of following phonemes – and not only in relation to /m/. A following bilabial plosive can cause it to shift to /m/, as in *ten places* and *ten bricks*. Followed by a dental fricative ('th'), it is made with the tongue-tip against the teeth, as in *tenth* and *in this*. Followed by a velar plosive, it tends to move in a velar direction, as in *include* and *enquiry*, which *can* be pronounced carefully as *in-clude* and *en-quiry*, but are more usually said as *ing-clude* and *eng-quiry*.

/ŋ/ is the nasal where we find most variation, both regionally and (especially) socially. In some areas, such as the British Midlands, we hear it end with an audible /g/, so that *ringing* sounds like *ring-gingg*. It's a pronunciation that was common in Shakespeare's day. In Cockney, and occasionally elsewhere, words ending in *-thing* add a /k/. In Charles Dickens' *Great Expectations* (Chapter 58), Joe Gargery uses two in quick succession:

> 'I ain't a-going,' said Joe, from behind his sleeve, 'to tell him nothink o' that natur, Pip. ... God knows as I forgive you, if I have anythink to forgive!'

But the main variation in the use of /ŋ/ has, since the eighteenth century, been social in character, when it is replaced by /n/ in an unstressed syllable (as in *nothin'*), and especially in the inflectional ending of verbs (as in *runnin'*). Because of our awareness of spelling, this is usually referred to as 'dropping the *g*', though in fact no /g/ sound has been dropped at all.

The irony is that, historically, it would be more accurate

to talk about *g*-adding rather than *g*-dropping. The origins of the *-ing* ending on verbs in Middle English show forms in /n/ only. Even when the *ing* spelling developed, the pronunciation stayed as /n/, as can be heard in many rhyming couplets from the eighteenth century and later, as in Byron's *undoing* and *ruin* or *scoffing* and *coffin* (both from *Don Juan*). But once the *ing* spelling became established, people began to privilege a pronunciation that reflected it, so that by 1800 the elocutionists of the day were insisting on /ŋ/ as the only acceptable form. John Walker, the compiler of the first *English Pronouncing Dictionary* (1791), demands it, allowing as exceptions only those cases where there are two /ŋ/s in succession – as in *singing*. However, even these cases were soon brought under the rule, so that during the nineteenth century /ŋ/ became the educated norm, and /n/ became a sign of 'vulgar' speech. Repeatedly, in the novels of the period, we see lower-class characters identified by *g*-dropping (and *h*-dropping, p. 139) – a famous example is in *David Copperfield* (Chapter 8) where Barkis the carrier *is waitin' for an answer* from Peggotty: his marriage proposal, *Barkis is willin'*, entered the quotation books. The opposite effect also happened. Lower-class characters, aware that there was something 'posh' about the use of /ŋ/, began to overuse it, replacing /n/ in all sorts of words that never had an /ŋ/ in their history, saying *captain* as *capting* and *garden* as *garding* – an example of what is technically called *hypercorrection* (when a speaker goes beyond the norm of a target variety because of a desire to be correct).

If things had stayed that way, with /ŋ/ being the educated norm and /n/ considered vulgar, the situation would have been typical of the social divide illustrated by the presence or absence of /h/. But during the nineteenth century something very unusual took place: the very top end of society also began to drop their *g*'s. It was a practice that generated a catchphrase describing the aristocratic users: those who went *huntin'*, *shootin'*, *and fishin'*. The pronunciation lasted well into the twentieth century, and even though it is little heard today, the memory of past usage is still with us. An episode of the BBC sitcom *Absolutely Fabulous* in 2003 was called 'Huntin', Shootin', & Fishin''.

The novelists captured the fashion, and sometimes even comment on and mock it, as in this extract from one of John Galsworthy's novels in *The Forsyte Saga* (*Maid in Waiting*, 1931, Chapter 31):

> 'Clare, you're lookin' thin; are you slimmin' too?'
>
> 'No. I've been in Scotland, Aunt Em.'
>
> 'Followin' the guns, and fishin'. Now run about the house. I'll wait for you.'
>
> When they were running about the house, Clare said to Dinny:
>
> 'Where on earth did Aunt Em learn to drop her g's?'
>
> 'Father told me once that she was at a school where an un-dropped "g" was worse than a dropped "h". They were bringin' in a county fashion then, huntin' people, you know. Isn't she a dear?'

The satirists noticed it too. Several cartoons in *Punch* bemoan the fate of 'Poor Little G' in the fashionable speech of the period (p. 156). And the aristocrats were often criticized for setting a bad example.

Why did it happen? The decades around 1800 were notable for their linguistic self-consciousness. They saw the rise of the prescriptive approach to language, the growth of the elocution movement, and the publication of the first dictionaries and manuals of pronunciation, written to show a new and aspiring middle class, anxious to avoid criticism from upper-class polite society, how to speak 'correctly'. Of

POOR LETTER "G."

The Duchess. "Yes; Skatin' would be charmin', if it weren't for the Freezin' stoppin' the Huntin'!"

Lord Charles. "Yes; and ain't Sleighin' toppin' fun, except for the Snowin' spoilin' the Skatin'!"

course, for those who were already senior members of the upper class, these anxieties were way beneath them. The new rule books were not for them. And if the lower classes were being schooled in the use of /ŋ/ as the everyday pronunciation of -*ing*, then upper-class usage would show its superiority by doing the opposite. Hence, huntin', shootin', fishin'.

G-dropping is less socially divisive today. Everyone does it, in varying degrees. The established trend still exists, of course: the lower the social class, the more likely we will hear *g* being dropped. But several sociolinguistic studies have shown how well-educated people also vary in their use of /ŋ/. In formal speech, or when reading aloud, they are likely to keep it; but in informal speech it is very often dropped, with some words dropping it much more than others – *going to* becoming *gonna*, for instance. Even the most fastidious /ŋ/-user will occasionally offer someone a cheery colloquial *g*-dropped greeting: *mornin', evenin'*.

Auditory check 8

Here are twelve words each containing a final consonant; six of them are nasals. Can you identify them? You can check your decisions on p. 278.

	Nasal	Not a nasal
in		
eel		
cub		
same		
fine		
big		
wing		
love		
at		
team		
song		
odd		

20

The approximant family

The plosives and fricatives (with their affricate cousins), along with the nasals, are the main types of consonant in English, making up 20 of the 24 items in the English consonant inventory. The remaining four – /l/ as in *lip*, /r/ as in *rip*, /w/ as in *well*, and /j/ as in *yell* – have always presented a bit of a problem, because of their distinctive phonetic character.

Sixteenth-century writers on pronunciation noticed the continuous, 'flowing' nature of /l/ and /r/, and called them 'liquids', along with /m/ and /n/. We can keep these phonemes going as long as we like, as when we say a hesitant *well-l-l* or *r-r-r-right*. I once heard an actor playing Sherlock Holmes say *elementary* to Dr Watson, and he held the *l* for over a second, adding a noticeably dismissive tone. And some of the most noticeable *r*'s emanate from the mouths of opera singers, trilling the consonant for all they're worth. In present-day phonetics, /m/ and /n/, as we've seen, have a separate classification as nasals. But /l/ and /r/ are still sometimes called 'liquids'.

A different history surrounds /w/ and /j/, which were usually ignored by early writers on pronunciation because they sounded like vowels. We can see why if we pronounce a word like *well* and hold the first phoneme: *wwwwwell*: it sounds exactly like the /uː/ vowel in RP *do*. Similarly, if we hold the first phoneme in *yell* it sounds exactly like the /iː/ vowel in *see*. In Old English, such words were sometimes even spelled that way, with a *u* or *i*. Not surprisingly, then, these two phonemes have been called *semi-vowels*.

But /w/ and /j/ aren't vowels. Nor are /l/ and /r/, despite their flowing vowel-like sound. They are consonants, because they behave in words in a typically consonantal way. For instance, they can be used at the beginning of a word before a vowel: we say *too, do, zoo, shoe, moo*, and so on, and also *you, woo, rue*, and *loo*. They are preceded by *a* and not *an*: *a well, a yell, a lip, a rip* (compare *an egg, an oak*, etc.). And they perform in clusters of consonants in the same way as others do: we can say *spin, stick, skin, smile*, and also *slip, swim*, and *suit* (as /sjuːt/), and occasionally /sr/ (as in *Sri Lanka*); and we hear similar clusters in many other words, such as *plum, trip, tweet*, and *tune* (as /tjuːn/).

Eventually, phoneticians came up with a way of classifying these phonemes that tied in with the other modern ways of talking about consonants. Clearly, they are all phonemes that can be lengthened, just like fricatives, except there is no audible friction, so they have been described as *frictionless continuants*. They are all usually pronounced with vocal fold vibration. They are all oral, not nasal. And they have one crucial thing in common: they are made with the vocal organs coming very close together, so that the airflow comes out through a narrow aperture. In the 1960s, the term *approximant* was suggested to capture this notion: the vocal organs 'approximate' but do not actually meet.

This is most obvious for /w/, where we can see the way the lips come close together, forming a slightly protruding, rounded shape, while (less obviously) the back of the tongue is raised towards the velum – a *labial-velar* approximant. With /l/ the tip of the tongue is pressed against the teeth ridge, and the air flows around the sides – laterally – hence this is usually described as a *lateral* approximant. With /j/, the front of the tongue is moved close to the hard palate, and the air flows diffusely through the narrow gap – a *palatal* approximant. And with /r/, the air flows through a gap a little further forward, usually in an area just behind the teeth ridge – a *post-alveolar* approximant – though there are several variations in position depending on the accent (see below).

It's probably the vowel-like character of /j/ and /w/ that enables them to appear early in children's speech, usually well before three. /l/ is also early, at the beginning of words like *look* and *light*, but takes longer to be established in the middle and end: *ball* will often be heard as 'baw' and *yellow* as 'yeyow'. /r/ is much later: even at around age five, many children will be heard replacing /r/ by /w/ or /j/ – 'wed' or 'yed' for *red*.

From a phonaesthetic point of view, the approximants are typically soft, smooth sounds, and their ability to lengthen appeals to anyone who wants to introduce a layer of gentle, leisurely lyricism into their speech. Poets love them. The opening lines of Tennyson's *The Lady of Shalott* introduce a refrain using /l/ and /r/ that recurs throughout the poem:

> On either side the river lie
> Long fields of barley and of rye,
> That clothe the wold and meet the sky;
> …
> 'Tirra lirra, tirra lirra:'
> Sang Sir Lancelot.
> …
> A longdrawn carol, mournful, holy,
> She chanted loudly, chanted lowly,
> Till her eyes were darken'd wholly,
> And her smooth face sharpen'd slowly,
> Turn'd to tower'd Camelot

Hopkins' 'Inversnaid' focuses on /w/ and /l/:

> What would the world be, once bereft
> Of wet and of wildness? Let them be left,
> O let them be left, wildness and wet;
> Long live the weeds and the wilderness yet.

The gentleness is instinctively recognized in the notion of a *lullaby*, whose phonetic form reflects the word's purpose. Some lullabies use approximants to an almost hypnotic level, such as the Irish 'Toora, loora, loora, / Toora, loora, liy ...' When we sing, without the words, it is generally using laterals: *la la la* ... *La-La Land* raises them to (almost) Oscar level. And they provide the auditory basis of several pleasure noises, such as *yum yum*, *yummy*, *LOL*, *lolz*, and *lovely jubbly* (that one chiefly in British English).

We would therefore expect these sounds to figure in literature in the names of people who are 'good guys', especially those who are gentle or amiable in character. Examples include Dickens' *Lillyvick*, *Lammle*, *Langdale*, and *Lenville*, or *Wardle*, *Weller*, *Winkle*, and *Wopsle*; *Star Wars* gives us *Yoda* and *Yaddle*, the *Ewok* race, with *Wicket W. Warrick*, *Warok*, and others, and the droid family whose most famous member is *R2* (though that /r/ isn't audible in all English accents).

Softer or more effete swear words or exclamations tend to begin with approximants: *Lord*, *Lawdy*, *lawks*, *lummy*, *yipes*, *yikes*, *yaroo*, *waa*, *well*, *woops(y)*, *wow*, *wowee*, *wowser(s)*, *woo hoo*, and not forgetting Eeyore's *worra worra* (in *Winnie the Pooh*), and older English *lo*. We don't expect approximants to figure much in aggressive settings, such as a fight, in which the noises that characters supposedly make (in comics, for example) are ones like *krak* and *ka-thok* (my source is *Street Fighter Legends*) and not *yal* or *ra-wol*.

Approximants also tend to be found in responses and

exclamatory noises of a generally positive character: *yes, yea, yeah, yup, yo* (*ho*), *yay, right* (*-o, -io, -y*). Here they can be quite energetic: *yippee, yee-haw, yahoo, ye gods, yoo hoo, yoicks, yah* (*boo*), *ra ra ra, wham, whee, whew, whoa, whoop*(*ee*), *whoosh*. As always, there are exceptions, such as exclamatory *woe* (*is me*) and (from Middle English) *wailaway*.

It makes an interesting phonaesthetic experiment to test the hypothesis that approximants are 'nice' consonants. Ask people to rate the following alien races in terms of their likely friendliness, knowing only their names: *Wilorians, Zibokians, Tishopians, Gritosians, Yirolians*. The *Wilorians* and *Yirolians* invariably come out top. Approximants (and nasals) also tend to be dominant when people say (without knowing any-thing about the place other than the name): 'That sounds like a nice place to live.' And why else are they so common in the names of fairy-tale characters? *Cinderella, Rapunzel, Thumbe-lina*, Princess *Aurora* (the Sleeping Beauty), *Ariel, Belle, Goldi-locks, Hansel and Gretel, Little Red Riding Hood* …

/l/ has several sound symbolic associations. Many words with a final /l/ preceded by a short vowel and a single con-sonant, convey uncertain or repeated movement: *bubble, fiddle, joggle, nibble, sniffle, wobble* …; others with this struc-ture suggest lack of size or importance: *dabble, freckle, niggle, pebble, speckle* … With a long central vowel preceding, there's a suggestion of roundness: *curl, furl, swirl, twirl* …, an effect also heard when there's a combination of /r/ and /l/, as in *barrel, roll*, and *spiral*. A *gl-* cluster suggests brightness and light: *glare, glass, gleam, glimmer, glint, glossy, glow* … As with other uses of /l/, there are exceptions (such as *glove* and *glue*, in relation to the last sequence), but the trends are nonethe-less intriguing.

Variation in usage is never far away when talking about approximants. /r/ is in fact the most regionally varied of all the English consonants: its phonetic form shifts from one end of the mouth to the other. In RP, the tip of the tongue, as mentioned above, moves towards a position just above the alveolar ridge. In the south-west of England, the tip curls back further to produce a 'darker' sound, and it is this *ret-roflexed* articulation that is heard in most Americans, or in varieties of English around the world influenced by American speech. It becomes really noticeable when it occurs after a vowel, in words like *bird*, where the tongue curls back during the vowel as well, adding a distinctive '*r*-colouring'.

In the north-east of England, an old pronunciation, called a *burr*, can still often be heard, where the root of the tongue vibrates against the uvula, producing a sound that is familiar to anyone who knows French. In Scotland and Wales, the /r/ is commonly rolled, or trilled, making the tip of the tongue vibrate rapidly – something that can also happen in other accents in a declamatory style of speaking. This pronunciation was often called in Latin a *littera canina* (a 'doggy' sound), because of its resemblance to a *grrr*. According to John Aubrey, in *Brief Lives*, this is how John Milton spoke: he 'pronounced the letter R very hard – a certain sign of a satirical wit'.

There is a great deal of individual variation. Some people have what is impressionistically called a 'weak *r*', in which the tongue doesn't move firmly towards the roof of the mouth, so that what emerges is a /w/-like sound. In earlier periods, it was thought fashionable to vary /r/ in this way, in Victorian times even to the extent of replacing it completely with /w/ – a habit that the satirists in *Punch* regularly parodied. In an 1875 cartoon, a clearly upper-class gentleman asks a lady 'Do you evah wink?' 'What *do* you mean, sir?', she replies, horrified. 'Well', he replies, 'skate, if you pwefer the expression'. In the early decades of the twentieth century, an affected uvular articulation had a similar cachet, a classic example being the aesthete Anthony Blanche in Evelyn Waugh's *Brideshead Revisited*, portrayed in the BBC television series with a distinctive uvular /r/ (and a stammer). These pronunciations would be considered speech defects today.

But the pronunciation of /r/ varies even within an accent. When it's preceded by /d/, the plosive articulation pulls the /r/ towards the alveolar ridge so that we begin to hear some friction – in effect, it becomes a fricative. When it occurs between vowels, in such words as *sorry* and *very*, the tip of the tongue makes a rapid flick, called a *tap*, so that /r/ sounds like a very short /d/. And all the approximants change their character when they occur after /p/, /t/, /k/, as in *price, clean, twice,* and *tune*: the voiceless nature of these consonants causes them to follow suit and they lose their voicing. An artificial emphasis can restore the voicing, as can often be heard from presenters on Classic FM – or, as they say, 'Cuhlassic FM'.

/r/ may be the most variable of all the consonants, but the other approximants are also geographically distinctive. The chief variation that affects /l/ is caused by the vowels that accompany it. If these are front vowels, especially those made high in the mouth, near the hard palate (p. 28), the /l/ has a palatal resonance, usually described as a 'clear *l*'. We hear this in such words as *leap* and *peel*. If these are back vowels, especially those made high in the mouth, near the soft palate, the /l/ has a velar resonance, usually described as a 'dark *l*'. We hear this in such words as *look* and *pool*, or in the last syllable of *puddle*. Try the 'breathing-in' strategy (p. 121) to feel the different place of articulation.

But in some accents, these patterns are disregarded. Most Americans, Scots, Australians, and New Zealanders use a dark *l* most of the time. Most Irish people and Tynesiders use a clear *l* most of the time. In Cockney, a final dark *l* has become so dark that it sounds like an /o/ vowel, and it becomes difficult to hear a distinction between, say, *pull* and *pool*. The final /l/ may disappear completely, so that *wall* sounds like 'waw'.

/j/ is the least variable of all the approximants. The most noticeable effect is when it is dropped, producing one of the most distinctive differences between British and American English: *news* is /njuːz/ in Britain and /nuːz/ in the United States. But it's occasionally regional within a country too: in East Anglia, words like *beautiful* and *music* are often pronounced without a /j/: /ˈbuːtɪfʊl/, /ˈmuːzɪk/. There's also a great deal of social and individual variation in the use of /j/, in such words as *absolutely*, *assume*, and *suit* – for example, /sjuːt/ vs /suːt/ – with upper-class pronunciation favouring the /j/ articulation. And some speakers introduce an audible /j/ between syllables in words like *happier, Australia*, and *saying*, so that they come out as 'happiyer', 'Australiya', and 'say-ying'. The effect is to add a syllable: 'Aus-tra-lia' vs 'Aus-tra-lee-ya'.

/w/ likewise has little regional variation, other than in words beginning with *wh*, where it can become voiceless – said as an isolated noise, this 'wh' is what we hear when blowing out a match or a candle. As a consonant, it's heard around the Celtic areas in the British Isles, so that speakers make a distinction between *Wales* and *whales*. All the *wh*-interjections above would be pronounced that way. It's my normal pronunciation. And Shakespeare's (p. 250).

Auditory check 9

Here are ten words each containing an initial consonant; four
of them are approximants. Can you identify them? You can
check your decisions on p. 278.

	Approximant	Not an approximant
see		
lay		
my		
he		
rip		
yes		
no		
two		
way		
zoo		

Beautiful sounds

Approximants also have a high level of association with words that native speakers consider to be beautiful. My favourite example here is the poem that John Kitching wrote following a *Sunday Times* competition in which readers were asked to submit the 'most beautiful sounding word in the English language'. A large number of words were sent in, and he brought together those that got most votes. This is the poem, which he called 'Sunday Words'. I underline the approximants:

I like to think of words with lovely sounds
That I can ease around my Sunday tongue –
– Like velvet, melody and young,
Gossamer, crystal, autumn, peace,
Mellifluous, whisper, tranquil, lace,
Caress and silken, willow, mellow,
Lullaby, dawn and shimmer, yellow,
Silver, marigold and golden,
Dream and harmony and olden,
Blossom, champagne, sleep and dusk,
Magic, hummock, love and mist,
Darling, laughter, butterfly,
Charity, eiderdown and sky,
And parakeet and rosemary,
Froth, gazebo, ivory,
And syllabub and vacillate,
Mesmerism, echo, fate,
Jacaranda, harlequin
And chrysalis and violin,
Enigma, tart and sycamore.
Pomp, chinchilla, truffle, myrrh,
Bewildered, claret, akimbo, fur,
Flamingo next and celandine,

Ominous, tantalize and wine,
Antimacassar, jewel, skill,
Russet, buckram, delight and thrill,
Clavichord and didgeridoo,
Doppelganger, fractious, zoo.
I don't know what they mean. Do you?
But I like to have them in my head
And dandle them and handle them
Like Wedgwood china. What finer?

In RP, 55 of the 81 words contain an approximant – sometimes more than one – and if we include accents where /r/ is pronounced after a vowel the figure rises to 64 (80 per cent). (Nasal consonants play an important part too.)

21

Words of one syllable

We can now answer the question I posed at the end of Chapter 1: how do we describe English pronunciation? It is a combination of all the tones of voice in chapters 5 to 10, all the vowels in chapters 11 to 15, and all the consonants in chapters 16 to 20. Everything works together to produce the words, phrases, and sentences of what we call 'connected speech'.

But there's one further thing. To make this happen, the individual sounds, or *segments* – the vowels and the consonants – have to combine to make speakable units. As we saw on p. 81, words rarely consist of a single segment, and some consonants (the plosives and affricates) can't be articulated at all without an accompanying vowel. So it makes sense to focus attention on the mechanism that allows vowels and consonants to combine to make words: the *syllable*.

Syllables are combinations of vowels (V) and consonants (C) articulated as a single rhythmical beat. I outlined the main types at the beginning of Chapter 11. Here they are again, but now showing all the ways that consonants can cluster, each with an illustrative word. In English, there can be up to three consonants before the vowel and up to four afterwards:

V: I
CV: me

CCV: crow
CCCV: straw
VC: in
VCC: apt
VCCC: asks
VCCCC: angsts
CVC: dog
CVCC: pigs
CVCCC: jumps
CVCCCC: sixths
CCVC: trip
CCVCC: stink
CCVCCC: trumps
CCVCCCC: twelfths
CCCVC: stroll
CCCVCC: strips
CCCVCCC: sprints
CCCVCCCC: splintst

That last type is rare: my example is from the sixteenth century, when a writer asks why his heart is breaking (splintering). It uses a shortened form of the *-est* verb ending after *thou*: 'why splintst (thou)?'

But, as these CCC- examples suggest, not all consonants can appear in all combinations. For instance, the CCC- cluster before a vowel has to begin with /s/, be followed by /p/, /t/, or /k/, and then have one of the approximants, /l, r, w, j/. Three of these combinations don't occur: there are no words in English beginning with /spw/, /stl/, and /stw/ (though children do go through a stage of saying *stwing* for *string*). And CCj- occurs only before /u:/ or /ʊə/, as in *stew* and *skewer*. Children's authors develop a keen sense of what is normal and what isn't. A name like *Mr Gloimp* would appeal precisely because that sequence of sounds fits the general pattern of English syllables while breaking the normal expectancies of which vowels go with which consonants. The study of the possible sequences of sounds in a language is called *phonotactics* (from Greek *taxis*, meaning 'arrangement').

All sorts of phonotactic restrictions exist, and these have to be acquired by children and second-language learners alike. For example, initial /p/ and /k/ are happy before /l/, but /t/ isn't: there are many words along the lines of *please* and *click*, but no words beginning with *tl-*. Final /s/ is happy before /p/, /t/, /k/, but final /z/ can be followed only by /d/: there are many words like *lisp*, *list*, *ask*, *buzzed*, but no words ending in *-zb* or *-zg*. The missing combinations of course make them ideal choices for names of alien beings in sci-fi stories: a really weird alien might well be called *Tlizg*.

These are frequency effects that crossword-puzzle and Scrabble enthusiasts soon develop an intuition about. How many everyday words are there in a concise English dictionary beginning with /pr/? Hundreds. And with /mw/? Just one (*mwah* – if that counts as a word). /sv/? Just four – *svarabakhti* (a linguistic term), *svedberg* (a physics term), *svelte*, and *Svengali*. /tw/? About 50 – until Twitter came along, and the twitterati began to exploit the expressive potential of the unusual combination of /t/ and /w/, inventing such playful words as *twaffic*, *twend* (a friend on Twitter), and *twacklog* (a backlog of tweets). You can find them all in the online *Twictionary*.

Our intuitions would be seriously tested in a pronunciation crossword (p. 177), where the answers would all have to be written in a phonetic transcription. Imagine a puzzle where three of the answers contain five vowels or consonants, and you have found just one of the consonants in each, as shown below. You want to fill in the blank that follows the known consonant with another consonant. Which one will be easiest?

- - - d -
- - - s -
- - - l -

The answer is /d/, because the only consonant that can follow /d/ at the end of a word is /z/. The next easiest is /s/, because that can be followed by only /p/, /t/, and /k/. But /l/ gives you very little help, as this can be followed by as many as fourteen consonants: /p, t, k, b, d, ʧ, ʤ, m, n, f, v, θ, s, z/.

When I was describing the consonant system, I mentioned the main constraints affecting consonants: /ŋ/ doesn't occur at the beginning of words, apart from in a few rare loanwords (such as *ngultrum*), and /ʒ/ (as in *genre*) is also uncommon; /h/, /j/, and /w/ don't end words, and there's no final /r/ in RP; /ʒ/ is also rare at the end of a word (*rouge*), and /ŋ/ is used only after four vowels: /ɪ, æ, ʌ, ɒ/, as in *sing, sang, sung,* and *song*. All vowels can be used at the beginning of a word, but in most accents four of them are never used at the end: /e/, /æ/, /ʌ/, /ɒ/. There are no such words in RP as /sɪte/, and so on, though a pronunciation like this will be heard in some regional accents – *city* in Lancashire, for example.

The table on p. 175 shows the (rounded) percentages of vowels and consonants in Received Pronunciation, after a survey made by Peter Denes (pronounced /ˈdeneʃ/) in 1963, based on transcriptions of British English conversation. A similar study carried out on General American would show some differences: /r/ is pronounced after vowels, so the percentage would rise to around 10 per cent; the diphthongs in *sheer, share,* and *sure* would become pure vowels (followed by /r/), so the totals for /ɪ/, /e/, and /ʊ/ would be higher; and there would be some discrepancies over the figures for /ɑː/ and /ɒ/, because of the different treatment of words like *lot*, *cloth*, *bath*, and *palm*. But the general impression would be the same. Whatever the English accent, /ə/ always comes top and /ʒ/ always comes bottom.

When tables like this one show differences, it's usually because they have used different sources of data. Some have based their survey on the headwords in a dictionary, in which case the figure for /ð/ (to take just one example) will be much lower, because in the dictionary words like *the* and *this* turn up only once as headwords, whereas in everyday speech they are very frequent. Similarly, a study based on colloquial conversation will show some differences compared with one based on formal speech. And regional accents will show some differences too: for example, the percentage of /h/ in Cockney will be much lower.

We can of course pronounce other sounds that aren't part of the English phonemic system. Take the sound of disgust or disapproval that we usually write down as *tut tut* or *tsk tsk*. It's a click sound, made by tapping the tongue-tip against our teeth. It doesn't use air from the lungs (we can breath in and out quite happily while going *tut-tut-tut*). In some languages, such as the Khoisan languages of Southern Africa, these sounds act as phonemes; but they don't in English. They exist on their own, outside the sound system. And the same point applies to other isolated sounds – the interjections I described in earlier chapters (as on p. 81) – such as the 'gee-up' click we use to a horse (or sometimes an admired human being), the *brrr* lip trill we make when we're cold, and the whistling noise through our lips that we make when we're expressing weariness, relief, disgust, and so on, often written as *phew*. Sounds from outside the sound system don't inter-fere with communication, because they aren't brought into our pronunciation when we're talking normally. But what if we're talking abnormally?

Column 1	as in	per cent
/ə/	the	9.04
/t/	to	8.40
/ɪ/	it	8.25
/n/	no	7.08
/s/	so	5.09
/d/	do	4.18
/l/	lie	3.69
/m/	me	3.29
/ð/	the	2.99
/k/	kin	2.90
/aɪ/	my	2.85
/e/	set	2.81
/r/	run	2.77
/w/	we	2.57
/z/	zoo	2.49
/b/	be	2.08
/v/	view	1.85
/i:/	see	1.79
/p/	pie	1.77
/əʊ/	no	1.75
/f/	few	1.73
/ʌ/	cup	1.67
/h/	hi	1.67
/ɒ/	not	1.53
/j/	yes	1.53

Column 1	as in	per cent
/æ/	cat	1.53
/eɪ/	day	1.50
/uː/	do	1.42
/ŋ/	ring	1.24
/ɔː/	law	1.20
/g/	go	1.16
/ɑː/	ah	0.78
/ʊ/	put	0.77
/aʊ/	now	0.77
/ʃ/	shoe	0.70
/ɜː/	bird	0.67
/θ/	thin	0.60
/ʤ/	jump	0.51
/eə/	fair	0.43
/ʧ/	chew	0.37
/ɪə/	fear	0.29
/ʊə/	sure	0.14
/ɔɪ/	boy	0.09
/ʒ/	genre	0.05

Phonemic torture

A phonemic crossword would look rather different from conventional puzzles. Only symbols from the IPA would be allowed. The clues wouldn't work for all accents, so it would be important to specify which accent the puzzle represents. The simple one below (with apologies for the rather boring clues) is for RP, though it would work just as well for General American with the change of just one vowel symbol. I can imagine the phonemic torture that would be produced by a phonetically inspired Ximenes or Torquemada.

Across
1 What I did 'with my little eye' (4)
4 What we obey (2)
5 Possess (2)
7 Name of a pumpkin eater (4)

Down
1 A gentle hill (4)
2 A passageway in a church or theatre (2)
3 Female offspring (4)
6 What you bend when you kneel (2)

The solution is on p. 278.

22
Speaking with your mouth full

Sharing a sound system means that we will normally be able to understand each other. 'Normally' is an important qualification. Speech usually takes place with the mouth empty, so that the sounds emerge unimpeded. But there are several situations where something gets in the way, and pronunciation is dramatically altered, even to the extent that what is said may not always be understood. Many are due to mouth-filled speech.

I suspect that we all do it, from time to time, especially in informal eating situations when there's an urgent need to make a point, and despite the fact that we've probably been trained not to do such a thing from an early age. 'Don't talk with your mouth full' is one of those linguistic prohibitions that we learn from our parents at around age three. There's more at stake than politeness. There's a risk of choking – and unintelligibility. But etiquette is a dominant factor in English. Some people, if asked a question at exactly the point where they have taken a mouthful on board, simply refuse to speak until they have swallowed, which can produce an awkward silence in the conversation (though the mouth-filled one will usually use facial expression or hand gesture to explain what's happening). Listeners understand the problem if they've been brought up in that way.

Eating is only one of the mouth-filled situations, though it's probably the most frequent because people tend to chat a lot during a meal. Somewhat less common, though just as interesting, is speech uttered while brushing your teeth. I recall a member of my family being asked a question while in the middle of this task, and replying 'I don't know' with a mouth full of brush and toothpaste. I just about understood the muffled words. Actually, they were hardly words at all – more pulsated approximations of words, three throbs with the first one neutral, the second a bit higher, and the third ending on a high falling tone. Since the words 'I don't know' are used so often in English, it wasn't difficult to guess the meaning. I imagine that, for any language, the most common words and phrases, even if intonated in such a 'muddy' manner, would still be understood because of their familiarity and frequency of use.

Once we start looking for mouth-filled situations, we come across them everywhere. Here's a selection:

– speaking while holding a writing implement in the mouth (while the hands are otherwise engaged), as in business meetings
– speaking (or trying to) when the dentist, just having filled your mouth with implements, asks you if you had a nice holiday
– and relatedly, speaking after having had your gum filled with anaesthetic
– speaking with pins in the mouth, while sewing
– speaking with a pipe or cigarette in the mouth
– speaking with a hand or finger in the mouth, as when sucking it better after a hurt or removing something tasty (such as ice cream) from the fingers
– speaking with ill-fitting false teeth
– speaking while keeping a dummy (pacifier) in the mouth, as observed in little (and sometimes not so little) children

– speaking with a decorative item in the mouth, for example with a pierced tongue

– for boxers, speaking with a gumshield

– speaking with something covering the mouth, as with surgeons (during operations), people avoiding smoke or poor climatic conditions, and Darth Vader (all the time)

– in old-style elocution, speaking with a pebble in the mouth to improve one's pronunciation (a technique supposedly used by Demosthenes to overcome a stammer)

– more dramatically, speaking with a gag in the mouth, as in the movies

– or speaking while someone else is in your mouth, as with a passionate kissing scene.

These situations are common enough to have made me role-play mouth-filled speech in listening comprehension exercises, when I used to teach on summer schools for foreign learners. Solo, I hasten to add, in view of the last example.

Which phonemes are most affected? That will depend a lot on what is in the mouth, and which parts of the mouth are involved. Lip movement, for example, won't be much affected by food, but pin or pen-holding will. Vowels will be less distorted than consonants. Presumably stress and intonation (chapters 6 and 7) will be retained, but speech rate and rhythm are likely to be slower and jerkier. There will be an odd pausing pattern. And other tones of voice will probably be absent. I can't imagine whispering while eating, for instance.

Phoneticians have had little to say about these effects, presumably because the situations are unusual, and good-quality recordings are difficult to get hold of. Some of the first transcriptions of body behaviour that were made in the 1960s (in the field of semiotics) include symbols for such effects as 'speaking through clenched teeth', 'speaking while licking one's lips', and 'speaking with mouth pursed'. However, these were just general markers. I don't know of any detailed phonetic descriptions, segment by segment. When I was transcribing everyday conversations in that decade, working on the Survey of English Usage at University College London, I analysed many hours of speech and never heard a single example of mouth-filled utterance. Our tape recorders simply weren't present in bathrooms or dining rooms at the relevant times, it seems. Perhaps we should have spent more time in dental surgeries.

Mouth-filled speech occasionally gets into the press. Anna Pickard in *The Guardian* (27 April 2006) begins an article like this:

> Fankky, i's ow-wajus. I fine i' affo-uuti owajus. Va figiss ... hangom, suwee, nee to swa-oh. Frankly, it's outrageous ...

This is difficult to process visually. But try saying it out loud, and it's much clearer. She goes on:

> And what, I ask, is so wrong with talking with your mouth full? In an age where multitasking is a marketable skill, surely the ability to eat and keep up your end of the conversation at the same time should be positively commended.

She specifies three benefits:

> **Time management** There simply isn't time in the day to set aside a separate amount for eating and for talking. By combining the two activities, an incredible amount of time can be saved. Also, none of your companions will ever need to ask what you had for lunch again. They will know, because they can see.

Portion control The process of eating while talking can do wonders for the figure. Anatomically speaking, the act of sucking in air for the talking while holding food in the oratory position should, in theory, bring more air into the food, thus inflating it, and making you feel more full (if slightly gassy). While this hasn't been scientifically proven as far as I know, speaking as a university graduate, it certainly sounds like a convincing theory. My degree is in dramaturgy.

Characterfulness By the simple act of talking while eating, you can easily ensure that you will be memorable to everyone you meet. While what you were saying might have been otherwise forgettable, no one will ever forget you if you gave them a good eyeful of bolognese while you were saying it.

Writing it down

Is mouth-filled speech ever used for literary effect? The phenomenon does turn up from time to time, but writers usually gloss what's happening and leave the actual phonetic effect to the listener's imagination. Take this example, from J. M. Barrie's *A Widow in Thrums* (Chapter 3):

'Ye daur to speak aboot openin' the door, an' you sic a mess!' cried Jess, with pins in her mouth.

The character has that accent throughout the book; no special effort is made to represent the effect of the pin-holding. Nor do we get any phonetic detail in George Eliot's *Scenes of Clerical Life* (Chapter 1):

'So,' said Mr. Pilgrim, with his mouth only half empty of muffin, 'you had a row in Shepperton Church last Sunday.'

That sentence would certainly have sounded differently. And even Charles Dickens, so good at depicting the idiosyncrasies in an individual's speech, leaves this effect to the imagination of the reader, as in *Nicholas Nickleby* (Chapter 5):

'This is the way we inculcate strength of mind, Mr Nickleby,' said the schoolmaster, turning to Nicholas, and speaking with his mouth very full of beef and toast.

But there are examples of authors trying to represent the pronunciation exactly.

Douglas Adams, *Mostly Harmless* (Chapter 18):

They munched for a bit.
    'It's quite good in fact,' said Ford. 'What's the meat in it?'
    'Perfectly Normal Beast.'

'Not come across that one. So, the question is,' Ford
continued, 'who is the bird really doing it for? What's the
real game here?'

'Mmm,' ate Arthur.

J. K. Rowling, *The Order of the Phoenix* (Chapter 11), in
which Ron is 'eating roast potatoes with almost indecent
enthusiasm':

'Ow kunnit nofe skusin danger ifzat?' said Ron.

His mouth was so full Harry thought it was quite an
achievement for him to make any noise at all.

'I beg your pardon?' said Nearly Headless Nick politely,
while Hermione looked revolted. Ron gave an enormous
swallow and said, 'How can it know if the school's in
danger if it's a Hat?'

Terry Pratchett, *Sourcery* (p. 29):

A thing with a goblin's face, harpy's body and hen's legs
turned its head in a series of little jerks and spoke in a
voice like the peristalsis of mountains (although the deep
resonant effect was rather spoiled because, of course, it
couldn't close its mouth).

It said: 'A Ourcerer is umming! Eee orr ife!' [A Sourcerer
is coming! Flee for your life!']

Dorothy L. Sayers, *In the Teeth of the Evidence* (Chapter 1):

'Ah—ow—oo—oo—uh—ihi—ih?' inquired Wimsey
naturally enough.

'How do I come into it?' said Mr. Lamplough [Wimsey's
dentist], who from long experience was expert in the
interpretation of mumblings.

A. A. Milne, *The House at Pooh Corner* (Chapter 2):

> But Tigger said nothing because his mouth was full of haycorns …
>
> After a long munching noise he said:
>
> 'Ee-ers o i a-ors.'
>
> And when Pooh and Piglet said 'What?' he said 'Skoos ee,' and went outside for a moment.
>
> When he came back he said firmly:
>
> 'Tiggers don't like haycorns.'

Alan Bradley, *A Red Herring Without Mustard* (Chapter 16):

> 'Good for you!' I said, clapping my hands together with excitement and shaking my head in wonder. 'What a super idea.'
>
> 'Don't say "super," dear. You know the Colonel doesn't like it.'
>
> I made the motion of pulling a zipper across my lips.
>
> 'Oon ewdge?'
>
> 'Sorry, dear. I don't know what you're saying.'
>
> I unfastened the zipper.
>
> 'Who else? The other Hobblers, I mean.'

23
Connecting words

Phonemes combine to make syllables. Syllables combine to make words. Words combine to make phrases ... Pronunciation has to keep pace with all of this. Literally, keep pace. When we speak, we don't talk a-sin-gle-syl-la-ble-at-a-time, or even a – single – word – at – a – time. We run our syllables and words together, especially when we talk quickly, causing some phonemes to change their form and influence each other in unexpected ways.

Some of these effects have already been mentioned in earlier chapters, when talking about *assimilation* (pp. 137, 152). That's the technical term for describing what happens when one phoneme causes an adjacent phoneme to change. In a careful, formal style of speech, we would say *good morning* with a clearly articulated /d/. But in fast or casual speech the brain and the vocal organs anticipate the bilabial /m/ and turn the /d/ into a bilabial, so that *good* comes out as either /gʊb/ or /gʊm/. *Goo'morning*, a novelist might write.

The consonants made in the alveolar area are especially prone to changing their form in that way. *That bag* becomes /ðap bag/, *that game* /ðak geɪm/, *good boy* /gʊb bɔɪ/, *ten people* /tem piːpl/, *ten cups* /teŋ kʌps/, *this year* /ðɪʃ jɪə/, *has she* /haʒ ʃɪ/, and so on. Sometimes both of the adjacent consonants change their form: *would you* becomes /ˈwʊʤuː/, *what you* becomes /ˈwɒʧuː/, commonly spelled *watcher* in popular writing. Avoiding these assimilations is something most radio presenters try to do, though they also have to avoid the opposite problem, as carefully articulating every consonant disturbs rhythm and makes speech sound artificial.

The same dilemma – making speech sound natural without it becoming too colloquial – is presented by the other thing that happens to some phonemes in connected speech: they are dropped. The technical term is *elision*: the phonemes are *elided*. Once again, /t/ and /d/ are the most commonly affected, especially when there is a sequence of two. If we say *next day*, it takes quite an effort to pronounce the /t/ in front of a /d/: people normally say /neks deɪ/. *Old man* comes out as /əʊl man/, informally written *ol' man*. Only the most careful of articulations pronounce the *t*'s in such phrases as *shouldn't go* and *doesn't Mary*, and some of these elided forms have been given a standard written form: *want to* > *wanna*, *going to* > *gonna*, *give me* > *gimme*, *got to* > *gotta*. They are all listed in the *Oxford English Dictionary*, each with a written history dating from the 1800s. 'Lemme just try', says Ben in Mark Twain's *Tom Sawyer*; 'I've gotta use words when I talk to you', says T. S. Eliot's Sweeney; 'gimme a light', says Keller in Rudyard Kipling's short story 'A Matter of Fact'. And that title, said rapidly, illustrates another elision, for most people would drop the *e* in *matter* and the *f* of *of*: /ˈmatrə ˈfakt/.

The unstressed vowel schwa (p. 117) turns up all over the place in connected speech, whether formal or informal. We do not say the indefinite article *a* as /eɪ/ unless we are really emphasizing it; it's always /ə/; and similarly *are, her, or,* and *of* regularly reduce to a solitary schwa. Some of the *of* elisions have achieved written permanence, as with *pinta* (milk) and *cuppa* (tea); and we regularly see *and* reduced to /n/ in such phrases as *fish 'n' chips* (sometimes written with just one apostrophe). The fact that *have* reduces to /əv/ or /ə/ in the same way as *of* has led to one of the most noticed errors of English spelling, when people write *I should of gone*.

Listener complaints to the BBC (p. 1) aren't only about colloquial elisions – generally described as 'sloppy' or 'careless' pronunciation – but also about the opposite effect, where a word that would normally be pronounced with a schwa is given its full form without there being any semantic reason for it. *A* and *the* are the two main culprits, according to my letter collection – the public speaker who says 'thee' for *the* or *a* as if it were 'ay' (as in *day*) when the context doesn't require any emphasis. Normally we say *the* as /ði:/ only when we are singling something out (*that is the car for me*) or hesitating (*It's the … main reason*), so when an announcer says *That was the symphony number 5 in D* – presumably in an attempt to add some liveliness to the voice – some listeners evidently find the effect distracting and irritating rather than appealing.

But, in the area of connected speech, most listener irritation is focused on one phoneme only: the way /r/ is used to connect words. In phonetics, this is the subject of *liaison* – adding a sound to make a sequence of words easier to say. In RP, the history of *r*-liaison is the story of how one thing has led to another.

As we saw in Chapter 3, RP is an accent that doesn't pronounce /r/ after a vowel. But in certain words, when there is an *r* in the spelling, and the next word begins with a vowel, then the /r/ *is* pronounced. It's called a 'linking *r*'. Which words? Those where the vowel before the /r/ is one of the following:

/ɑ:/ My <u>car is</u> being repaired.
/ɔ:/ She bought <u>four eggs</u>.
/ə/ His daugh<u>ter is</u> six today.
/ɜ:/ We gave <u>her a</u> present.

/ɪə/ I h<u>ear a</u> noise.
/ɛə/ Th<u>ere is</u> no need.
/ʊə/ I'm <u>sure of</u> it.

Early in the history of English, this pattern was extended to other word sequences where the first word ended in one of these vowels and the second word began with some other vowel, as in *Afric<u>a a</u>nd Asia* or *the very ide<u>a of</u> it*. *Africa* was pronounced 'Africar' and *idea* as 'idear'. Because there is no *r* in the spelling, the /r/ came to be called *intrusive r*. And this is the phenomenon that has attracted most condemnation by those who feel that pronunciation should faithfully reflect spelling.

It's a curious situation, as even the complainers are never totally consistent in their usage. They do routinely notice the intrusion when words end in the very open vowels – /ɑː/ in *the sp<u>a is</u> lovely* and *the Sh<u>ah of</u> Persia*, /ɔː/ in *l<u>aw and</u> order* and *I s<u>aw it</u>*, as well as within a word, such as *draw(r)ing*. *Law and order* is the expression that has become iconic, presumably because it has been used so often on the radio: listeners named it *Laura Norder*. The message got across. I have seen newsreading scripts where the presenter has underlined *law and order*, to make sure that no intrusive *r* slips in.

The irony is that the same people who complain about the open vowels tend not to notice the effect when the more central vowels occur – and indeed often use an intrusive *r* themselves without realizing it. I used to carry out experiments in which I gave *r*-complainers a set of newsreading sentences such as this:

There has been a complete breakdown of law and order this week in Northern India and Southern Pakistan.

The almost universal response was to read the sentence with

a careful avoidance of /r/ in *law*; but hardly anyone then noticed that there was another instance later in the sentence, in *India*, which they unconsciously pronounced with an /r/ as /ˈɪndɪər ən pækɪˈstɑ:n/. The reality is that an intrusive *r* makes pronunciation easier, especially when speech rate increases, and it takes some effort to suppress it. But, whether people are successful in avoiding it or not, it is a present-day socio-linguistic fact that intrusive *r* is considered by many people to be a 'bad' pronunciation.

But that led to a second irony. As people became sensitive about using /r/ when there is no *r* in the spelling, they transferred their anxiety to the cases where the spelling does contain an *r* – the linking cases illustrated above. So they began to drop the /r/s in those places too, replacing them with a pause or a glottal stop. That's why we often hear such pronunciations as *car is* /kɑ:ˆɪz/, *four eggs* /fɔ:ˆegz/, and so on (where the ˆ shows a slight pause). And those who have developed this habit now run the risk of being criticized for, once again, not respecting the spelling.

These problems are largely restricted to RP. People tend not to worry about intrusive /r/ in other accents where /r/ is normally pronounced after vowels, such as in most American English or in the British West Country. And even in those accents which, like RP, don't pronounce /r/ after vowels, such as much of northern England, there isn't such social pressure to follow spelling, so people use it without any self-consciousness or a feeling that they need to conform to pre-scriptive tradition.

Might there be any literary support for the assimilations and elisions in connected speech? I would cite Hamlet, in his speech to the players at the opening of Act 3 Scene 2 of *Hamlet*:

> Speak the speech, I pray you, as I pronounced it to you,
> trippingly on the tongue: but if you mouth it, as many of
> your players do, I had as lief the town-crier spoke my lines.

Trippingly. An apt characterization of natural connected
speech.

24
Accents welcome

Speaking with your mouth full may interfere with the sound system so much that speech becomes unintelligible. But are there any situations where the mouth isn't physically obstructed and yet the pronunciation is so deviant that we fail to understand what is being said?

Here's one. Daughter Lucy, aged about five, was watching a Mickey Mouse cartoon on television. She understood Mickey's high-pitched voice, and Goofy's swallowed sounds, but when Donald Duck spoke she turned to me for help – and even I had some trouble. It's quite a tricky sound effect to produce; few people are as skilled as the voice's originator, Clarence Nash. You have to push air into one of your cheeks, make it build up pressure, and then release it while your tongue and lips form the sounds. The larynx isn't involved at all. Because the cheeks are used as the source of the air-stream, it's called *buccal* voice (from the Latin word for the cheek, *bucca*).

Other cartoon voices tend to be more intelligible, even though many characters suffer from some sort of speech defect. Daffy Duck has a slushy *s*. Porky Pig has a marked stutter. Bugs Bunny is hypernasal. Elmer Fudd has trouble with his *r*'s (famously in the episode *What's Opera, Doc?* (1957), popularly known as 'Kill the wabbit ...' because of its parody of Wagner's 'Ride of the Valkyries'). Evidently the cartoon companies wanted their characters not just to look funny but to sound funny as well. And that meant deviant.

There is of course a serious, not to say poignant, side to deviant pronunciation, and that is when we encounter children and adults who are unable to pronounce speech well because of some medical condition. Sometimes the reason for the disability is obvious from the person's anatomy, as when we see a child with a cleft lip and palate. Such children are extremely difficult to understand until the clefts are surgically repaired and speech therapy helps them develop a normal sound system. Another condition is any form of muscular paralysis affecting the vocal organs, which can result in a slow and slurred speech, with many approximate articulations – again, difficult to understand until the listener gets used to it. The condition is called *dysarthria*, from Greek *arthron*, meaning 'articulation'.

These are just two of the several conditions that can interfere with normal speech production. Others include stammering, cluttering (speaking so rapidly and irregularly that sounds tumble over each other), poor or clumsy speech coordination (known as *dyspraxia*), and a range of developmental conditions where children simply fail to acquire phonemes normally, so that they sound immature for their age. I mentioned difficulties with some individual phonemes (such as /s/ and /r/) in earlier chapters (pp. 134, 161). Such problems are all part of the stock-in-trade of the profession of speech therapy – also called speech and language therapy, or (in the USA, Canada, and Australia) speech pathology (see further, Appendix).

These are special cases. Is there ever unintelligibility among people (or cartoon characters) who have no handicapping condition (and who aren't under the influence of drink or drugs)? This is where the notion of regional accent once again comes to the fore. In Chapter 1, I stressed the importance of seeing accents as a critical index of personal and community identity. Everyone has an accent that shows something of their geographical, social, or occupational background. It is the regional dimension that attracts most attention: we listen to someone speaking, and try to work out where they're from. And it's a common experience that sometimes we can do this without understanding everything they're saying.

Accent familiarity breeds content. That's how we know we're talking about different accents and not different languages. We can listen to French for hours, but if we've not learned the language we'll not understand the speaker. By contrast, if we're unfamiliar with the way people speak from Glasgow, or Newcastle, or Brooklyn, or India, or the Caribbean, then a period of exposure to the accent will soon help. It's when people suddenly encounter an unfamiliar accent differing greatly from their own that they talk (usually jocularly) about needing an interpreter – or, in the case of films, ask for subtitles. Ken Loach's film *I, Daniel Blake* (2016) was given subtitles when shown at Cannes because producers feared the audience wouldn't understand the Newcastle accents, and several other British and American films using broad accents have been dubbed for an international audience. The problem, of course, is not just one for the UK and USA; it arises whenever any local accent, from any part of the English-speaking world, is so broad that it defeats the normally rapid process of 'tuning in'. In a face-to-face situation, we can ask the speaker to slow down, and that usually helps. We can't do that when watching the characters in a movie.

Accents are there to express different cultural (regional, social, political, religious ...) identities. That is why there are so many of them. And that is why they arouse such strong emotions. Dialects, which are primarily a matter of local vocabulary and grammar, do the same thing. But accent is more important than dialect, as an index of identity. Dialect features are intermittent: they consist of local words (such as the name of a type of bread roll: *bap, cob, bride, batch, oggie* …) and local grammatical constructions (*we were sat here, she jamp over the wall*), which turn up in speech only every now and again. But *every* word and sentence has to be spoken in the local accent. Accents are always in front of our ears.

Behind every accent there's a piece of social history. People speak like they do because of a long sequence of events that might go back hundreds of years. There are so many accents in England because of the way different groups of immigrants, from various parts of northern Europe, arrived in Britain during the fifth and sixth centuries, bringing with them the accents of their homeland. We call them all Anglo-Saxons today, but they could never have been a homogeneous group, from the point of view of accent or dialect, given that they originated in places as far afield as (modern) Denmark and northern France. They settled in locations all along the south and east coast, as far north as the River Humber, and soon beyond that and into the midlands, bringing their different accents with them. Contact between the communities would have been sporadic, so local speech differences would have become more marked as time went by. Other influences then affected different parts of the country in different ways: a few centuries later, Danish settlers arrived after the Viking raids; a couple of centuries after that, French settlers arrived following the Norman Conquest. And so it has continued over the years, each influential group leaving its phonetic mark on some sections of the population, but not in the same way on all.

As long as the country was fragmented, lacking a national identity and means of communication, accent and dialect divergence would continue without pause. But as soon as there was a strong political will to unify, there was a corresponding need to develop a way of talking and writing that everyone would use and understand. This is the force for intelligibility that I described in Chapter 1, and it is the force that led to the development of a standard written English, first in Britain, and then throughout the English-speaking world. It didn't happen overnight. It took some 400 years, roughly between 1400 and 1800, to get everyone writing the language in more or less the same way, in spelling, punctuation, and grammar.

Pronunciation never achieved the same kind of standardization, despite the best efforts of influential writers on language in the 1700s. In earlier centuries, there was no such thing as a 'standard' accent – a pronunciation used by everyone. People spoke in different ways, reflecting their regional backgrounds, regardless of their social class. In Shakespeare's day, having a broad regional accent didn't stop you becoming powerful in the kingdom, as illustrated by Francis Drake and Walter Raleigh, both said to have had strong Devonshire accents. Here's John Aubrey's account, written around 1680:

> Old Sir Thomas Malett, one of the Justices of the King's bench *tempore Caroli I et II* [in the time of Charles I and II], knew Sir Walter, and I have heard him say, that notwithstanding his so great Mastership in Style and his conversation with the learnedest and politest persons, yet he spake broad Devonshire to his dying day.

Indeed, you could become king with a regional accent, as happened in 1603, when James VI of Scotland became James I of English, and suddenly the entire court echoed to the sound of a Scottish accent. Francis Bacon described James's speech as being 'in the full dialect of his country'.

There was no such thing as RP in Jacobethan England. People in the south-east – the home of the Court, the Church, and Oxford and Cambridge universities – of course considered their accent(s) to be superior to those spoken elsewhere. Shakespeare in *As You Like It* (3.2) has Orlando noticing the disguised Rosalind's accent, finding it odd to hear it from a supposed shepherdess in the middle of a forest, and making her think quickly to maintain her disguise:

ORLANDO: Your accent is something finer than you could purchase in so removed a dwelling.
ROSALIND: I have been told so of many; but indeed an old religious uncle of mine taught me to speak, who was in his youth an inland man …

The basis of this 'finer' accent would have been no more than the London accent of the time – it may even have been Cockney-like – but filtered through literacy. As we know from characters such as Shakespeare's Holofernes in *Love's Labour's Lost*, there were people around in his day (as today, with intrusive *r*, p. 189) who thought the best speech was that which accurately reflected the spelling. So Holofernes is horrified when he hears Don Armado say the word *debt* without sounding the *b*. Shakespeare is satirizing contemporary pedantry, of course. But the characterization tells us something about attitudes to pronunciation at the time.

Nonetheless, the accent of the court, as it subsequently evolved, and despite the arrival of monarchs with various regional accents (such as William III with a Dutch accent, and George II with a German one), gradually became the pronunciation to imitate, if one was to appear cultured in England. But even as late as the middle of the eighteenth century, there was uncertainty about it: Dr Johnson, for example, found pronunciation so unpredictable that he made one of the aims of his *Dictionary* to 'fix' it forever (an ideal he subsequently abandoned).

By the end of the century, the notion of a 'posh' accent had begun to emerge, as a result of the elocution movement, promoted by Thomas Sheridan (the father of the dramatist) and others, which was intended to satisfy the demands of the up-and-coming middle class who wished to speak in a way that would not be criticized by polite society. It made Sheridan a rich man. The period also saw the first dictionary of English pronunciation, published by John Walker in 1791 (p. 52), who talks in his Preface about the prestige of the London accent, and introduces the term by which it later came to be known:

> For though the pronunciation of London is certainly
> erroneous in many words, yet, upon being compared with
> that of any other place, it is undoubtedly the best; that is,
> not only the best by courtesy, and because it happens to be
> the pronunciation of the capital, but best by a better title;
> that of being more generally received.

By 'received' he meant the kind of pronunciation that had come to be socially accepted because it had been passed down by the 'higher orders' in society from one generation to the next. And it was this sense of 'received' that later appealed to the phonetician Alexander Ellis, who in 1869 described the English cultured accent as *Received Pronunciation*. The term became really well known when it was taken up by Daniel Jones some decades later, and widely abbreviated (as in this book) to *RP* (p. 21).

Walker made it very clear in the Preface to his dictionary that this cultured accent needed to be clearly distinct from other regional accents, and his recommendations showed speakers how they could maintain the divide, by stressing words in the 'right' way, and giving vowels and consonants the 'right' value. If Cockney speakers dropped their *h*'s, then speakers of RP should not. If people in Scotland (and elsewhere) pronounced their *r* after a vowel, then speakers of RP should not. The actual character of RP came about as a partly conscious and partly unconscious attempt to differentiate 'polite' speakers from those of the 'lower orders'. It was as clear a linguistic index of class division as it was possible to imagine. And it became the voice of English worldwide after it became the preferred pronunciation in the public schools, and after the products of those schools – the missionaries, diplomats, and military officers – took the language around the world during the formation of the British Empire.

In 1922, when the BBC was founded, Lord Reith recognized the status of RP as a unifying force. Although himself a Scot, he realized that broadcasting needed to use an accent that would be the most widely understood, and the only one that could achieve that aim was the one that had become the educated norm. It would certainly be the accent that would be expected among those people who could afford to buy one of the new wireless sets. But there was no narrowly rigid interpretation of what RP was.

Arthur Lloyd James, in *The Broadcast Word* (1935), looks back on the early history of the BBC and describes how announcers were selected. Applicants were required to pass a test before a microphone where they had to read a short news bulletin, an SOS in French, a programme of music in French, German, and Italian, and a piece of unprepared prose. The results were listened to by a board of officials, including a phonetician, to determine whether (as he described it):

the voice is suitable;
there are speech defects, however small;

the dialect of English is suitable;
the standard of pronunciation of the foreign languages is
moderately good;
the candidate can read aloud intelligently.

Lloyd James goes on to say: 'Most candidates fail.' And
he singles out the main reason: 'their English accent is
unsuitable.'

Now at this point a modern reader will assume that he
was thinking of broad regional accents. But that is not what
Lloyd James had in mind:

usually it is too aggressively modern, too much like what is
sometimes called 'haw-haw'– the sort of speech that certain
comedians love to play with. Oftentimes the candidate's
speech is indistinct, suffering occasionally from those
laxities of articulation which, while of minor importance in
ordinary conversation, make seriously for unintelligibility
over any but the best receiving apparatus.

It is the exaggerated upper-class accent he singles out, not
regional varieties. And then he makes the general point – one
that any modern elocutionist would make – that it is delivery
that counts, which is entirely a matter of breath control, intonation, rate, rhythm (a 'critical factor'), and the other tones
of voice described in Chapter 5. It is an educated accent that
counts, not the region it comes from:

The B.B.C. insists that all its speakers, official or otherwise,
as far as possible, shall speak a variety of educated English;
it may be the educated English spoken by a Scotsman, or
a Welshman, or an Irishman, or an Englishman, but it has
to be educated, unless there are very powerful reasons,
political or social, why this proviso should not apply.

And he adds that even among the staff with an impeccable public school and Oxbridge background, they 'do not talk the King's English in the same way'. It is a recognition of diversity that would soon come to be lost, with a single 'BBC accent' becoming the norm during the 1940s, to the extent that it took an official report in 1977 (the Annan Report) to draw attention to what had happened, and to say, as if the point was being made for the first time: 'We welcome regional accents.'

Myths about accents

Every now and then there's a media story that tries to explain why a regional accent has its distinctive phonetic quality. We read claims like these:

- the Liverpool accent is the result of mists and fog in the River Mersey (see picture), causing colds and nasal catarrh, which led to its characteristic adenoidal twang
- the accents heard in the Appalachians developed because the people lived in the mountains, which led to a higher and more sweeping range of intonation patterns
- the Birmingham (UK) accent arose because people didn't open their mouths much in order to avoid the dirty air of the industrial Midlands, so over time their accent became very nasal
- the Australian accent arose because the first convict settlers were regularly drunk, resulting in many

so-called 'lazy' diphthongs, such as the /aɪ/ sound in words like *day*
- the South African accent arose because many people settled on the farmland of the low plains, leading to flat intonation patterns and a staccato rhythm

I suppose such explanations spread because they are simple and easy to understand. But none of them stand up to examination. They are all myths. There's no simple correlation between accent and features of the physical environment.

If British sea mists cause a nasal twang, why don't we hear it in the accents of Newcastle, Bristol, Hull, Belfast, and all the other often-foggy ports of the nation? If the black smoke of industry causes nasality, why don't we hear a similar twang in all the industrial towns and cities, such as those in Lancashire and Yorkshire? If high-pitched lilting intonations are caused by mountains, why do we hear such tunes in the accents of the plains, such as the lowlands of Scotland or the American South? If we hear staccato (syllable-timed) speech in the lowlands of South Africa, why do we also hear it in the mountains of Jamaica?

The reality is that accent distinctiveness is nothing to do with physical environment, but a result of the combination of regional and social factors that have influenced the emergence of a particular community. The distinctive accent of Liverpool is the result of its unique social history – waves of immigrants from Ireland in the nineteenth century brought a range of Irish accents, which combined with the already existing Lancashire speech of the area. Welsh accents added to the mix, with over ten per cent of the population in the early decades of the century coming from Wales – to the extent that Liverpool was often called 'the capital of North Wales'. Even if there was a high level of respiratory disease on Merseyside, there's no reason to suppose that speakers would find it socially desirable to continue to use features of their illness-pronunciation when they recovered.

Australian speech is another amalgam, the result of inter-action between the British accents of the original settlers, both convicts and free, many of whom came from all over England, Ireland, Scotland, and Wales, but especially London. If the wide diphthong of *day* is the result of drunkenness, then we would have to say that the entire Cockney popula-tion of London was drunk, for the same diphthong is heard in their speech. And there is nothing lazy about it: the move-ment of the tongue in pronouncing the /aɪ/ of *day* is actually greater than that needed for the /eɪ/ of *day* in Received Pro-nunciation. It involves more energy, rather than less.

Each of the myths about the influence of environment on accents can be exploded along similar lines. It's very rare indeed for a form of pronunciation to emerge as an adap-tation to specific physical surroundings. An example where this has happened is the 'whistled speech' that has occasion-ally developed around the world to help shepherds, hunters, and other members of isolated communities to communicate across mountain valleys or in dense forests. Having discov-ered that whistling carries further, a wide range of calls has evolved, based on the sounds of the local language, to express everyday notions. For example, in the island of La Gomera, in the Canary Islands, the Silbo Gomero ('Gomeran whistle') is based on the local Spanish dialect, with different pitches rep-resenting a small number of vowels and consonants. Systems of this kind have been called 'speech surrogates' – substitutes for the real thing. But they are a world apart from the charac-ter of English accents.

25

Being accommodating

Pronunciation changes in three ways: it varies from one part of a country (or one country) to another; it changes from one individual to another; and in each of these countries and individuals it changes over time. Pronunciation has never stood still and it never will. Some people find that thought unappealing, but it is one of the facts of linguistic life.

Time is the really great changer. It isn't that people get fed up with a pronunciation, so they decide to change it. Rather, they find it desirable to change their pronunciation, either because they like the new sound or because they feel it enables them to identify more closely with a social group they admire. And when I say 'they', I don't mean that everyone does this at the same time and at the same rate. Sociolinguistic research has shown that new pronunciations enter a language at very different times and rates. Gender is a particularly important factor, along with age and social class: women are usually at the forefront of any accent change, favouring the more widely used or prestige pronunciations that are around, whereas men tend to favour more vernacular forms that convey local identity. So when a change of pronunciation takes place, it can take years for it to spread through the whole community; and at any one time, there will be differences among the population – differences that may make some people reach for their pen or keyboard and write to the BBC about it.

All this usually goes on in a totally unconscious way, of course. And the process starts early in life. Many parents have had the experience of moving from one part of the country to another, sending their three-year-old to a local crèche, and hearing the youngster come home pronouncing some words in a different way. It can make them feel quite upset, especially if the new pronunciation is one that has attracted criticism in the past. A friend of mine, having moved to London from Wales, worried about the way her little boy Michael was now saying *bo'le* for *bottle*. He had picked up the glottal stop (p. 130) within a few hours of attending his nursery group for the first time. 'Should I correct it?', she asked.

To answer this question, we first have to appreciate what is going on. Michael is having his first community experience of what sociolinguists call *accommodation*. It's something he will continue to do throughout his life. Everyone accommodates in their behaviour when interacting with others. What this means is that they are influenced by the behaviour of the person they are talking to. Two big trends in pronunciation have been repeatedly reported. If people from different regions like each other, and are getting on well, then their speech patterns converge: each person picks up some features of the other's way of talking. It might be an intonation pattern, a difference in rhythm, a vowel or consonant quality, a particular assimilation or elision, or just an overall level of loudness. People with a particularly good ear or a strong capacity for empathy can slip into another person's accent almost immediately.

But the crucial point is: as long as they're getting on well. If this rapport is lacking, and the relationship is one of disagreement or outright antagonism, then the speech patterns do the opposite: they diverge. One of the first research studies of accommodation showed this effect. A group of people who were learning Welsh were asked to respond to a survey, while sitting in the booths of a language laboratory so that their responses could be recorded. The questioner whom they heard through their headphones spoke in RP. When he asked questions that were emotionally neutral, the students replied in their everyday voices, most of which showed a mild Welsh accent. Then (deliberately) he asked them why on earth they wanted to learn Welsh, asserting that it was a dying language with no future. The learners responded indignantly, as we would expect, but – and this is the interesting point – they broadened their Welsh accents when replying. In other words, they increased the linguistic distance between their accent and that of the questioner.

It's the sort of thing we all do, without being conscious of it. And it's something we have done from our earliest days. I talked above about Michael's first 'community' experience. In fact, he has been accommodating at an individual level almost from birth. During his first year of life, when all he could do was cry, coo, and babble, he accommodated to the speech around him. Researchers of child language acquisition have found that, when infants babble while interacting with their mother, the babble is at a higher pitch, reflecting her 'soprano' voice, than during interaction with their father, when it takes on a lower pitch, reflecting his 'bass' voice. A little later, when toddlers are role-playing at being 'mums and dads', their voices are higher when being mum and lower when being dad.

Accommodation is a permanent presence in our lives. If people are having an argument, and one voice is raised, then it is likely that within seconds the other voices will be raised. It takes a real effort of will not to do so. In a jocular interchange, if one person puts on a silly voice, it's very likely that someone else will too. In my book *Language Play*, I reported an occasion in a pub when I overheard a student at a nearby table switch from his normal accent into a mock Irish accent, and suddenly everyone else around his table was doing the same thing. Just as people walking together in the street will adopt the same rate and style of leg movement, so that they are in synchrony, so it is when they communicate. All aspects of communication are affected: if we are in a rapport-building situation, if I smile, you will smile; if I nod my head, you will nod; and if I use a high rising intonation on statements (p. 49), you will too. Convergence promotes social intimacy, integration, and identification. It is a way of signalling a willingness to support, approve, and cooperate. And if there is no desire to achieve these goals, the result will be the opposite: divergence.

Of course, it isn't always the case that our relationships with others are as black and white as this. Sometimes people object when they sense convergence. They may feel that the converger is 'taking the mickey' out of their accent. Or they may interpret the convergence as insinuating or pushy (as with some shop salespeople). But the bottom line is that everyone has the option of shifting their accent as occasion arises, and has the ability to do so, though the ability (or perhaps the motivation) seems to decrease somewhat as we grow older. The important point is to be sensitive to the occasions when accommodation becomes a conscious process and people notice it – as with Michael's mother.

So I wouldn't want to 'correct', in Michael's situation – to give him the impression that there was something 'wrong' with his new pronunciation. If his parents want him to assimilate comfortably into his new learning environment, then they have to recognize that this will involve accent change. They will of course continue to provide him with home role models that are different from those outside, talking in their parental

accents, but it's important to do this in a natural and unemotional way. Michael will eventually come to learn that there
is an 'accent of the home' and an 'accent of the school', and
(as he learns new outside vocabulary and grammar) become
capable of switching between them – become *bidialectal*. It's
the sort of thing that actors do all the time, and in a sense,
when we leave our home environment and present ourselves
to the world at large, we all become actors.

Accommodation explains a lot. It even explains the way
that pronunciation changes when people are not face-to-face,
as on the radio. When local radio began in the UK, during
the 1960s, one of the immediate signs that it was 'local' was
the way the different stations employed presenters whose
accents reflected the region. I now expect a Liverpool-sound-
ing voice if I tune in to Radio Merseyside, and would find
it very strange if I heard RP there. But the issue had been
discussed several decades earlier. In a radio discussion called
'The voice of Britain', reprinted in *The Listener* (2 March
1939), one of the participants makes the point: 'when I tune
in to any station, I like to think I'm there; when I tune in to
Wales, I like to hear that inflection at the end of the sentence
that you get from the Welsh', and he objects to the uniformity he hears in the emerging 'BBC manner'. The linguistic
adviser to the BBC, Arthur Lloyd James (p. 60), responded
somewhat acerbically:

> Well, one of my jobs is training the announcers. Now, as far
> as I'm concerned with these men, I never train them to do
> anything of the sort you're suggesting. I have to teach them
> to read aloud in a reasonable way, but as for *grooming* them
> – well, I just don't do it.

But uniformity in pronunciation did become the norm, as we
saw in the previous chapter. And accents still don't reflect the

region in many walks of life. It's a lesson that still needs to be learned by the makers of automated systems that speak to us. I recall entering a busy lift at a store in Manchester, and heard the voice telling me that doors were opening and closing in a very posh-sounding RP. The Mancunians in the lift laughed when they heard it – hardly the reaction the makers intended. And this raises a very general question: what pronunciation should we give our robots?

26

Where are you from, robot?

Robot inventors usually give their creations a standard educated accent from the region in which the robot (or film) was
made. The robot butler in *Robot and Frank*, voiced by Peter
Sarsgaard (born in Illinois) has a gentle General American
accent. C-3PO in *Star Wars* has an elegant Received Pronunciation, voiced by Anthony Daniels (born in Wiltshire). Computer voices are the same. HAL in *2001* has a soft, reassuring
Canadian accent, voiced by Douglas Rain.

These are friendly robots. What should inventors do
when they create robots – or any alien life forms – that are
unfriendly? They need to give them pronunciations that
are very different from educated standards, but also different from recognizable regional norms. It would be just as
implausible for a Dalek-like being to speak in broad Yorkshire
or in a Texan drawl as it would be to have it speak in Received
Pronunciation or General American. At the same time, these
beings have to be intelligible, if film-viewers are going to
understand them. How is the dilemma to be managed?

The problem disappears when we recall the two dimensions that comprise pronunciation: the segments and the
tones of voice (Chapter 5). Segments are the primary means
of conveying intelligible speech. The primary function of
tones of voice is to add emotional, aesthetic, and social properties to speech. So, if we want to create an intelligible but
evil alien, all the creator has to do is use normal vowels,

consonants, and syllables, and replace normal patterns of pitch, loudness, rate, rhythm, and timbre by abnormal tones of voice. Perhaps have them speak in a loud monotone, with abnormal rising lilts, and a staccato, syllable-timed rhythm, often with lengthened syllables. Add a distinctive timbre, acoustically generated, that no human voice could ever achieve. The result? A Dalek. *Cry-stal must be ex-ter-mi-na-ted.*

The pantheon of enemy aliens provides a fascinating example of phonetic deviance at work. Abnormal voice qualities are the norm, from the harsh high-pitched haranguing tone of the Daleks to the low-pitched hoarse breathiness of Darth Vader. Some aliens have altered their pronunciation over the years – for example, different generations of Cyber-men in *Doctor Who* have changed their pitch, loudness, and timbre, partly reflecting the increased options made available through acoustic technology. We can be sure of one thing: if we hear a being with a strongly nasal, creaky, or hoarse voice, with flat intonation and erratic rhythm, or with all of these effects combined, they are definitely not on our side.

At present, in real life, robotic voices stay within the parameters we would expect to hear from a normal human voice. But now the question is: which one? We want to hear a pronunciation which is not just intelligible but one which is pleasant to listen to and which conveys associations that make us feel comfortable. The makers of GPS audio car navigation systems were among the first to realize that the choice of accent is important, because it can affect the driver's concentration and state of mind. As one firm puts it: 'Awful GPS voices make for awful drives.' So they went in for celebrity voices (including cartoon characters), either real or impersonated. It is possible to have your car directions given by Homer or Marge Simpson, as well as by Arnold Schwarzenegger, Sean Connery, Clint Eastwood, Kim Cattrall, and many more. One firm uses Darth Vader, so he can't be all bad.

When asked in surveys, people say that they want their robot voices to sound warm, friendly, intelligent, competent, trustworthy, even sexy. Given a choice of accents, they go for ones that they feel convey these values. In a 2009 survey carried out by the British hands-free car-kit firm Bury Technologies, almost half of the people they asked (some 3,000 respondents in all) found regional accents to be sexy. Irish and Scots came top. Other surveys have produced similar results, with some accents being judged in very positive terms and some very negatively. Inner-city accents traditionally tend to rank low.

But times change, and so do attitudes. An accent that is viewed with distaste by one section of society may become accepted and even admired over quite a short period. Take the difference in popular attitudes towards Scottish and Welsh accents. Scottish accents have long been given positive ratings in surveys – and are frequently encountered in call centres as a consequence – probably because of the prestige associated with Scotland's ancient historical status as a kingdom, and its corresponding role in England after 1603. Welsh accents, on the other hand, have traditionally been given negative ratings – a view which also has a long history: in *A Hundred Merry Tales*, printed in 1526, a popular collection of stories about stupid people who did silly things, seven are about Welshmen; none of the tales are about Scotsmen.

Move on four centuries or so, and we find people trying to explain the failure of the Labour Party to win general elections in the 1980s. In a section headed 'Why Labour lost' in a Fabian Society pamphlet (no. 554, 1992), political adviser David Lipsey wrote about Tredegar-born Labour leader Neil Kinnock: 'Had he been born to a Scottish rather than a Welsh accent, he might have been prime minister today.' It's unlikely that this would be a factor nowadays: the Welsh accent has steadily increased its general popularity ratings, thanks primarily to its increased presence in the media (such as encountered in the voice of Huw Edwards on BBC television).

Welsh is not alone. Regional speech generally achieved a greater public presence during the later decades of the twentieth century. Call centres and television commercials provide convenient indications of change. Formerly, the voice answering the phone at a national enquiry centre would have been RP, with local accents heard only in regional offices (and not always then). During the 1990s, there was a noticeable increase in the use of local accents at national level. The voice you would hear in enquiring about car insurance or a mortgage would very likely be Edinburgh Scots or Yorkshire (the two most preferred accents). Not all regional speech was favoured: in particular, some urban English accents, such as Birmingham, still generated negative reactions. And when companies outsourced call centres to India, the accents were controversially received, with some listeners finding them difficult to understand (because of their staccato, syllable-timed rhythm, p. 54), some finding them unpleasant, some finding them quite attractive, and some not noticing anything at all. It remains to be seen whether the reactions to these accents will diminish as people become more familiar with them.

The news isn't all positive in relation to regional accents. There are pockets of resistance to the general trend, some quite influential. A report in the *Independent* (7 March 2017) was headed:

Banking jobs denied to young people due to having 'wrong accents'

A YouGov survey carried out on behalf of the Sutton Trust and Deutsche Bank found that 80 per cent of banking leaders thought candidates from disadvantaged backgrounds were less likely to secure a job in the finance sector because of how they presented themselves in interviews, regardless of their ability and experience. It wasn't just accents: wearing the wrong clothes – and apparently brown shoes – had a negative impact too. But it was accent that generated the headline.

At least the problem is being recognized, though how long it might take to change attitudes within an industry that places such store on conformity is anyone's guess. It is an anomaly, given that sociolinguistic research since the 1980s has clearly identified two major trends: an increase in positive attitudes towards certain regional accents, and an increase in negative attitudes towards RP. The methodology is to use reaction studies. People are invited to give their opinion of an accent using a wide range of questions, such as whether it sounds 'educated', 'sincere', 'honest', 'friendly', 'warm', 'intelligent', and so on. Traditionally, RP has been the accent that attracted all the positive values; regional speech would typically attract negative ones, with urban accents in particular being poorly rated.

The turnaround has been quite dramatic. Several regional accents now achieve strongly positive ratings such as 'warm' and 'customer-friendly'; whereas RP has begun to attract negative ratings such as 'insincere' and 'distant'. Organizations that rely for their income on voice presentation have noticed the change. We rarely now see characters in television commercials using RP (a marked difference from the plummy accents selling washing powder on our screens in the 1950s). The voice agent of my actor son Ben was unequivocal, when he interviewed her for *You Say Potato* in 2014: requests from commercial clients for RP were now 'a rarity'. And the BBC

newsreader Charlotte Green, once voted the 'most attractive female voice on national radio', said at around that time:
'Received pronunciation is on the wane ... The BBC's days of
employing people who sound like me are more or less over.'
The attitude surveys bring to light such comments as 'RP
is customer-unfriendly', 'distant', 'cold', 'out of touch', even
'untrustworthy' – a surprising comment, but understandable
when we consider the habit in American movies of having
RP used by the bad guys – several Bond villains, for example,
or Khan (Benedict Cumberbatch) in *Star Trek into Darkness*
(2013).

It isn't just a question of attitude. RP continues to have
a strong presence in public broadcasting, but its phonetic
character has changed. Accents never stand still, and indeed
radio is the chief medium where accent change can be traced.
Anyone listening to radio programmes made in the 1920s and
1930s cannot fail to be struck by the 'plummy' or 'far back'
sound of the RP accent then – when *lord* sounded more like
'lahd' – but even the accents of the 1960s and 1970s sound
dated now. And changes continue to affect RP. If we compare
the voice of the Queen, as classically heard in a speech for
the opening of parliament or a Christmas message, with the
voices of Prince Harry or Prince William, two generations
on, we find many differences. The Queen would never, for
example, replace the final consonant in such words as *hot*
with a glottal stop; the youngsters often do. But even the
Queen's accent has changed, with her open fronted vowels
in words like *man* and *cup* more centralized. All of this has
led to a dramatic change in terminology, for the label RP has
been replaced in the latest edition of the most widely used
textbook on English pronunciation, A. C. Gimson's *Introduction to the Pronunciation of English* (p. 80). The current editor,
Alan Cruttenden, explains:

despite many attempts to say that RP has evolved and
includes variation within it, non-phoneticians and
even some British linguists and phoneticians, persist
in identifying RP as a type of posh, outdated, falsely
prestigious accent spoken, for example, by senior members
of the Royal family (e.g. Prince Charles, but compare Prince
Harry's much more modern pronunciation). Because of
this narrow use by many of the name RP, and the frequent
hostility to it, the name of the accent described in this book
has been changed to General British (GB).

The parallel is with the way in which American English pronunciation is described, General American. Cruttenden adds
that it is important to be clear that GB is not a totally different accent, but 'an evolved and evolving version of the same
accent under a different name'.

Individual accent histories will affect the way we relate to
our robots, as well as to other people, especially in domains
where our personal welfare is concerned, such as health
and financial services. In a 2011 study from New Zealand,
researchers used a healthcare speaking computer whose role
was to assist in measuring blood pressure. They gave it three
synthesized accents (British, American, and New Zealand),
presented different groups of New Zealand listeners with
each of the voices, and asked them to judge the quality of
the performance. Although exactly the same information was
being presented in each setting, the computer was judged to
be doing better when it spoke in the local accent. We trust
our robots more if they talk like us, it seems. We like robots
that know how to accommodate.

It's a message that has to be taken on board by manufacturers of robotic equipment, which is already becoming
routine – recorded voices giving instructions at the other
end of a telephone, intelligent personal assistants such as

Apple's Siri, unintelligent advisers such as those who can only tell you which floor you've reached in a lift (p. 210). Manufacturers need to be aware of the factors that influence our judgements about pronunciation. If it pays companies to employ people with certain accents in call centres, or use these accents in television commercials, it will pay them to think about programming their robots in similar ways.

They also need to think globally. The New Zealand study illustrates a general point: the number of English accents in the world is increasing, as a consequence of English becoming a global language. With over two billion people speaking English today, spread throughout all the countries of the world, the development of new regional accents expressing local identity is an inevitable outcome. And because so many people have become highly mobile, travelling between countries on a regular basis and moving house several times in a lifetime, mixed accents have become more frequent than at any other time in English linguistic history.

Once, phoneticians were able to say, with some confidence, where someone was from, based solely on the accent. This is Henry Higgins again (p. 11):

> The science of speech. That's my profession, also my hobby. Anyone can spot an Irishman or a Yorkshireman by his brogue, but I can place a man within six miles. I can place him within two miles in London. Sometimes within two streets.

Six miles? It could hardly be done now. A century ago, most people lived their entire lives in one place, and only occasionally heard speakers from elsewhere. A village community would have displayed little if any variation in pronunciation, so anyone who had made a study of English accents would be able to say with some confidence where a person came from, within a few miles. Today, the more typical scenario is to find a mixture of antecedents in someone's pronunciation. These can sometimes be unravelled, as we'll see in Chapter 30, but as often as not the way that the different influences have interacted has resulted in new mergers of sounds that make the task of localization impossible. In any case, it's hardly a sensible question to ask people where they are from if they have spent most of their lives living in places other than the one they were born in.

We can still, as Higgins claims, locate accents in a very general way. Most people can identify the main accent distinctions in a region – in the British Isles, the chief Celtic accents (Wales, Scotland, Ireland) or those from large areas such as 'the West Country' or 'the North' or those spoken in major cities such as Newcastle, Liverpool, and Birmingham. But ability becomes less as the locations become more specific. If you don't know the area, it's not so easy to tell the differences between, say, Lancashire and Yorkshire, or Cornwall and Devon – in other parts of the world, between Texas and Arkansas, or South Carolina and Tennessee. The bigger the country, the more difficult it is to identify origins. That is why a man who could do this in the USA has to be considered the supreme champion of all pronunciation detectives.

The accent detective

WHERE ARE YOU FROM???

CINCINNATI? NEW YORK?
PITTSBURGH? MOBILE? HOUSTON?
NORFOLK? OKLAHOMA CITY?

IF *ON* IS pronounced *ahn*, that is, with relatively little rounding, the speaker is from 'north of the 40th parallel. If *awn* is heard with considerable rounding the speaker is from south of 40 degrees. It's all very confusing — but it's all very entertaining.

EVERY WEDNESDAY at 8:00 p. m., E. S. T., at the New Amsterdam Roof, "Mutual's" playhouse in New York, Dr. Henry Lee Smith, professor at Brown University, lines up a score of people—Americans all —and guesses where they're from. And he never met or saw any of them before.

IT ALL STARTED when Maurice Dreicer (Right) holding manuscript, was possessed with an idea for a radio program. Mr. Dreicer seems to be possessed with an awful lot of ideas, for we discovered that he is concerned with no less than fifteen broadcasts per week over the "Mutual" chain. Anyhow, he met Dr. Smith, who, by the way, won his doctorate with a thesis on linguistics, and thus we have "Where Are You From." (Right) Dreicer scouts the audience for contestants who are sent up to Dr. Smith. (Above) for a word before the broadcast.

In 1940 Henry Lee Smith – a 27-year-old professor of English at Brown University, Rhode Island – began to present a weekly radio series in New York City called 'Where Are You From?' A group of people whom Smith had never met were selected from the audience. He gave them a set of twenty words to pronounce, such as *very*, *any*, *wash*, and *on* – words that he knew varied around the country – and including word sets such as we see in this little jingle:

> Said Mercenary Mary
> The man that I would marry
> Must be merry and adroit about the house

He must not take it easy
While the dinner pots are greasy
The simple cheerful man that I'd espouse.

On the basis of their responses, Smith would tell them where they were from. If he was exactly right, a peal of five tubular bells would be rung. If he was almost right, four. It was rare for fewer than three bells to be heard. He was correct seven out of ten times.

The radio series was a huge success, continuing for several years, with later broadcasts being transmitted on local television stations. An article in the magazine *Radio Parade* called Smith's ability 'uncanny', and labelled him a 'voice detective' – though he always pointed out that any well-trained phonetician who had specialized in English accents would be able to do what he did. True then, but much more difficult today.

27

Which century are you from?

Time-travelling science fiction always presents speech historians with a problem. Doctor Who (or whoever) travels back to medieval England, and we see the drama department taking pains to provide a setting that is a plausible reconstruction of every aspect of social life and behaviour – apart from pronunciation. The language might even contain examples of archaic vocabulary (*verily, forsooth* ...) and grammar (*he hath, thou knowest* ...), but we hear all this in decidedly twenty-first-century accents.

I suppose we have to make allowances, in the interests of telling an intelligible story. Certainly, the further back in time we go, the more the pronunciation differences accumulate. We would have little difficulty understanding Shakespeare; rather more understanding Chaucer; and listening to Beowulf would be a huge challenge – though that would be largely because of his Germanic vocabulary, most of which died out at the end of Anglo-Saxon times.

We can trace changes in pronunciation back as far as the very beginning of the English language, in the fifth century AD, when the first boats of Germanic settlers arrived in Britain. How is it done? It's intricate detective work, based chiefly on a careful analysis of the spellings in old texts, the rhymes used by poets, and the commentaries made by observers of the language of earlier periods. The period is 1,500 years, more or less, and it is bounded by two points about which we can be fairly confident. We know how we speak now. And we can make a fairly confident guess about how they spoke then, based on how the missionaries first wrote English down.

Put yourself in their position. Here's a language that needs to be written down for the first time – so that people can read the Bible, among other things – and the only tool you have available to do it is the alphabet that has been used for writing Latin. So you'll use the Roman alphabet as far as you can. If a word in English has a /p/ in it, you'll use the Roman letter *p* to write it down; if it has an /e/, you'll use Roman letter *e*; and so on. Your problem will come when you encounter phonemes in English that don't exist in Latin, such as the 'th' of *thin* and *this*, or are slightly different, such as the 'a' in *man*. The missionaries solved this by using letters from the ancient runic alphabets to do the job. That is why the orthography of Old English looks unfamiliar, to modern eyes.

However, that is the story of English spelling, which I've told in *Spell It Out*. From the viewpoint of pronunciation, the innovations clearly convey a desire to write down the language as phonetically as possible – one sound, one letter. The missionaries weren't entirely successful: some Old English letters, such as the one we now write as *g*, had several values, and they didn't manage to work out a good system for distinguishing long and short vowels (Chapter 13). But on the whole it's fairly straightforward to read Old English aloud.

So there we have the two end points. In Modern English we have *stone*, pronounced /stəʊn/ in RP, with variants such as /stoːn/ in other accents. In Old English we see it usually written *stan*, and occasionally *staan*. In one of the earliest Old English texts, the Corpus Glossary, compiled in the eighth century, we find a Latin word *crustula similis* (referring to a flat cake with a very hard crust) glossed as *haalstaan*, the double *a* clearly suggesting a long vowel. That's the kind of evidence we need, and it's supported by the way this word is pronounced with a long vowel or a diphthong in related languages of the time. It was written *stein* in Old High German, *steinn* in Old Icelandic, and *stains* in Gothic. Note that only the vowel poses a problem, in this word: the /s/, /t/, and /n/ have stayed the same over the centuries.

That defines the task for historical phonologists: they know the beginning point and the end point. All they have to do is work out how to get from the one to the other! Fortunately, along the road, there are several signposts. And the experience of studying sound change in modern times provides a theoretical framework. Audio recordings of English date from late Victorian times (see below), and phonetics as a research domain is also over a hundred years old. The accumulated wisdom that has come from a century of detailed analysis has given us a pretty good understanding of the nature and rate of pronunciation change. Because we now know how the vocal organs work, we expect some sound changes to be more likely than others – for example, the various kinds of assimilation and elision (Chapter 23). We know the ways stress moves about in words (Chapter 7). We know how a change in one part of the sound system has knock-on effects for other parts of the system (Chapter 15). So we make an assumption: that human vocal organs and behaviour haven't changed all that much in 1,500 years, and that the way a sound system worked then is going to be the same, in salient respects, as the way it works now. Then we look for the evidence – the signposts – that support this assumption.

There are plenty of them. Spelling is the main one. Left to themselves, people will spell their words as they pronounce them. It's a simple solution, which works well when different accents develop in isolation from each other, as happened in Old English, with communities living very far apart and with minimal contact. We can tell from the spellings that the way the Anglo-Saxons spoke in Kent was different from the way they spoke in Northumbria – for example, the word for *work* was spelled *weorc* in the south and *werc* in the north. Individual scribes had their personal preferences, many of which seem to have reflected local pronunciations. And this kind of deduction continued throughout the Middle English period. Even as late as Shakespeare, around 1600, we see idiosyncratic spellings, reflecting the way individuals spoke.

However, as already mentioned in Chapter 24, the growth of national political unity led to the need for a standard language, part of which would involve a standard spelling system. The writing system gradually stabilized – but pronunciation continued to change, so that over the centuries spelling became unreliable as a guide to pronunciation. Regional accents become less visible in the written record. And we end up with the situation we have today, where modern spelling tells us about the way English is pronounced only in very limited ways (as all schoolteachers are very much aware, striving to find the best methods for teaching children to read).

We can't use spelling as a reliable guide to pronunciation after the eighteenth century; but before that it's an invaluable source of information. So, for example, in working out Shakespearean pronunciation, we can see from the spelling *philome* for *film* (in *Romeo and Juliet*) that the word must have been pronounced with two syllables – much as it still is today in some regional accents, 'fillum'. And similarly, such spellings as *aparision* for *apparition* and *murther* for *murder* give us clues as to how these words would have been sounded. We have to build up a case, of course. Isolated words could be simply flukes of misspelling or erratic typesetting. But when we see a spelling turning up dozens or hundreds of times, and sets of associated words spelled in the same way, we can be confident that something systematic is going on.

Occasionally, we find a gold mine of spelling evidence. In the twelfth century, a monk from Lincolnshire, Orrm, compiled a collection of homilies that he called the *Orrmulum*. He turns out to have been the first English spelling reformer. He decided that he would show that words contained a short vowel by doubling the following consonant; words with a long vowel he would leave with a single consonant. (We follow the same principle today: *ridding* has a short vowel; *riding* has a long one.) So we know from his spelling of *annd* that it has a short vowel, and *boc* 'book' has a long vowel, otherwise he would have written it *bocc*. The principle becomes really illuminating when we read words that have changed their pronunciation since his time: *nemmnedd*, for example, is modern English *named*. The sound is long today, but short in Orrm's time.

What other signposts are there? Rhymes help enormously from the Middle English period onwards (rhyming wasn't something that Old English poets did). Chaucer, in the Prologue to *The Canterbury Tales* (line 197), describes the Monk as having a special pin holding his cloak:

A love-knotte in the gretter ende ther was. [greater]
His heed was balled, that shoon as any glas. [head ... bald ... shone]

The vowel in *glass* was short (it's often spelled *glasse*, with a double *s*); so *was* must have been pronounced /wæs/, and not as today, /wɒz/. Another example: in a fourteenth-century Northumbrian poem *The Prick of Conscience* (line 8380), we find *love* rhyming with *prove*:

> Salle be frendschepe and parfyte love [Shall be friendship
> and perfect love]
> þat ues mare þan ever man moght here prove. [That was
> more than ever man might here prove]

The analysis of thousands of rhyming couplets like these
provides a solid body of evidence about the pronunciation of
many words.

But there remains an ambiguity. In the case of *love* and
prove, which way did the rhyming go? Did *love* rhyme with
prove, with a long vowel, or did *prove* rhyme with *love*, with
a short vowel? To resolve this, we need to examine further
cases of *love* and *prove* and see which other words in the language they rhymed with. And we need to take into account
the comments about pronunciation made by contemporary
writers. By Shakespeare's time, there were many such commentators, known as *orthoepists* because of their interest
in spelling reform. If you wanted to reform English spelling, you had to have a thorough grasp of English pronunciation, and that meant describing the qualities of vowels and
consonants.

Ben Jonson's *English Grammar*, written in the early 1600s,
is a useful source of evidence (I like to think that playwrights
are good listeners and have sharp ears). In his description of
letter *O*, we read:

> In the short time more flat, and akin to *u*; as
> *cosen, dosen, mòther,*
> *bròther, lòve, prove*

and he contrasts this sound with long-vowel usages such as
in *do* and *go*. This doesn't exclude the possibility that other
accents of the time could have pronounced *love* with a long
vowel – after all, Elvis Presley did – but it does give us a clear

sense of direction when we try to work out why so many rhymes don't work in a modern English reading of the poetry of the time.

In Shakespeare's *Sonnets*, for example, *love* rhymes with *prove* (in Sonnet 10, 32, 39, 72, 117, 136, 151, 153, 154), *move* (47), *remove* (116), and *approve* (42, 70, 147), *loved* with *proved* (116), *beloved* with *removed* (25), and *loving* with *moving* (26) and *reproving* (142). Then, as if to underline the point, in Sonnet 110 he rhymes *love* with *above* – a word that has never had a long vowel in English. The only way to say these lines so that the rhymes work is to adopt a perspective that respects OP – 'original pronunciation'. That's one of the reasons that so many present-day actors, directors, and early music enthusiasts have developed a fresh interest in the reconstruction of earlier periods of English.

Carrying this perspective through to later centuries, we find pronunciation coming closer and closer to what we know today, as we would expect. But even in the eighteenth century there were many differences, which we can easily explore because there is now another source of evidence: the dictionaries. Dozens of dictionaries were published in the century following Samuel Johnson's ground-breaking work in 1755, and many give pronunciations. John Walker's *Pronouncing Dictionary* (1791) brings to light hundreds of fashionable pronunciations that differ from modern RP. I've mentioned some of the variations in stress in Chapter 7. Here are half a dozen from his letter A that affected the segmental pronunciation. Walker recommends that:

> the *o* in *adorable* is pronounced as in *no*
> the second *a* in *average* has the same vowel as in *fate*
> *alert* has the *e* of *met* (as in modern Scots)
> the *h* is pronounced in *annihilate*

the *d* in *arduous* is an affricate, /ʤ/, as in *judge*
the *th* of *asthma* is pronounced /t/

Some words are so different from today that they would cause modern listeners some uncertainty, if heard out of context: the first vowel in *china* was the same as in *fate*, and the second as in *me*, so we get /ˈʧeɪniː/; *gold* had a close vowel, /guːld/. He notes that 'most frequently, if not universally', *chart* is pronounced like *cart*, though he himself prefers the former.

Some of his recommendations anticipate usage disagreements of later times. He pronounces *asylum* with an /s/, not /z/, and *Christianity* with a /ʧ/ for the first /t/. He has *alternate* with the first *a* as in *fat*, but *almanac* beginning with /ɔːl/ and *almond* dropping the /l/ – /ˈɑːmənd/. In his condemnation of pronunciations he doesn't like, we actually get a great deal of useful information about variations at the time: *authority* with a /t/ for the *th*; *bracelet* with the *a* both as in *fate* and in *fat* (the latter especially in Ireland, he says); *southern* with the first vowel as in *south* as well as in *sub*; and *duke* has to be /djuːk/, avoiding the 'vulgar' /duːk/ and /ʤuːk/.

The waves generated by the two pronunciations of the *i* in *oblige*, with /iː/ or /aɪ/, continued until well into the nineteenth century. In a popular collection of anecdotes about personalities between 1810 and 1860 (*The Reminiscences and Recollections of Captain Gronow*, published in 1900), we hear a story that was repeated in *Punch* magazine, and many times thereafter, about the English actor, John Kemble and the Prince Regent (the future George III):

> John Kemble had the honour of giving the Prince of Wales some lessons in elocution. According to the vitiated pronunciation of the day, the prince, instead of saying 'oblige,' would say 'obleege,' upon which Kemble, with much disgust depicted upon his countenance, said – 'Sir,

may I beseech your Royal Highness to open your royal jaws, and say "oblige"?'

So, based on a detailed reconstruction of the way the sound system developed between Old English and the present day, we would be able to answer the question 'Which century are you from?' And the question applies as much to the future as to the past, for pronunciation will continue to change. Doctor Who would have a similar problem travelling centuries forward in time.

RP 130 years ago

In 1890, the Light Brigade Relief Fund was established to provide support for destitute veterans of the Crimean War, no government money being available. One of the fundraising ideas was to make a sound recording of some famous voices, using the technology invented by Thomas Alva Edison in 1877. Three wax cylinder recordings were made: a veteran trumpeter sounding the charge as heard at Balaclava; Lord Tennyson reading his poem about the event; and a message from Florence Nightingale to the veterans, recorded on 30 January 1890 at her home in London. (They can all be heard on the British Library CD, *Voices of History*.)

We hear Nightingale saying her name and the date, and then: 'When I am no longer even a memory, just a name, I hope my voice may perpetuate the great work of my life. God bless my dear old comrades of Balaclava and bring them safe to shore. Florence Nightingale.' Her accent is reminiscent of the voices heard in early BBC recordings of the 1920s. She says *thirtieth* with the first vowel close to the one in modern *car*. *Ninety* ends with a short open vowel, rhyming more with modern *say* than *see*. *Shore* is very open, moving towards *Shah*. But the overall impression is that her RP was very close to what would have still been heard in the mid-twentieth century.

How did Isaac Newton speak?

Most famous people from the past don't write about their pronunciation; but Isaac Newton did. An unpublished notebook, now in the Pierpont Morgan Library in New York, contains his observations on such diverse topics as recipes and astronomical tables – and a scheme for spelling reform which gives a remarkable amount of phonetic detail. It was compiled probably during his last year in school, or perhaps his first year at Cambridge University, 1661–62, when he was about nineteen.

It seems to be a private set of notes. It doesn't show the influence of earlier seventeenth-century writers on language, such as John Wallis, and contrasts with most of them by its precise phonetic descriptions, which bear comparison with any modern textbook (y^e is the abbreviation of *the*, and wch of *which*):

A vowel is turned to v when ye breth passeth difficultly through ye lipps. v turned to b by shutting ye lipps & b to m by opening the nose. ...

The quavering or jarring of toungs end against ye fore parte of palate changeth a vowel into r, that quavering ceasing r turns to z (ye breath vibrating against ye teeth wch passeth by ye toungs end), z is turned to l if ye tongues end & palate close & ye breath so passe by ye tounge sides as to vibrate against ye cheekes. ...

Newton lists all the English vowels and consonants and gives examples of their use, as well as a piece of continuous prose in his new spelling. They show several features of his own accent – born in south Lincolnshire, and at school in Grantham – some of which are still present in the area today. He writes *ever* as *iver*, *come* as *coom*, *truly* as *triuly*. *Why* is spelled *huoy*, suggesting the voiceless sound (p. 166). *But* and *must* have the same vowel as *good* and *full*; *health* has the same vowel as *say*; *weigh* has the same vowel as *sea*. Interestingly, *and* has the same vowel as *care* (still heard in a very conservative RP). He isn't totally consistent. *Too* appears both as *tu* and *tuu*, perhaps because of a difference in stress.

The most distinctive notation can be seen in the diphthong in such words as *I* and *thy*. He writes *I earnestly desire* as *Oy ernestloy dizoir*. This suggests a rounded vowel (common in many modern regional accents), but more open than the one in *boy*, for he shows three different diphthongs:

au, as in *how*, *out*, *doubt*
oy, as in *thy*, *I*, *pride*, *bite*
ωy, as in *boy*, *joy*

That suggests /bʊɪ/ for boy, rather than present-day /bɔɪ/. On the other hand, he also uses ω for *furre* and *turne* as well as for *frogg* and *dog*, which suggests that he is having trouble distinguishing the vowels in the mid-central/mid-back region.

Did he write all this while at school? Possibly, but more likely while an undergraduate:

The filling of a very deepe flaggon wth a constant streame of beere or water sounds yᵉ vowells in this order w, u, ω, o, a, e, i, y.

It is an exercise modern phonetics students might well appreciate.

28

Where is English pronunciation going?

We can reconstruct the accents of the past, and hear the accents of the present – but what of the future? Is it possible to predict how people will sound in a hundred years' time? Or 50? Or even next year? Predicting the long-term future of a language is a notoriously dangerous thing to try to do. Who, for example, would have thought, 1,000 years ago, that Latin would no longer be the language of education? But even short timescales present problems. Pronunciation change is almost entirely the result of social change, so to predict the future here is to predict changes to the way in which English-speaking society will evolve, and who in a post-Brexit/Trump age, would ever dare to do that?

As we saw in Chapter 26, two major changes have affected English accents in Britain over the last 50 years. The attitude of people towards accents has altered in ways that were unpredictable 30 years ago; and some accents have changed their phonetic character very significantly over the same period. The main change in attitude has been a rise in the prestige of many regional accents. In 1980, when the BBC made its first attempt to use a regionally accented announcer on Radio 4, the decision aroused such virulent opposition that it was quickly reversed. Susan Rae, the Scots presenter in question, was withdrawn. Today, her voice is regularly heard reading the news, and not only on Radio 4. And in

August 2005 the BBC devoted a whole week to a celebration of the accents and dialects of the British Isles.

The 'Voices' project, as it was called, was an attempt to take an auditory snapshot of the way Britain was sounding at the beginning of the new millennium. Every BBC regional radio station was invited to take part, and local presenters arranged recordings of the diversity within their area, as well as programmes which explored the history and nature of local accents and dialects. The impact of the project was considerable, and can still be seen (through the archive website at www.bbc.co.uk/voices). 'Voices' signified institutional recognition of a fundamental change in attitudes to regional speech which had taken place in Britain. There is now a much greater readiness to value and celebrate linguistic diversity than there was a generation ago.

As far as broadcasting was concerned, it was the rapid growth of local commercial radio during the 1980s that fostered the new linguistic climate. Regional radio gained audience (and national radio lost it) by meeting the interests of local populations, and these new audiences liked their presenters to speak as they did. At the same time, national listening and viewing figures remained strong for such series as *The Archers* and *Coronation Street*, where local accents were privileged. The trend grew in the 1990s, and developed an international dimension: alongside the London accents of *EastEnders* were the Australian accents of *Neighbours*. Soon, non-RP accents began to be used as part of the 'official' voice of national radio and television, most noticeably at first in more popular contexts, such as on Radio 1 and in commercial television advertisements. Some regional accents from the time even became part of national consciousness, widely mimicked in the manner of catchphrases – such as the 1977 Campari ad in which Lorraine Chase responded to the come-on line 'Were you truly wafted here from paradise?' with the immortal response, 'No, Lu'on airport'. Before long, regional voices were heard presenting other channels, and are now routine. Non-indigenous accents, especially from the West Indies and India, began to be used. Old attitudes die hard, of course, and there will still be those who mourn the passing of the days when a single accent ruled the British airwaves. But they are a steadily shrinking minority.

The BBC, or any other national broadcaster, does not introduce language change. Rather it reflects it, and thereby fosters it, by making it widely known. This has been the case with so-called 'Estuary English', a variety which became noticed when it attracted media attention in the early 1990s, though the phenomenon had been evolving over many years. The estuary in question was that of the River Thames, and the people who were noticed as having an Estuary accent lived on either side of it, chiefly to the north. The variety is characterized not only by accent, but also by certain words and grammatical constructions, such as the use of *right* as a tag question (*It starts at six, right?*) or *innit* ('isn't it?'). Phonetically it can be roughly placed as a set of accents – note the plural – intermediate between RP and Cockney. Nationally known figures who use it include Jonathan Ross and the two characters played by Pauline Quirke and Linda Robson in the television comedy series *Birds of a Feather*. The accents of these three are not identical, and that is important. 'Estuary' is a broad label, covering a number of closely related ways of speaking. (RP was never homogeneous either.)

One of the most noticeable pronunciation trends has been to hear the way in which features of Estuary English have radiated from the London area to other parts of the country. They have travelled north towards Yorkshire and west towards Devon, and they are widespread in East Anglia,

Kent, and along the south coast. It is not that they have replaced the local accents of these areas (though this sometimes happens); rather they have modified the phonetic character of those accents, pulling the vowels and consonants in different directions. Old-timers in a rural village now sound very different from the younger generations who live there. As part of the 'Voices' project, a television documentary was made (called *Word on the Street*) about four generations of a family living in Leicester. One could hear the changes from old to young: an East Midlands accent was present in all of them, but in several different forms.

It is this proliferation of accents which is the national pattern today. People sometimes claim that 'accents are dying out'. What they have noticed is the disappearance of old rural ways of speech as the people who used them pass away. But the people who now live in these localities still have accents, although very different in character. The Estuary English heard in Hampshire is very different from that heard in Leicestershire. Intonation and rhythm, in particular, remain distinctive. Nor is Estuary English the only contemporary pronunciation trend. In the major population centres of the country we hear a new phenomenon: a remarkable increase in the range of accents within the community, brought about largely by the influx of people of diverse ethnic origin. In Liverpool, there used to be only 'Scouse'; today we can hear Chinese Scouse, Jamaican Scouse, and an array of accent mixes reflecting the growing cosmopolitan character of that city. London, of course, is where this trend is most noticeable. There are well over 300 languages spoken in London now, and the English used by these ethnic communities inevitably reflects the linguistic background of the speakers. New combinations of sounds, words, and grammatical constructions can be heard, such as the mix of Bengali and

Cockney used by members of the Bangladeshi community in East London. Every British city today displays such accent and dialect mixes.

To understand why Estuary English has spread so widely and so rapidly we have to appreciate that it is the result of two complementary trends. First, an improved standard of living for many people formerly living in London's East End allowed them to move 'upmarket' into the outer suburbs and the townships of the home counties. As they began to interact with their new neighbours, their accents naturally accommodated to them (Chapter 25). In a case where people want to 'fit in' to a society which speaks in a different way, and where careers and success can depend on the incomers developing a good relationship with the incumbents, the direction of the accommodation is largely one way. Thus East Enders began to adopt features of Essex or Kent or Hertfordshire speech, when they moved into those localities, rather than the other way round. At the same time, people from counties further afield were commuting to London in increasing numbers, their travel facilitated by the new motorway system and faster rail connections. With cities such as Hull, Leeds, Manchester, and Bristol now only a couple of hours away, huge numbers of people arrived in London with regional accents and soon found themselves accommodating to the accents of the city. It was now the Midlands and West Country commuters who adopted some of the London ways of speaking. And when these commuters returned home, they brought those London features back with them. And thus the accent spread.

Cutting across the Estuary influence is an unknown set of other trends, all prompted by the increased mobility of the working and playing population. The BBC programme about Leicester showed some members of the family attending a biking convention elsewhere in the country. Bikers were there from many counties, and presented a huge range of accents. When they talked to each other it was possible to hear their accents accommodating – often in a conscious and jocular way, as when one speaker mimicked another. An individual short-term encounter of this kind is unlikely to have a long-term effect, of course; but in contexts where people routinely interact in this way, accent change is normal. And commuters, by definition, have routine.

It is not that one accent replaces another. Rather, features of two accents combine to make a third. When an RP speaker is influenced by a regional accent, or vice versa, the result has been called 'modified RP', and there is modified Scouse, modified Geordie, modified everything these days. I myself am a heavily modified speaker, using an accent which is a mixture of my original North Wales (where I spent my first ten years), Liverpool (where I spent my secondary-school years), and the south of England (where I worked for twenty years). Apart from the overall auditory impression of my accent, which is difficult to 'place', it displays certain features characteristic of all modified accents, such as inconsistency – for instance, I sometimes say *example* and *bath* with a 'short *a*', and sometimes with a 'long *a*' (*exahmple, bahth*). And because I accommodate to my (now grown-up) children, who have been influenced by a more recent set of trends (such as American English), I sometimes say *schedule* with a *sh-* and sometimes with a *sk-*. There are dozens of such variant forms in my speech.

Mixed accents are the norm these days. Even if you don't travel, you're not immune from accent shift. Innumerable voices enter your home every day through radio, television, the telephone, and the internet. In 2013 a team of researchers from the University of Glasgow published the results of a study in the journal *Language* which showed that certain features of the typical Glasgow accent were changing among young people partly as a result of prolonged exposure to the London-based BBC TV soap, *EastEnders*. They were increasingly replacing /θ/ with /f/ (in words like *tooth* and *think*) and replacing /l/ by a vowel (so that *milk*, for example, comes out more like 'miuk'). It might seem strange to think of a TV programme causing accents to shift, but when we think of the amount of listening involved, it's perhaps not so surprising. Half-hour episodes go out four times a week, with repeats and an omnibus edition – and there have been over 5,400 episodes at the time of writing. The programme is watched by almost a third of the UK population, and the topical scripts ensure that it surfaces regularly in everyday conversation.

So there is some widespread levelling in the UK at the moment – and in other English-speaking countries too – but this doesn't amount to a total replacement of one accent by another. Rather, what we hear is one accent being 'coloured' by another. Young people in Glasgow still sound Glaswegian even if they do replace /θ/ with /f/. The new features are changing the character of the accent, certainly, but the local identity is still being distinctively expressed, especially in the intonation. And RP has been affected in the same way. When people hear radio or television announcers speaking in a regional accent, they are quick to identify it as Scottish or Welsh or whatever; but what they fail to notice is that the accents have been pulled in the direction of RP. It is accent colouring rather than accent replacement.

American influence on British English has been notable in new vocabulary and idiom, but so far it has been quite limited in respect of pronunciation. There are only a few dozen examples like my *skedule* one, affecting vowels and consonants, but they are noticeable (at least, to the older generation) when they occur, and are one of the main topics in letters to the

BBC. I've noted several differences between the two varieties in my earlier chapters on vowels, and in relation to pop singing (Chapter 12) Here are some current changes:

anti – rhyming with *by* rather than *be*
lieutenant – 'lootenant' instead of 'leftenant'
mall – rhyming with *fall* and not *pal*
progress – with the *o* as in *not* rather than *no*
route – with the vowel of *now* rather than *too*.
zebra – with *e* as in *see* rather than *set*
tomato – with the *a* as in *say* rather than *palm*

These changes are not all taking place at the same time, and some are affecting sets of words in different ways. The American pronunciation of *lever*, for example, has the first *e* as in *set*, whereas traditional British pronunciation has it as in *see*; but the commonest British pronunciation of *leverage* these days has the *set* vowel. It's presumably only a matter of time before this extends to *lever*. On the other hand, there is little sign (yet) in British English of *clerk* rhyming with *lurk*, of *vase* rhyming with *face*, of *leisure* with a long 'ee', and of *herb* without the *h*.

Rather more widespread is the phenomenon noted in Chapter 7, where stress has shifted from one syllable to another, as in *frontier* and *research*. It would be a mistake to think that these forms are used only by young people. They may have started out among the young, but American English has been influencing British for several decades, so those youngsters are now middle-aged or older. Many have also achieved positions of power in society, or are regularly heard in the broadcasting media, where celebrity culture – including its most demotic forms, as seen in such programmes as *Bake Off* and *Top Gear* – has been a significant factor in the rapid spread of these pronunciations.

That is why it is so difficult to predict the future. Who knows which programmes, and which personalities, are next going to capture the public imagination? What will be the effect of a new social order in which people from other countries play different roles? Which countries will be the dominant economic, political, or religious players in the next century, so that the way their people speak will become attractive? Will the influence of the 'New Englishes' of the world – the way the language has evolved in such places as India, Singapore, Jamaica, and over 50 other countries – increase or decrease? We have already seen the way in which one of these countries – Jamaica – has made syllable-timed ('rat-a-tat-a-tat') speech rhythm (Chapter 7) popular among young British people through hip-hop and rap performance; and there are clear signs of this rhythm transferring into their everyday speech, and replacing the stress-timed ('tum-te-tum-te-tum') rhythm characteristic of traditional British accents. Might this trend continue, so that in a hundred years' time we will all be speaking in a syllable-timed way? Or will there be a reaction against it?

Doubtless word stress, for example, will continue to see-saw backwards and forwards in polysyllabic words, as it has always done, but as to which words will be affected is anyone's guess. There are as many questions to be asked in relation to pronunciation as in any other area of futurology, and just as few answers.

29

Pronouncing Purcell (and others)

We can never reconstruct an earlier period of pronunciation with 100 per cent certainty. One reason is that proper names are notoriously unpredictable. We only have to look around at modern spellings to see that this is the case. Some of the really irregular ones are well known, as in *Beauchamp* ('Beecham'), *Buccleuch* ('Buck-loo'), *Crichton* ('Cry-ton'), *Mainwaring* ('Mannering'), *St John* ('Sin-jin'), and *Wodehouse* ('Wood-house'). Often there is no single modern pronunciation: we hear *Marjoribanks* as both 'Marchbanks' and 'Marshbanks'; *Cowper* with both 'Cow-' and 'Coo-'; and *Fetherstonhaugh* in a handful of different ways, from 'Fanshaw' to 'Feather-stone-huff'. Even first names can be affected: *Ralph* is frequently 'Rayf'; *Neil* might be 'Neel' or 'Nye-al' (the latter especially in Ireland, where it is usually spelled *Niall*).

Unpredictable pronunciations are there for a reason – usually because a particular family decided to pronounce its name in a particular way, perhaps to reflect its historical origins (often, in France), or just 'to be different'. It's not difficult to imagine upper-class families in the Middle Ages underlining their status by deliberately adopting a distinctive pronunciation for their name. People would show they were from the same social group by knowing how to pronounce it, whereas outsiders would get it wrong. The reasons may also be bound up with other changes taking place in the language. If your name included the element *Cock*, such as

Cockburn, and *Cockshot*, you might well wish to change its pronunciation as the impolite usage developed at the end of the sixteenth century. You might want to change its spelling too, turning *Cocks* into *Cox*, or *Cockburn* into *Cohburn*. Or you might stay proud of the original form, and keep it. We are talking about identity now, not intelligibility (Chapter 1), and the issues are full of passion.

People get very upset if their name is mispronounced, and take pains to correct the mispronouncers. Many of the enquiries and complaints received by the BBC Pronunciation Unit relate to personal names, with foreign names increasingly a problem: *Mahmoud Ahmadinejad, Kofi Annan, Vitaly Churkin, Erkki Tuomioja* ... Getting it right requires an understanding of both the language of origin as well as any personal preferences. Often the phoneticians have to ask the people themselves, or listen to the way in which they pronounce their own names. As Catherine Sangster of the BBC Unit neatly put it, commenting on a query about the UN secretary-general (BBC Archives, 2006):

> The pronunciation is KOH-fi AN-an, with the stress on
> the first syllable of the surname. We have the best possible
> source for this pronunciation; it is how he said his name
> himself during his swearing-in ceremony in 1996.

But current events can make their efforts a thankless task. When I was presenting *English Now* in the 1980s, I interviewed newsreader Richard Whitmore about these matters. He told me how it had taken him ages to master the pronunciation of the prime minister of Nigeria, Sir *Abubakar Tafawa Balewa* – 'and then they shot him'.

Taking the trouble to ask those who know is routine procedure for living personalities. But what if they are beyond living memory? People are often uncertain about the pronunciation of such surnames as Henry *Purcell* and Andrew *Marvell*. Here is a typical enquiry (sent to my blog in 2011):

> In preparatory school I was taught to place the stress on the first syllable of Purcell and the second syllable of Marvell, always assuming that to be correct. However, I frequently hear the former pronounced with the stress on the second syllable and the latter with the stress placed on the first. Was my English instructor correct? And do American and British usage conform or differ? Has the stress shifted historically?

When establishing an earlier pronunciation, as seen in Chapter 27, there are several kinds of evidence to look for – rhymes, puns, metre, spelling, and comments by contemporaries. In the case of *Purcell*, we find clear evidence of the stress falling on the first syllable from contemporary spellings. Before spelling standardized, the vowel in an unstressed syllable would be written in different ways. So when we find such spellings as *Pursal*, *Purcel*, and *Persill* in the seventeenth century, an initial syllable stress is clearly suggested. It's reinforced by the ode John Dryden wrote on the death of his friend, in which the metre requires the stress to be on the first syllable:

> So ceas'd the rival Crew when Purcell came ...
> Now live secure and linger out your days,
> The Gods are pleas'd alone with Purcell's Lays.

The same stress pattern is found in a rhyme in a poem by Gerard Manley Hopkins, who rhymes *Purcell* and *reversal*. That was 1918. So there doesn't seem to have been any historical change.

Nor is this just a British pronunciation, as American dictionaries say the same thing. William Cabell Greet's *World*

Words, compiled in association with the Columbia Broadcasting System in 1948, gives initial-syllable stress for both *Purcell* and *Marvell*, but adds, after *Purcell*, 'As an American family name the last syllable is often accented'. The *Random House Dictionary* confirms this. It lists three Purcells: Edward Mills (the US physicist), Henry (the composer), and a town in Oklahoma. The first and third, it says, have the stress on the second syllable; for Henry, the stress is on the first. And the very next entry is for the Purcell Mountains in British Columbia and Montana, with, once again, the stress on the second syllable. American intuitions are thus split down the middle, with Henry apparently in the minority, so it's hardly surprising that people assume he is like everyone else.

However, intuitions in Britain are split too. Because it's never possible to anticipate the strange ways in which the English like to pronounce their surnames, when we encounter a surname ending in *-ell* there's no way of predicting the stress pattern. There are several examples of *-ell* surnames which have the stress on the second syllable, such as the Irish politician *Charles Stewart Parnell*. This end-stress is a typical feature of polysyllabic words in Irish English. But even here there are problems, because in *Parnell Square* the stress usually reverts to the first syllable (a similar alternation to what we find with *he's sixteen* and *sixteen people*: see p. 57). And Parnell himself preferred to say his name with the stress on the first syllable.

So we get the result we see in, for example, the *Cambridge English Pronouncing Dictionary*, where we find both pronunciations given, in both British and American English. And because linguistic uncertainty is always contagious, it's not surprising to find other surnames vacillating. No dictionary I've looked at gives any other pronunciation for *Marvell* than one with the stress on the first syllable, and similarly for the members of the famous *Durrell* family; but we do hear the alternatives, especially from American speakers, from time to time. *Cornell*, on the other hand, is usually second-syllable stressed, as in the name of the university – reflecting the name of the founder, whose ancestors came from south-east England.

The origin of the *Purcell* confusion lies in the name's etymology. The surname is French, from *pourcel*, 'little pig' – a (probably affectionate) occupational name for a swineherd – and the name is attested in records from the twelfth century. It would therefore be the normal pattern of stress in French, where the last syllable of a word is prominent. This conflicts with the English norm, which is to place the stress earlier in a word (Chapter 7). So, gradually, there was a stress-shift, though it would have been resisted by speakers who were at pains to draw attention to their noble ancestry.

My correspondents with the surname tell some interesting stories. One reports that the members of his own family always say *Purcell*, whereas his in-laws often say *Purcell*. Another, who married an Irishman, has the stress on the first syllable when in Ireland; but when in the UK she switches. Why? Because otherwise, she says, when she says her name people think she's talking about the washing powder, *Persil*! That trend may have been around for a century, as the product dates from 1909.

Such a change is really a kind of naming euphemism – avoiding the unpleasant associations of a word. It's actually quite common with surnames, where the original meaning has been forgotten and a modern association interferes. The phonetician Jack Windsor Lewis, in a blog post in 2009, gives examples of the many ways in which people have manipulated the pronunciation of their surnames in order to avoid an unwanted connotation. Several involve shifting the stress, as in *Twaddell* and *Waddell*. Probably today, with the advent of Lidl stores, some people will shift from *Liddell* to *Liddell*. But it's not just the *-ell* ending that is affected. The *OED* lexicographer C. T. Onions pronounced his name like the vegetable, but it's also common to hear it as if it were *O-nions*. Names like *Ramsbottom* often replace the *tt* by a *th*. And the Scots surname *Smellie* can shift to forms like *Smiley*. We are back with *Cockburn* again. Windsor Lewis calls them *euphonic* pronunciations.

Pronouncing Shakespeare

How would Shakespeare have pronounced his name? It's a tricky question, because there are many variations of the spelling of Shakespeare's name in the literature of his time. According to David Kathman, who collated them all, we have the following references to a Shakespeare surname between 1564 and 1616 (the ~ indicates an illegible mark):

Schaksp 1	Shackespeare 7	Shackespere 5
Shackspeare 12	Shackspere 6	Shagspere 1
Shak-speare 2	Shake-speare 1	Shake-speare 21
Shakespe 2	Shakespear 19	Shakespeare 190
Shakespere 31	Shakespheare 1	Shakp 1
Shakspe 1	Shakspe~ 2	Shakspear 2
Shakspeare 23	Shaksper 2	Shakspere 9
Shaxberd 4	Shaxpeare 1	Shaxper 1
Shaxpere 1	Shaxspere 3	Shexpere 2

What are we to make of this?

For the first syllable, there are clearly two types, with an *-e* and without an *-e*, and this is an important difference, as the presence or absence of an *-e* was one of the signals of the contrast between a long and a short preceding vowel. The *Shakespeare* spelling is overwhelmingly the predominant one. *Shake* rhymes with *make*, *take*, and *quake* in the canon, which clearly suggests a long vowel, and this would in original pronunciation be a mid open front vowel, approximating to a long version of the modern vowel we hear in RP *pet*: /ɛ:/. On the other hand, the *Shak*, *Shack*, *Shax* series clearly suggests a short front vowel, as in RP *back* today.

How can we reconcile the difference? There are many spelling variations in Elizabethan writing which suggest that the short vowel of *back* was higher at the front of the mouth than it is in RP today, closer to the short /e/ of *bet*: we see, for example, *acts* written as *ectes*, and there are several other instances, such as the two instances of *Shexpere* above. There are also many rhymes which show that the short /a/ vowel must have been close to short /e/, such as *back* rhyming with *neck* in *Venus and Adonis*.

If we start with *Shake*, with its long /ɛ:/ vowel, we can expect – as with all long vowels – that it would sometimes have been pronounced rapidly, and be heard as a short vowel, and spelled accordingly. If we start with *Shak*, this would have had a short vowel such as /ɛ/ or the slightly more open /æ/, but – as with all short vowels – it would sometimes be pronounced slowly, and be heard as a long vowel, and spelled accordingly. Either way, we end up with the same result – a vowel sound which is roughly what we hear in *share* in RP. There's also the option that a Warwickshire regional pronunciation would have affected the length, but there's no firm evidence about that.

For the second syllable, we first need to eliminate the

versions that are clearly abbreviations, such as *Schaksp*, and the odd *Shaxberd*, which must be an idiosyncratic spelling by someone who probably misheard the name. When the tip of the tongue is curled back for a retroflex *r* (p. 164), its end point is very close to the position of the tip when making a /d/. Some listeners might have imagined a /d/ to be there, and in some speakers the release might have been audible.

The main point to note is that the /r/ would have been pronounced at the end. All sources agree on that. As for the vowel, the spellings suggest a long vowel, as in *spear*. But when we look at *spear* (and similar words) we find that it could rhyme with *there* (in *The Rape of Lucrece* and *Venus and Adonis*, for instance) and similar-sounding words, and it is this which doubtless motivated such spellings as *-pere*, *-berd*, and so on in the name. The vowel may also have had a shortened and centralized form, being in an unstressed syllable. So it would have been roughly what we would hear today in (long) *spare* or (short) *spur*.

In short: I would say the evidence points to /ˈʃɛːkspɛːr/ or /ˈʃɛːkspɛr/, when the name is spoken slowly or emphasized, and /ˈʃɛkspər/ or /ˈʃækspər/ as more rapidly spoken alternatives. But not modern /ˈʃeɪkspɪə/.

30

Never heard of it

If personal names present us with a pronunciation problem, place names are far worse.

I was driving along a country road in Norfolk wanting to get to Happisburgh on the coast. My daughter had just moved there, and it was my first visit. I reached a crossroads and was at a loss – no signpost. But there was a bus stop nearby with some people waiting at it. I asked them if they knew which was the road to /ˈhæpɪzbərə/. They grinned. 'Never heard of it,' they said. I showed them the name. 'Oh, you mean /ˈheɪzbrə/.

They were, I suspect, having some fun at the expense of a foreigner in those parts. It wouldn't have been the first time they had heard someone mispronouncing the name of that coastal village. Either way, there was a linguistic lesson in the exchange. If they *were* being naughty, it dramatized the close link between pronunciation and identity; and if they weren't, it highlighted the extraordinarily unpredictable nature of English place names.

As I got to know Norfolk, I discovered that *Happisburgh* was by no means alone. There was *Wymondham* /ˈwɪndəm/ and *Hunstanton* /ˈhʌnstən/; and over the border into Cambridgeshire there was *Godmanchester* /ˈgʌmstə/. Several online sites now present selections from around the country. They include such names as *Lympne* /lɪm/, *Mousehole* /ˈmaʊzəl/, *Leominster* /ˈlemstə/, *Cholmondeley* /ˈtʃʌmlɪ/, *Marylebone*

/'mɑːlɪbən/, *Brougham* /bruːm/, and *Gotham* /'goːtəm/ – a surprise for fans of Batman, where *Gotham* City is /'gɒθəm /. There's often an overlap with personal names (Chapter 28), as a surname frequently derives from the place where a person lived.

Britain is full of such pronunciation anomalies, most of which have come from the way that colloquial speech readily drops phonemes and syllables, especially in the unstressed parts of a word (Chapter 23), and spelling has consequently ceased to be a guide. With a language that has evolved over 1,500 years, the changes may have begun many centuries ago, and become fossilized. The city of *Leicester* means 'the fortified town (*ceaster*) of the people called the Ligore', and we see it as *Ligoraceaster* and similar spellings in the tenth century, clearly a full pronunciation. But by the 1600s we see such spellings as *Leceter* and *Lester*. Similarly we find *Worster* for *Worcester* and *Gloster* for *Gloucester*. A will written in 1454 refers to 'the Friars of Gloster'. It's also the usual spelling in Shakespeare's First Folio.

Which phonemes are likely to be dropped, as colloquial pronunciation takes a hold? Any of them. A comprehensive survey of English place names would bring to light examples of every consonant being elided somewhere or other. And when consonants go, adjacent vowels elide, modify, or combine. A single consonant went in *Aldeburgh*, where the omission of /d/ before /b/ led to /'ɔːlbrə/, and that /d/–/b/ simplification is seen again in *Kircudbright* /keɹ'kuːbriː/. A double change is seen in *Alnwick* /'anɪk/ – an interesting example, because it brings together two of the commonest elisions, of /l/ and /w/. /l/ goes in *Belvoir* /'biːvə/, *Folkingham* /'fɒkɪŋəm/, *Mytholmroyd* /'maɪðəmrɔɪd/, and London's *Holborn* /'hoːbən/; /w/ goes in *Berwick* /'berɪk/, *Cudworth* /'kʌdəɹθ/, *Fowey* /fɔɪ/, and *Norwich* /'nɒrɪtʃ/ – locally even more reduced, to /nɒrtʃ/. It's perhaps not surprising to find that the approximants – the most vowel-like of all the consonants – should disappear so readily. At the same time, we have to recognize that not everyone may concur about a colloquial pronunciation. In several places we find locals disagreeing about how their town should be said, with some wanting to follow the spelling: in and around *Bedworth*, Warwickshire, we hear both /'bedəθ/ and /'bedwərθ/; in *Topsham*, Devon we hear both /'tɒpʃəm/ and (especially among older people) /'tɒpsəm/.

But it's not just Britain. Any part of the English-speaking world is going to present place names with unpredictable pronunciations. If Americans have problems with *Gloucester* and *Leicester*, Brits have problems with *Connecticut* /kə'netɪkət/ and *Tucson* /'tu:sɒn/, let alone *Des Moines* /də'mɔɪn/, *Albuquerque* /'albʊkəɹki:/, *Boise* /'bɔɪzi:/, and *Arkansas* /'ɑːɹkənsɔ:/. Any European is going to mispronounce borrowed city names such as *Bethlehem* in Pennsylvania /'beθləm/; *Berlin* in New Hampshire /'bɑ:rlɪn/; *New Prague* in Minnesota /nu:'preɪg/, *Versailles* and *Vienna* in several states /vəɹ'seɪlz/, /vaɪ'enə/; and *Athens* in Illinois, Kentucky, or Vermont /'eɪθənz/. The *Thames River* in Connecticut is /θeɪmz/. In Canada we find *Delhi*, Ontario /'delhaɪ/. In Australia *Wagga Wagga* /'wɒgə 'wɒgə/.

Pity the poor linguists at the BBC (and other broadcasting stations) who have to keep pace with these things. Their remit goes well beyond English place names, of course. They have to work out what to do with foreign names, and especially decide whether to use the foreign pronunciation or (if it exists) an anglicized form. Some English forms are now totally standard: no presenter would ever pronounce *Paris* as 'Paree'. But there is a great deal of variation when the place is less established in people's minds – for example, saying

Stuttgart with an initial /s/, as it would be in English, or with an initial /ʃ/, as it would be in German.

Much depends on the linguistic awareness of the presenter. The issue isn't going to be very problematic with a relatively familiar language such as German, where the shared historical background of the two Germanic languages means that pronunciations are not going to be too far apart. But names from more distantly related or unrelated languages – Polish, Hindi, Chinese, for example – pose a much greater difficulty, especially if the letters in the names have values that are markedly different from those in English. *Łódź* in Poland is a case in point: in several dictionaries aimed at English readers the name is given as /lɒdz/ or something similar, whereas in Polish it has a pronunciation that is more accurately represented as /wʊʤ/.

Programme content and participation are additional factors influencing the choice of a particular pronunciation. There is a greater likelihood that names will conform to the source language in programmes to do with the arts and humanities, for instance, perhaps because artists, authors, actors, musicians, critics, and other professionals in these fields are aware of their international reach, and are more ready to engage with issues of identity. And if there is a discussion in which some of the participants are native speakers of particular languages, others are likely to accommodate to them (Chapter 25). I recall a programme in which a presenter introduced a guest musician as coming from *Calcutta* /kalˈkʌtə/. The guest also mentioned his home city, but pronounced it /kɒlˈkata/, reflecting the city's new name (since 2001), *Kolkata*. The presenter used that pronunciation thereafter.

The nature of the listening audience also needs to be taken into account. A few years ago, newsreaders on BBC Radio 4 might have used the /lɒdz/ pronunciation without receiving any complaints. On the other hand, newsreaders on the BBC World Service would have been wise to use the Polish pronunciation (or as close to it as they could get), given its transmission across Europe. But times change. With Polish these days being the main foreign language spoken in England, I can imagine that an English pronunciation of *Łódź* on home radio might generate a degree of criticism which would not have been experienced before.

Do people deliberately change place names, as they sometimes do their personal names (Chapter 28)? It's unusual, but it has happened, for political reasons, once again to do with identity. When Kenya became independent, /ˈkiːnjə/ became /ˈkenjə/. And in Wales, we now hear some places using a pronunciation that sounds 'more Welsh', such as *Conwy* /ˈkɒnwiː/ in place of *Conway* /ˈkɒnweɪ/ and *Rhuthin* /ˈr̥ɪθɪn/, with a voiceless /r/ as well as a vowel change, in place of *Ruthin* /ˈrʌθɪn/. Unpleasant associations may also cause a change. In 2010 the City Council in Bettendorf, Iowa, agreed to change the name of one of its streets, Falmouth Court, to Lilly Court, because residents were unhappy about the pronunciation. They felt it was too close to 'foul mouth'.

New brand pronunciations

In 2009, the Korean car firm Hyundai ran an advertisement during the US Super Bowl which focused on the pronunciation of its name. You can watch it online: it's called 'Angry Bosses'. We see a group of executives from competing car brands getting increasingly furious at the sight of a new Hyundai model, and screaming the company name. There's a sudden moment of quiet and we hear a voice say: 'Win one little award and suddenly everyone gets your name right. It's Hyundai, just like Sunday.'

The problem had evidently been that the Korean pronunciation of the company name, /'hjʊndeɪ/, wasn't transparent to the general car-buying public outside Korea. People said it in several different ways, and the firm was concerned that these versions might cause a confusion with its Japanese competitor, Honda. So, in order to solve the problem, in the USA the company opted for an old and well-tried remedy: rhyme. They dropped the /j/ and made *Hyundai* rhyme with *Sunday*. In the UK, they went for a different solution: there, the ads aimed at British sales pronounce the name as /haɪ'ʊndaɪ/.

Hyundai isn't the only firm to face the problem of uncertain or competing pronunciations. Popular variants exist alongside official versions for many brands: *Porsche, Nike, IKEA, Givenchy, Zenith*, for example. *Adidas* also has US and UK versions, with Americans usually stressing the second syllable, /ə'diːdas/, and the British usually stressing the first, /'adɪdas/. European practice follows the German source, where the name is a blend, after the company's founder, Adolf (nickname Adi) Dassler. The stress was always on the first syllable. But in 1986 the US hip-hop group Run-DMC used a different pronunciation in its hit single 'My Adidas', repeatedly stressing the second syllable, as this extract illustrates:

> We travel on gravel, dirt road or street
> I wear my Adidas when I rock the beat
> On stage front page every show I go
> It's Adidas on my feet high top or low

That pronunciation spread, and – as so often happens in popular culture – the American version fed back into Europe. But more than pop influence was involved. The hip-hop version conforms more to the stress-timed rhythm of English (Chapter 7), and this seems to have made it more appealing. It may well be the more frequent form in the UK now.

31

Using phonetics

Three general perspectives operate in linguistic study. We can study *languages* (and groups of languages); within a language, we can study *dialects* (and accents); and within dialects we can study *idiolects*, the way in which individuals use language. This last perspective is of especial interest in relation to pronunciation. To take further the point I made in Chapter 1, an idiosyncratic use of particular words or grammatical constructions is going to manifest itself only every now and again, in the stream of speech, whereas pronunciation is there all the time. So if someone has a personal mannerism it is likely to be frequently encountered.

This is the principle that fuels one of the most interesting applications of the study of pronunciation: *forensic phonetics*. There is a surprising number of instances where the analysis of the way someone speaks is relevant to the solving of a crime. Someone might receive an anonymous threat over the phone, or in a recording. They think they know who it is. So a comparison is made of the speech of the suspect with the recorded voice. The analysis can be either auditory, using the trained ear of a phonetician, or technological, using acoustic equipment to determine the physical properties of the voice, or both. The assumption is that no two voices are exactly the same, and this belief has motivated the term *voiceprints*, on analogy with fingerprints.

We have to be cautious. Just because no two people have

yet been found to have the same fingerprints, we can't say that this is impossible. Nobody has recorded the fingerprints of everyone who is alive on the planet; and even if they did, we can't study the fingerprints of the billions who have died. So it remains an assumption. And the same caution applies to voiceprints. But when we think of all the anatomical variables that are involved in speech production (Chapter 4), and realize that even a slight difference in anatomy will alter the characteristics of the air flowing through the vocal organs, we can see how voice qualities could be as distinctive as facial features, if not more so. Our ability to recognize people we know without seeing them is based on their individual voice quality – plus, of course, all the features that are found in their accent.

Probably the most famous forensic case of recent times was that of Peter Sutcliffe, the so-called Yorkshire Ripper, who was eventually convicted of killing thirteen women between 1975 and 1980. By mid-1979, the police had made little progress. Then a series of handwritten letters arrived, claiming to be from the killer, followed by an audio cassette. 'I'm Jack,' the tape began, 'I see you are still having no luck catching me.' It went on for three minutes and sixteen seconds. The detective in charge of the case was sure that the tape was genuine, and set up Dial-the-Ripper phone lines. The public could ring in and listen to the voice, and the hope was that someone would recognize it. It was all a waste of time. When Peter Sutcliffe was eventually caught, in 1981, his accent was not at all like the one on the tape.

The police turned to two phoneticians from the University of Leeds, Stanley Ellis and Jack Windsor Lewis, in order to establish where the tape voice came from. It was fairly obvious that the speaker came from the north-east of England. The media had already dubbed him 'Wearside Jack'.

But which part, exactly? The phoneticians identified the voice as coming from Sunderland, and then visited the pubs and clubs of the town to narrow it down. They concluded that the voice was of someone who had been brought up in the Castletown or Southwick districts, just north of the river.

The voice was certainly distinctive, and the phoneticians were sure it would have been quickly recognized. One word had an unusual quality for the sound [l], and the word *sorry* had a lengthened *s*, suggestive of a residual stammer. If this man had been living in Yorkshire, where the murders took place, his voice would have stood out a mile. The man had to be living on Wearside, where the voice would not have been so identifiable. They concluded that it was a hoax, and advised the police accordingly, but their warning went unheeded. Suspects continued to be eliminated from enquiries if they had no Wearside accent.

Angry that their warnings had been disregarded, Windsor Lewis sent a detailed account of his reasoning to *The Yorkshire Post* (3 December 1980 – now available on his website). Here's part of his conclusion:

> There are hundreds of thousands of people with some degree of Geordie accent, but factors like the ones I have mentioned narrow down the field to tens of thousands and even to thousands. The accents, taken together with purely personal features – like the individual voice quality of the speaker and various little minor imperfections of articulation which are not marked enough to label as speech defects – suggest that we can think in terms of only a few hundreds of people who can sound anything near to exactly like this. ...
>
> His accent is so individual that I believe the man would have been brought to police attention if he were living in Leeds, Bradford or anywhere else but Wearside. ...

> I cannot believe (a) that the man is disguising his
> real voice and (b) that he can be living anywhere but
> the Sunderland area. This suggests that the only likely
> possibility is that this voice which has become so familiar to
> the nation is the voice of a super-hoaxer.

Events proved him right. Sutcliffe was caught soon after. He came from Bradford. The hoaxer was caught in 2005, using DNA evidence, and pleaded guilty at a trial a few months later. He had been living in Flodden Road, just south of the river, less than a mile from Castletown; and he had gone to school in Castletown.

This kind of research is invaluable, though hugely time-consuming. Every phoneme in every word has to be listened to repeatedly, and a picture of the individual sound system built up. But the Ripper case shows just how accurate a phonetician familiar with English accents can be – as also seen with Henry Lee Smith (p. 221). Given that Henry Higgins was the first to claim publicly that such identifications could be done (p. 11), this seems to be yet another instance of Oscar Wilde's dictum: 'Life imitates art.'

Forensic phonetics may be the most obvious example of interest in the personal properties of pronunciation, and the one that attracts most public interest; but it is by no means the only one. Speech therapists also deal with pronunciation individuality. A wide range of medical and psychological conditions can result in speakers developing an abnormal voice quality, having difficulties in articulation, or using a set of sounds that is so different from normal speech that it interferes with their intelligibility or makes them stand out in a way that they find unpleasant or upsetting. An obvious example is stammering. Another is the slurred speech that can come from some form of paralysis affecting one or more of the vocal organs (Chapter 24). Another is the breathy voice quality that can be the result of abnormal growths on the vocal folds that prevent them closing properly.

Rather less obvious are cases of delayed or deviant pronunciation in children, which may take some time to be noticed. A three-year-old might still be pronouncing words like an eighteen-month-old, using immature forms such as those described in Chapter 24. As the chapters on the different consonant and vowel families have shown, phonemes are acquired in particular sequences and at different rates. To assess the kind and degree of abnormality in a child, therefore, the therapist needs to make a detailed description of the phonemes being used and how accurately they are being articulated, note the ones that are not being used (for a child of that age), and plan a treatment programme that will help the child achieve a normal pronunciation. Corresponding programmes are needed for other speech conditions, in adults as well as children.

All the information in this book, and a great deal more, forms part of the routine training of speech therapists. It ought also to be routine in the training of teachers, as knowledge of the properties of the sound system is essential for any principled approach to the teaching of reading, and provides an important perspective in promoting oral fluency (oracy) and developing eloquence (see further, Appendix). Unfortunately, few teacher-training programmes include a course on phonetics.

Nor is phonetics routine in the training of actors. When teaching Shakespearean original pronunciation (Chapter 27), it's essential to use phonetic symbols to identify the differences between the Modern English and Early Modern English sound systems; but I was surprised to find that most of the actors and directors in the companies I was working with were unable to use the International Phonetic Alphabet or lacked confidence in applying it to different accents. Some, of course, have such a good ear that they don't need to analyse or transcribe before adopting an accent that is not their own – professional impressionists, I imagine, also fall into that category – and a good voice or dialect coach can make all the difference. But most actors need to think carefully about the way an accent works in order to master it – vowel by vowel, consonant by consonant, prosodic feature by prosodic feature. And that means understanding the basics of pronunciation, and how phonemes function together to form a sound system – which is what this book is about.

Anyone involved with public speaking would find their role enhanced by a modicum of phonetic training, and it is when this is absent that we most often encounter problems of communication. I'm thinking of the many domains where we struggle to understand what is being said in public announcements, such as at airports or railway stations, or in call-centre interactions. The problem may be one of an unfamiliar accent; more often it is a problem of delivery, especially someone speaking too quickly. Voice teachers, elocutionists, and operatic and theatrical dialect coaches are among the specialists who can offer assistance – and not only to the speech professions. Anyone who has to deliver a speech at a wedding, a talk to a society, or an address at a special occasion would do well to be informed about the nature of good delivery, as part of their preparation.

These are some of the areas where the study of pronunciation turns out to be especially useful, but an understanding of what is involved in this most natural of behaviours has a universal appeal, whether we are engaged in professional activities or not. One of the earliest specialists, Henry Sweet – another professorial antecedent for the character of Henry Higgins (p. 17) – called phonetics 'the indispensable foundation of all study of language'. But it is far more than an academic study. Pronunciation engages and arouses the passions in a way that other domains of language do not. For some, it is a source of delight in speech as an end in itself, when eloquent delivery, poetic performance, and evocative accents make it attractive: sounds appealing. For others, it is a source of discontent, when they encounter a way of speaking so unpalatable that they feel the need to complain about it to anyone prepared to listen: sounds unappealing. Both constituencies, I believe, can benefit from an increased understanding of how pronunciation works.

Epilogue:
Endless changes

The English language has such range,
Such rhymes and half-rhymes, rhythms strange,
And such variety of tone,
It has a music of its own.
With Milton it has organ power
As loud as bells in Redcliffe tower;
It falls like winter crisp and light
On Cowper's Buckinghamshire night.
It can be gentle as a lake,
Where Wordsworth's oars a ripple make
Or rest with Tennyson at ease
In sibilance of summer seas,
Or languorous as lilies grow,
When Dowson's lamp is burning low –
For endless changes can be rung
On church-bells of the English tongue.

From John Betjeman, the Preface to *High and Low* (1966)

Now there are such an infinitude of notes, tunes, cants,
chants, airs, looks, and accents with which the word *fiddlestick*
may be pronounced in all such cases as this, every one of 'em
impressing a sense and meaning as different from the others,
as *dirt* from *cleanliness* – that casuists (for it is an affair of
conscience upon that score) reckon up no less than fourteen
thousand in which you may do either right or wrong.

Laurence Sterne, on Mrs Wadman's expostulation; Chapter 25 of the
final book in *The Life and Opinions of Tristram Shandy, Gentleman* (1767)

Appendix:
Teaching pronunciation

As any teacher of English as a foreign language (EFL) will tell you, teaching pronunciation isn't easy. When it comes to replacing one sound system with another, it's difficult to change the habits of a lifetime. So it's no surprise that, even in the most fluent of English learners, with very few exceptions, there remain traces of the speakers' first language in their English accent. There was a time when that 'foreign accent' was something learners wanted to eradicate. These days, teachers tend to be more relaxed about residual accents – as long as they aren't so broad that they interfere with intelligibility – and learners are gradually coming to realize that they can be proud of them.

It is a further extension of the identity theme that I've been addressing throughout this book. Just as native speakers of English are happy to 'sound British, American, Australian ...', so second-language learners can feel happy to 'sound French, German, Japanese', and so on – again, as long as their speech is easily intelligible. Diversity is part of the richness of a language, and there's no reason why this should be restricted to native speakers. It's an inevitable consequence of a language being used globally that there will be an increase in the number of identifiable accents reflecting the countries of origin.

In mother-tongue settings, the issues are different, but not entirely. Large numbers of children in the schools of a multicultural society do not have English as a first language, and come from different linguistic backgrounds. Many who *are* native speakers find themselves, because of family house moves, in a school in a different part of the country from where they were previously brought up. Their accents are alien, for a while. The younger they are, the more they will accommodate naturally to the new setting (Chapter 25), but this process is greatly facilitated if they find themselves in schools where there is a comfortable acceptance of diversity. Such acceptance is not yet universal, especially in schools where RP is the norm: newcomers can feel that their regional accent is somehow inferior to the traditionally respected standard. But the negative phonetic climate at home is changing, as is the climate abroad. The achievement of fluent and eloquent intelligibility need not be at the expense of a proud and personal identity.

A certain amount of explanation in class about these two forces – intelligibility and identity – will help set the scene for teaching pronunciation, as it would for teaching grammar, vocabulary, and other aspects of language. It's important to point out that both forces rely on the same set of processes: the use of the vocal organs, several of which work together to produce the sounds of speech. An early goal should therefore be to familiarize students with the layout of the vocal organs, and the associated terminology (Chapter 4). There aren't many terms, and some – such as *lips* and *teeth* – will be part of their everyday vocabulary, so the focus needs to be on the less visible areas, such as the palate and larynx. Here, a three-dimensional anatomical model or an ENT (ear, nose, and throat) poster is well worth the purchase, providing a colourful analogue of the diagram on p. 28. (There are many companies online that provide these products.)

The earlier that students familiarize themselves with the

anatomy of speech, the better. Teaching about pronunciation is different from teaching about grammar or punctuation, where it's wise to postpone expounding the terminology until it's really needed in order to talk about how sentences work (the argument of the previous book in this series, *Making Sense*). The situation in phonetics is more like what we have to do when we teach spelling: students will not be able to proceed at all until they have learned the names of the letters of the alphabet.

That is the next step: to learn the International Phonetic Alphabet (IPA) – or, at least, as much of it as needed to transcribe an English accent. The core set of phonemic symbols is shown on pp. 21–3. Draw attention to the fact that the written alphabet has 26 letters (graphemes) whereas the spoken 'alphabet' has 44 phonemes (in most accents). The majority of the consonant symbols will need no explanation, as they are the same as the letters of the writing system: *b* in writing closely corresponds to the use of /b/ in speech (with just a few spelling exceptions, as in *debt*). The focus needs to be on those sounds where there is no equivalent – the two kinds of 'th', for instance, or the symbols that capture the consonants of *church* and *judge*. Introduce consonant symbols first, before dealing with the more complex issues raised by vowels.

In doing this, it's important to check whether there will be any interference from earlier terminology that has been encountered in relation to the teaching of reading. An obvious point is to make it clear that *phonetics*, in the sense of this book, is not the same thing as *phonics*, an approach to reading. Also make sure that the symbols are seen as representations of phonemes, and are not thought of as ordinary letters of the alphabet. Introduce the transcriptional convention of putting phonemes into slant brackets as early as possible: /t/, /e/, etc. Simple phonemic crosswords will reinforce the growing awareness of the difference between pronunciation and spelling (p. 172).

As soon as some symbols are in place, give students practice in the two dimensions of pronunciation: listening and speaking. In phonetic terms: *ear-training* and *performance*. Listening should always precede speaking, as is natural in child language acquisition. A dictation exercise is a typical procedure in an English phonetics course. Students hear the teacher say a sequence of words (minimal pairs, p. 15), such as /pat/, /pet/, and /pɪt/, and write them down using phonetic symbols. Then it is their turn to say them. The more frequent words in English should be used as much as possible – for example, when teaching /ð/, *they*, *then*, and *that* rather than *though*, *other*, or *breathe*. After a while, they are given short sequences, such as *that pet* – made as interesting to the age range as possible (one teacher, working with teenagers, got a great response by using the minimal pair *hip-hop*). Then there needs to be a slightly more testing exercise, to see just how carefully the students have been listening: an assimilation, perhaps, such as /ðap pet/ (Chapter 23).

This is a critical stage. Up to that point, students will assume that people speak as they write, with every sound relatable to the way in which a word is normally spelled. They will not be expecting a pronunciation which does not correspond to the usual spelling. They will expect there to always be a /t/ at the end of *that*, and a /v/ to be always at the end of *of* in *cup of tea* (*cuppa*). It is the moment when there needs to be a classroom discussion about formal and informal pronunciation. Teachers sometimes introduce role play at this point, such as contrasting the speech of a television newsreader with that of someone speaking colloquially. Again, the settings need to relate to the age range or background of the students.

It's also important, when bringing listening and speaking together, to take account of the accent(s) of teacher and student. If the accents are the same, there won't be an issue, as the sounds will coincide. But if the teacher has a different accent from the students, care needs to be taken to ensure that sounds aren't unconsciously introduced into the ear-training that the students wouldn't normally use in their own speech. For example, teachers (e.g. from Scotland) who unconsciously pronounced /r/ after a vowel (Chapter 20) would immediately introduce a confusion if working with a class where the accent is RP. An RP-speaking teacher in Scotland would experience the opposite problem. A session of in-house training, in which teachers ear-train each other, usually brings to light any such issues – an especially useful exercise in schools where the teachers come from a variety of accent backgrounds. Also useful is making an accent profile of each of the students. Apart from anything else, it brings to light any students who might have special pronunciation needs.

It should go without saying that, before any ear-training is begun, teachers should be satisfied that their students have normal hearing. A degree of hearing loss will usually have been picked up before a child arrives in school; but it is surprising how often it is missed. The loss may be very specific. For example, a child who has no problem distinguishing between /p/ and /t/ may have trouble with /s/ and /θ/ because of the higher acoustic frequencies of those sounds. The point can be checked by working through the contrasts in an *auditory discrimination test*. It is the sort of thing that speech therapists do routinely, but anyone can do it if they follow the procedure exactly. It typically involves showing students a pair of cards, say of a *thumb* and a *sum*, and asking: 'Which is the thumb?' or 'Which is the sum?' The ability to hear the difference needs to be checked for other parts of the word: 'Which is the *mouth*?' vs 'Which is the *mouse*?' Several publishers produce card sets of this kind. And doing the same sort of test for EFL learners can produce some surprising results. Even if hearing is normal, there may be a confusion because of interference from the sounds of their first language – as in the well-known difficulty Japanese learners have in distinguishing English /r/ and /l/.

When it comes to teaching English sounds from scratch, as happens routinely in EFL, or in a speech therapy setting where a child has a severe delay, a decision has to be made about the sequence in which sounds (both segmental and non-segmental, Chapter 5) are to be taught. Practice varies widely, though speech therapists, and many EFL teachers, respect the stages that have been established in normal child language acquisition, several of which I've described in outline in earlier chapters. Fuller accounts are available (see References). EFL teachers also have to take into account sounds that are the same in the learner's first language and in English, and those that are different – not only because they are unfamiliar sounds, but because they may be familiar sounds in unfamiliar places. Both English and German use the /ʃ/ phoneme, for example, but as illustrated in Chapter 29 (in relation to *Stuttgart*) German allows it before /t/, whereas English does not – and also before /p/: a German learner is likely to say 'shport' for *sport* (and an English learner of German likely to make the opposite error).

Of especial importance in teaching pronunciation is to work with minimal pairs *within sentences*: the critical task is not the ability to produce a sound in isolation but to use it in a word that is playing a meaningful role in a sentence. Children may have the ability to imitate /s/, but before this ability is linguistically useful, they need to be able to use it contrastively. That means more than contrasting two words (as in the auditory discrimination task). We need to hear those words in real sentences, because often the position of a word within a sentence causes a phoneme to vary its articulation (as seen in relation to assimilation). A danger is to over-articulate – for example, pronouncing *cup* as 'cup-uh', and *cub* as 'cub-uh'. Putting the words into sentences (*The cup is on the table*, *The cub is in the zoo*) helps avoid that.

The principle of teaching sounds through contrast also applies to the non-segmental dimension to pronunciation (Chapter 5). Again, a certain amount of ear-training is required. Most students will have no problem hearing the difference between loud and soft or fast and slow; but pitch contrasts will take more time. Although there are important differences between speech and music (Chapter 6), the task of teaching English intonation can be facilitated by tapping into students' musical awareness and preferences. (Be suspicious of anyone with normal hearing who says they are 'tone-deaf': it can happen, but it's extremely rare.) Several books on intonation provide methods for visually representing intonation patterns and describing in detail the tones that change meanings (see References).

It's wise to begin with settings where there is a clear pitch distinction conveying a semantic contrast that the students use all the time, such as in asking vs telling or uptalk (Chapter 6 and panel). British football-mad students will appreciate learning about the difference between a home win, an away win, and a draw, in the reading aloud of results on the radio, where the result can be predicted from the intonation used on the second team: 'Everton two, Chelsea –'. If the tone rises on *Chelsea*, it anticipates a higher score; if it has a lower level tone, a lower score; and if it falls in a glide, the same score. In an intonation textbook we might see these contrasts represented using a 'tadpole' transcription, in which parallel lines show the upper and lower limits of the voice, the black 'head' marks the stressed syllable, and the 'tail' the direction of the following pitch glide:

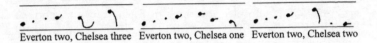

Everton two, Chelsea three   Everton two, Chelsea one   Everton two, Chelsea two

These are patterns that are used in everyday speech, as people convey different moods (excitement, as in the first result; gloom, as in the second; a sense of balance, as in the third), so the exercise has relevance that goes well beyond that sporting situation.

Child speech development can, once again, be a source of examples. From the early period would come the pitch contrast between statement and question. Somewhat later would be the contrast between a list that is complete and one that is incomplete:

> What did you buy in the shop?
> I bought some eggs, butter, and tea. [with a falling tone on *tea*, the list is complete: I bought three things]
> I bought some eggs, butter, and tea … [with a rising tone on *tea*, the list is incomplete: I bought other things as well]

At some point, work on pronunciation needs to tie in with work on grammar and punctuation (as the contrast between the period and ellipsis dots illustrates). When teaching relative clauses, for example, we need to show that the use of commas in writing is a consequence of the way different intonations and pauses occur in speech, as can be heard when these sentences are said aloud:

My son, who lives in Italy, has sent me a letter. [I have one son]
My son who lives in Italy has sent me a letter. [I have more than one son]

A perspective from child language acquisition also brings to light the importance of certain favoured pronunciation practices that can be used in teaching. Chief among these is the central role of repeated sounds (Chapter 9), which emerges most noticeably in the notions of alliteration and rhyme (Chapter 12). Rhythm too plays a critical role (Chapter 9). The consonant sequences and vowel contrasts described in earlier chapters (*Mickey Mouse, Bugs Bunny, Pink Panther*, etc.) illustrate some of the enticing possibilities. And interjections and nonsense words shouldn't be ignored, as they have considerable appeal, to young and old learners alike.

It was this last point that motivated one of the first teaching books I encountered in this field – Ronald James and R. G. Gregory's *Imaginative Speech and Writing* (1966). It was full of good ideas for promoting awareness in young children of the power of sound, and the same kind of initiative has since influenced many a subsequent approach. They began with a lesson on sounds made by things:

pretend you are a machine in a factory: decide what sort of thing you are going to make, and what sort of noise it will make ...
if these shapes could make a noise, what would it be: circles, wavy lines, jagged lines ...

They went on to sounds made by animals:

make the sound of a contented lion, an angry mouse, a wounded snake ...

make the sounds of an animal waking up, hunting, being
hunted, being hurt ...

Then sounds made by the human voice:

when somebody gives you an ice-cream, when somebody
treads on your toe ...
when you are watching a show and it is funny, exciting,
boring ...

Next came words to describe sounds, followed by sound
symbolic names:

make the sound of a clock, car horn, bell ...
write a poem about building a house using noise-words:
bang, clatter, buzz ...
what taste and what size would you give to sweets with
these names: Teenies, Wumps, Jelloc, Quangles ...

Later lessons brought words and sentences together, and
explored different kinds of poem.

It is a short step from here to more advanced kinds of oral
fluency (oracy), working with pitch, loudness, rate, and other
features of delivery, presenting good models of eloquence to
listen to and emulate, and providing opportunities to practise
(as in role play and classroom debates). It is how Winston
Churchill became a great orator – by listening to other orators
– a story I've told in *The Gift of the Gab*. As Chapter 30 has
illustrated, a knowledge of phonetics turns out to be relevant
in a remarkable range of everyday situations. It never ceases
to amaze me just how often I find myself tapping into this
knowledge, in responding to questions about language, and
students who have had even a modicum of phonetics training
will find themselves doing so too.

Quiz answers

Auditory check 1 (page 26)

Diphthongs: my, round, toy, toe, say, clear, there, sure
Monophthongs: soon, fur, mean, car, law, men, sit, hat

Auditory check 2 (page 96)

Long: moon, see, her, palm, saw
Short: pit, fell, tap, put, pot, cup, the

Auditory check 3 (page 104)

Rounded: look, paw, true, lot
Unrounded: men, feel, bird, sit

Auditory check 4 (page 115)

Close: see, shoe, pick, took
Mid: get, cut, the, bird, stop
Open: far, cat
Front: see, pick, get, cat
Central: bird, the, cut
Back: shoe, took, stop, far

Auditory check 5 (page 129)

Plosive: go, tie, key, pay, do, bow

Auditory check 6 (page 141)

Fricatives: say, vow, shy, they, zoo, fee, hi, thin

Auditory check 7 (page 148)

Affricates: char, jay, chip, joe

Auditory check 8 (page 158)

Nasals: in, same, fine, wing, team, song

Auditory check 9 (page 167)

Approximants: lay, rip, yes, way

Phonemic crossword solution (page 177)

Across:
1 spaɪd (spied)
4 lɔ: (law)
5 əʊn (own)
7 piːtə *or* piːtɚ (Peter)

Down:
1 sləʊp (slope)
2 aɪl (aisle)
3 dɔːtə *or* dɔːtɚ (daughter)
4 niː (knee)

References and further reading

Chapters 1–4

Clark, John and Colin Yallop, *An Introduction to Phonetics and Phonology* (Oxford: Blackwell, 3rd edn, 2006).

Collins, Beverley and Inger M. Mees, *The Real Professor Higgins: The Life and Career of Daniel Jones* (Berlin and New York: Mouton de Gruyter, 1999).

Fry, Dennis, *Homo Loquens: Man as a Talking Animal* (Cambridge: Cambridge University Press, 1977).

Laver, John, *Principles of Phonetics* (Cambridge: Cambridge University Press, 1994).

Mugglestone, Lynda, *Talking Proper: the Rise of Accent as Social Symbol* (Oxford: Oxford University Press, 2nd edn, 2003).

O'Connor, J. D., *Phonetics* (London: Penguin, 1973).

Scherer, Klaus R. and Howard Giles, *Social Markers in Speech* (Cambridge: Cambridge University Press, 1979).

Internet sources

Addresses are not always reliable. At the time this book went to press, the following links worked.

One of the first X-rays of the vocal organs in action, made by American phonetician Ken Stevens in 1962: https://www.youtube.com/watch?v=DcNMCB-Gsn8

An MRI (magnetic resonance imaging) video of an opera
soprano and an emcee/beatboxer: https://www.youtube.
com/watch?v=M2OdAp7MJAI

A laryngoscopic view of the vocal folds, from the Voice
and Swallowing Centre of Maine Waldo County
General Hospital, USA: https://www.youtube.com/
watch?v=Gv4evDGLgjQ

Ultrasound images of vocal fold movement: https://www.
youtube.com/watch?v=-2mesy5C914

The International Phonetic Alphabet is managed by the
International Phonetic Association: https://www.
internationalphoneticassociation.org

Chapters 5–10

Couper-Kuhlen, Elizabeth, *An Introduction to English Prosody*
(London: Edward Arnold, 1986).

Lloyd James, Arthur, *Broadcast English* (London: The British
Broadcasting Corporation, 1929); reprinted as *Society for
Pure English, Tract* 32.

O'Connor, J. D. and G. F. Arnold, *Intonation of Colloquial
English* (London: Longman, 2nd edn, 1973).

Pittenger, R. E., C. F. Hockett and J. J. Danehy, *The First Five
Minutes: A Sample of Microscopic Interview Analysis* (Ithaca,
NY: Martineau, 1960).

Wells, J. C., *English Intonation: An Introduction* (Cambridge:
Cambridge University Press, 2006).

Chapters 11–23

Burgess, Anthony, *A Mouthful of Air* (London: William
Morrow, 1992).

Cruttenden, Alan (ed.), *Gimson's Pronunciation of English* (London and New York: Routledge, 8th edn, 2014).

Roach, P. J., *English Phonetics and Phonology: A Practical Course* (Cambridge: Cambridge University Press, 4th edn, 2009).

Rockey, Denyse, *Phonetic Lexicon* (London: Heyden, 1973).

Chapters 24–30

Crystal, Ben and David Crystal, *You Say Potato* (London: Pan Macmillan, 2014).

Crystal, David, *Language Play* (London: Penguin 1998, now available at www.davidcrystal.com; Chicago: Chicago University Press).

Crystal, David, *Spell it Out: The Singular Story of English Spelling* (London: Profile Books; New York: St Martin's Press, 2012).

Crystal, David, *Making a Point: The Pernickety Story of English Punctuation* (London: Profile Books; New York: St Martin's Press, 2015)

Crystal, David, *We Are Not Amused: Victorian Views on Pronunciation as Told in the Pages of Punch* (Oxford: Bodleian, 2017).

Giles, Howard, Justine Coupland and Nikolas Coupland (eds), *Contexts of Accommodation* (Cambridge: Cambridge University Press, 1991).

Lloyd James, Arthur, *The Broadcast Word* (London: Kegan Paul, Trench, Trubner & Co., 1935).

Phillipps, K. C., *Language and Class in Victorian England* (Oxford: Blackwell, 1984).

Wells, J. C., *Accents of English* (Cambridge: Cambridge University Press, 3 vols, 1982).

Internet sources

Article in *Radio Parade* on Henry Lee Smith: http://www.otrr.org/FILES/Magz_pdf/Radio%20Parade/Radio%20Parade%201941%20March.pdf

British Library 'Voices of History': http://www.bl.uk/onlinegallery/onlineex/voiceshist/

David Kathman, 'The spelling and pronunciation of Shakespeare's name': http://shakespeareauthorship.com/name1.html

Hyundai 'Angry Bosses' commercial: https://www.youtube.com/watch?v=s0kGarkR1Ao

Jack Windsor Lewis blog post: http://www.yek.me.uk/ykpostart.html

Appendix

Cruttenden, A., 'An experiment involving comprehension of intonation in children from 7 to 10', *Journal of Child Language* 1, 221–31.

Crystal, David, *Listen to your Child* (London: Penguin, 1986).

Crystal, David and Rosemary Varley, *Introduction to Language Pathology* (London: Whurr, 1998; reissued by Oxford: Wiley, 2013).

James, Ronald and R. G. Gregory, *Imaginative Speech and Writing* (London: Nelson, 1966).

Knight, Dudley, *Speaking with Skill* (London: Bloomsbury, 2012).

Internet sources

International Association of Teachers of English as a Foreign Language (IATEFL), Pronunciation Special Interest Group: http://pronsig.iatefl.org

The British Voice Association: http://www.
   britishvoiceassociation.org.uk
Voice and Speech Trainers Association:https://www.vasta.
   org

Acknowledgements

Illustrations

Pages viii, 20, 130, 156, 220: author's collection.

Page 11: Photo 12/Alamy Stock Photo.

Page 19 (Henry Sweet): Paul Fearn/Alamy Stock Photo.

Page 28: drawing by Steve Panton.

Page 85: classicpaintings/Alamy Stock Photo.

Page 105: engraving by Sol Eytinge Jr (1871)/Philip V. Allingham/ The Victorian Web.

Page 202: Trinity Mirror/Mirrorpix/Alamy Stock Photo.

Quotations

Pages 4–5: 'I'll Hush If You'll Hush' by Ogden Nash, from *The Primrose Path*, John Lane The Bodley Head, 1936.

Pages 30–31: extract from *The Lesson* by Eugène Ionesco, © Editions Gallimard, Paris, 1954; English translation by Donald Watson. By permission of the Estate of Eugène Ionesco.

Page 79: extract from *The Caretaker* by Harold Pinter, from Harold Pinter, *Plays*, volume 2, Faber & Faber, 1991.

Page 151: extract from *Blackadder II*, 'Bells' episode, copyright © Richard Curtis and Ben Elton 1985, from *Blackadder: The Whole Damn Dynasty* by Richard Curtis, Ben Elton, John Lloyd and Rowan Atkinson, Penguin, 2009.

Page 266: extract from the 'Preface to *High and Low*' by John Betjeman (1966), from John Betjeman, *Collected Poems*, enlarged edition, John Murray, 1970.

Index